YALE PUBLICATIONS IN THE HISTORY OF ART, 32
George L. Hersey, Editor

Act of Portrayal
Eakins, Sargent, James

DAVID M. LUBIN

Yale University Press
New Haven and London

Designed by James J. Johnson
and set in Sabon Roman type by
Brevis Press, Bethany, Connecticut.
Printed in the United States of America by
The Alpine Press, Inc., Stoughton, Massachusetts.

Library of Congress Cataloging in Publication Data

Lubin, David M.
  Act of portrayal.

  (Yale publications in the history of art, 32)
  Bibliography: p.
  Includes index.
  1. Portrait painting—Psychological aspects.
2. Eakins, Thomas, 1844–1916. Sargent, John Singer,
1856–1925. 4. James, Henry, 1843–1916—Characters.
I. Title. II. Series.
ND1300.L8 1985   757'.01'9   85–2436
ISBN 0–300–03213–7 (alk. paper)

The paper in this book meets the guidelines for
permanence and durability of the Committee on
Production Guidelines for Book Longevity of the
Council on Library Resources.

10 9 8 7 6 5 4 3 2 1

Contents

List of Illustrations

Note to the Reader

My intention in the following chapters is to take three works of portraiture that originated in the 1880s and show that they were not completed then, nor are they complete now. The book is an attempt to trace not one but numerous paths and byways through these portraits, spreading bread-crumbs and making notches along the way. It is an attempted journey, without predetermined destination; the emphasis is not on where we end but how we go.

I am being vague . . . metaphoric . . . unscholarly. Although much in-debted to the work of many fine scholars, a number of whom I cite in footnotes, I must from the outset warn the reader not to expect here a "research" volume, at least not in the ordinary sense. Think of it instead as an act of searching and (re)searching the three texts, a continual dipping into them and extracting from them, but not, I hope, without giving some-thing back in return. Again I am being vague, but then this is only a brief note; in the textual analyses themselves, I am as specific as I can be. Yet even there vagueness makes an occasional appearance, and this is as it should be, for the last thing I want to do is package any one of these portraits, or any part of them, in a neat, airtight container. I do not ever, to use the key animating term of chapter 3, wish to "box" them in.

These portraits, as I started to suggest before, are not closed, immobile systems, static and academically hallowed relics, born (and subsequently deceased) a century ago. Rather they are fluid, ongoing, open systems that are recreated, created anew, whenever researched, or searched anew, with any sort of creative effort, intentional or otherwise. By this last phrase I mean that one need not *try* to be creative or original in one's engagement with any of these texts, for in any act of reading "mistakes" or "misreadings" will occur, as in daily life slips of the tongue, dreams, daydreams, faces and forms seen in clouds, and all sorts of odd, untoward, and often unwanted emotions will and do occur.

However. (Yes, here comes the however.) Despite all this emphasis on welcomed misprision, interpretive free play, creative engagement with the text, and so forth, I have no desire to be ahistorical. Rather than attempt, as some critics over the years have been interested in doing, to "liberate" individual works of art from the (perceived-as) dry and dusty realm of social and intellectual history, I am glad to let them linger there, but not languish. (And certainly, for every reader who finds too much history here, there will be others who find not enough.) The historical era I will be focusing upon is that of America between the Civil War and the turn of the century—more specifically, America in the middle of that period, America in the 1880s. Nevertheless, most of what emerges from my readings of the three 1880s portraits has more to do with industrialized nineteenth-century culture generally than with 1880s American culture specifically, inasmuch as, although the three portraitists were American citizens born of American parents, they all trained abroad, and two of them lived much of their lives there as well. Still, I have tried wherever possible to be clear on which factors contributing to the rise of the new portraiture can be traced not simply to general historical trends (urbanization or the drawing together of the nuclear family, for example), but also to the one specifically American event of the century, the Civil War.

Our present needs, concerns, and desires directly impose themselves on the past that we are observing, giving that past a definite present-hued tint that differs from the tint given to it in another period.[1] In other words, 1885 as seen in 1935 will have a certain thirties torsion to it, while the same year observed in 1985 will have a distinctly 1980s look. Once the historian accepts the inevitability of this cultural, perceptual relativism, he need not throw up his hands in despair; it has not become pointless to talk about recovering the past, so long as the past is not conceived of as some pristine object that must be had in its purest, most virginal form. Neither should it be treated as a previously abused woman whose redemption to a state of purity is the historian-husband's holy task. Such regressive Victorian idealism, false and destructive in marriage, is equally unfortunate when it sways one's approach to history. A preferable approach is to regard the past as that which determines the present, the present as that which deter-mines the past (as far as it can be known), and this organic, imperfect, and symbiotic relationship between the two as the most fruitful focus of our concern.

With this in mind I propose that the best way for us in the 1980s to know the 1880s through its portraiture is to read the portraits with a deliberate and ongoing consciousness that our present needs and values are unavoidably superimposed. In not only recognizing this superimposition but actually thrusting it into the foreground, we keep clear of the illusion—pleasant, but an illusion nonetheless—that it is possible to ascertain the life of the 1880s as it really was. Moreover, continually calling attention to ourselves as historically located readers presently engaged in a culturally determined act of reading is more than simply a way of keeping ourselves honest. It is a way of gauging distance. By saying "I respond to x, y, and z in this portrait," we are in effect saying, "The culture in which I am now actively reading this text and the culture in which it was previously pro-duced intersect at points x, y, and z." For it is at the points of intersection, and only at these points, that we in the present may go back to the past.

Thus the three following readings are deliberately self-conscious and deliberately present-tense. We shall view ourselves in the act of viewing. The portraits represent the artists' views of their protagonists. In each portrait, the protagonists are depicted in the act of viewing either them-selves or other fictive individuals (including the implied reader or implied viewer). Therefore, in the following pages we shall be viewing ourselves in the act of viewing the artist's act of viewing an individual who is himself or herself engaged in viewing. If this approach sounds nervously narcissistic and voyeuristic, perhaps it is, but that should not be surprising, given the times in which we live—as well as the neurasthenic age in which these portraits were produced. This is portraiture squared, cubed, or quadrupled; portraiture to the nth degree.

Hence the title, *Act of Portrayal*. We are looking not only at how Eakins, Sargent, and James construct portraits, but also at how the subjects within those portraits are the makers of portraits, and how we too, by our constructive, synthetic act of reading, are portrait-makers. At each level we are dealing with acts of portrayal; indeed, at all levels, with "active por-trayal." It will thus be appropriate to stop from time to time to take stock of our mode of perception and our method of construction. We will be asking again and again, how is it that this text (whether written or painted) enables us to perceive the differences between one character and another, or a character and his environment, or a character and himself at an earlier or later point? How is it that we can recognize, or think we recognize, an internal consistency in a character who is sufficiently true to life to be, as people in real life are, a tangle of inconsistencies?

The portraits to be examined are not presented here in chronological sequence. To have done so would have been to convey implicitly the notion that history is a simple unfolding "forward," a linear progression. Even if I do see the 1880s as being in a different place historically from the 1850s, say, or even the 1870s, I wish to avoid giving the impression that an artist in 1889 would be entirely free of cultural paradoxes, disunities, and anxieties that beset that same artist or his colleagues in 1881. The texts have been arranged, therefore, not by chronology but by my sense of which order works best for the development of issues common to all three that I wish to bring to light. As it turns out, the portraits occur here in a reverse chronology; if they are arranged in any forward order at all, it is only that of the alphabet: *The Agnew Clinic, The Boit Children, The Portrait of a Lady.*

Criticism, wrote Henry James, "talks a good deal of nonsense, but even its nonsense is a useful force. It keeps the question of art before the world, insists upon its importance, and makes it always in order."² Concerning the criticism that is about to follow, I set for myself two standards. Does this book succeed in opening new windows or doors on the works considered, letting in fresh air to invigorate the reader and perhaps even reinvigorate the works themselves? And does it succeed in making visible the submerged operations of text through which can be detected moral, sexual, and ideological fissures in a culture historically distinct, but not altogether different, from our own? How well I meet these standards each reader can judge.

*   *   *

Where money is concerned, to be in debt is never a happy experience; yet when the debt is not financial but intellectual, the opposite is true. Thus my joy knows no bounds. The following scholars are those to whom I am especially indebted: R. W. B. Lewis, who guided me graciously, thoughtfully, and always helpfully from the start of my academic interest in American portraiture; Jules Prown, a remarkably capable teacher, for his firm but kind insistence on visual, verbal, and intellectual precision (even when I was not willing or quite ready to give it to him); Bryan Wolf, for his ceaselessly creative, tough-minded, and energetic involvement; and Eddie Ayers, who batted my ideas back at me even faster and more skillfully than he returned my racquetball serves. Certainly each of these friends is well aware of my gratitude without needing to read it here, but all the same, what a pleasure it is for me to set down the words.

Others who have commented on parts of the manuscript at various stages along the way include Peter Brooks, Daniel Camp, Robert Carringer, Charles Feidelson, Jonathan Freedman, Barbara Heins, Elizabeth Johns, Michael Marlais, Judith Mayne, Angela Miller, Joel Pfister, Dianne Sadoff, David Simon, David Steinberg, Ann Warner, and my copyeditor, Nancy Woodington. For what is worthwhile in the following chapters, each of these readers deserves credit and thanks; none of them, however, should be held to account for the inadequacies.

Gerald Burns, Theresa Murphy, and Michael Smith, through friendship and many enjoyable conversations over the years, have done more than I can say to help me develop my ideas concerning the place of art in American history. My friend Bruce Robertson similarly has extended my thoughts about the place of portraiture in art history. Thanks also to Jean-Christophe Agnew, Richard Brodhead, Fredric Jameson, J. Hillis Miller, Alan Trachtenberg, and Robert Westbrook for other conversations I consider to have been important.

Colby College generously assisted me in the preparation of this manuscript. I spent many fine and not so fine hours there using and trying not to be done in by the marvels of word processing, whose technology continues to elude me. Colby's computer staff—and reference librarians, too, I might add—rescued me from peril more than once.

My editor at Yale University Press, Judy Metro, has been unsparing in her encouragement, her professional counsel, and, when tested, her patience. I feel fortunate to have had someone like her at the other end of my phone calls.

Finally, I wish to thank my family—the Lubins and Warners—and acknowledge here only a small part of my ever-growing affection for the person I live with, learn from, and love, my wife, Libby. This book is dedicated to her and to our daughter, Molly, who, born only a hundred hours ago, becomes by the minute stronger, wiser, and more alive.

ACT OF PORTRAYAL

CHAPTER ONE

Introduction

WHY PORTRAITURE? Some time ago I found myself wanting to explore three sets of differential oppositions in American art: (1) "masculine" and "feminine" character (nature, sensibility, what have you); (2) "past" and "present" notions concerning the first opposition; and (3) "verbal" and "visual" means of aesthetically reproducing that opposition.

My reason for putting the opposing pairs of modifiers in quotes is to emphasize from the start that these terms and the concepts they signify are not fixed points but rather directional arrows. Cleaving apart past and present, or dividing male and female, or determining when verbal ceases to be visual and visual verbal, is akin to establishing the difference in infinite outer space between east and west. Nonetheless, it is by means of such heuristic oppositions that portraiture as a historically specific act of writing, and the reading of portraiture as an equally history-bound act, can be theoretically articulated.[1]

My wish to draw together the first and third set of differences into a single empirical study has made it necessary to compare verbal and visual representations of men and women. In effect this means comparing an instance of character-oriented fiction (the psychological novel) to an instance (or instances) of character-oriented visual representation (as in psychological portrait painting).

The past/present differentiation is made by gathering from a single point in the past a handful of verbal and visual portraits and examining them in a variety of ways from a present-tense viewpoint that never fails to be conscious of its "presentism." For my point in the past, I have selected the 1880s because it was the decade when American novelists (especially Henry James and William Dean Howells) as well as painters (particularly Thomas Eakins and John Singer Sargent) began bestowing upon the artistic study of male and female character a depth and complexity hardly touched, or even considered, in the decades previous. True, a generation before, Nathaniel Hawthorne and Herman Melville had rendered fictional characterizations that were nothing if not compelling, and two or three generations before them John Singleton Copley and Gilbert Stuart had painted portraits still remarkable for the character insight they proffer. Nonetheless, in the case of those earlier novelists, characterization was subsidiary to moral allegory or aesthetic symbolism,[2] and for the portrait painters it was secondary to the goal of certifying social, moral, or political rank. Beginning more or less in the 1880s, however, characterization—particularly when performed by James or Eakins—became a primary goal in itself, equaled only by the goal of technically mastering the medium in which the characterization was being cast.[3] Yet this new breed of portraiture, whether written or painted, offers up something more than characterization-for-the-sake-of-characterization conjoined with the working out of technical and aesthetic challenges; it provides a social criticism as well. With certain of the new portraitists, the criticism was not superficial, not grafted on from without, but originated instead from the same impulse that compelled them to use characterization to strengthen technique, and technique to deepen characterization. Such social criticism contained "within" these portraits of the 1880s may very well have been an act, to borrow Fredric Jameson's term, of political unconsciousness, but regardless of how the criticism came into each work, decidedly its presence is manifest.

Finally there is the question of which works to analyze. The selection of a single written portrait is simple. With Henry James having entitled his first and perhaps most enduring masterpiece *The Portrait of a Lady,* one need look no further. Certainly other texts by James are suitable, but none more perfectly meets the specifications of the present endeavor. As that novel is so long and full, it might seem that half a dozen portrait paintings would be needed to effect a balance. A strong painting, though, can hold its own against a strong novel, especially if its scale or scope is similar to the novel's. Both Eakins' *The Agnew Clinic* and Sargent's *The Boit Children* fit the bill. The three portraits go together well. Each is a product of the 1880s; each manifests within itself a localized tension between verbal and visual expression; each, at its deepest levels of form and of content, is concerned with matters of sexual difference; and each, finally, is in some sense a metaportrait, a portrait *about* portraiture.

WHAT IS A PORTRAIT?

Whether a portrait is one-to-one (that is, represented figure to real-life figure), as with Sargent and Eakins, or composite (more than one model for a single portrait figure), as with James, a portraitist's implicit purpose is the revelation and interpretation of a specific, delimited human identity.[4] The means of achieving this is through depiction and analysis of the behavior, appearance, and "essence of character" that best make that particular identity decipherable. Yet even though portraits are usually intended as interpretations of a single individual, real or composite, we regard them as significant to the extent that they widen (or give us the sensation of having widened) our understanding of man in general.[5] By "man in general," what we are actually talking about is (a) distinguishable traits that are common to members of a discrete group or that belong transhistorically and transculturally to members of widely differing social groups, and (b) social, political, and psychological relationships that are also either group-specific or group-transcendent. We can therefore rephrase our earlier formulation thus: even though a portrait purports to allow us the close observation of a single, localized individual, we discern meaning in it to the extent that it appears to *reveal* something about general human traits and social relationships.

The Portrait of a Lady may be about a single, fictionally hypothesized woman named Isabel Archer, but as will be shown in chapter 4, Isabel, the fictional construct, is the locus for intersecting traits (idealism, guilt, obsessive propriety, narcissism, the desire for autonomy, and the equally weighted desire for fusion with a parent-object through submission to authority) and relationships typical of modern Western society (between rich and poor, fathers and daughters, mothers and daughters, actors and spectators, portrait subjects and portrait texts). *The Agnew Clinic* may be about a certain Dr. D. Hayes Agnew who actually lived and practiced in late nineteenth-century Philadelphia, but the Agnew of the portrait is, like Isabel, an aesthetically constructed entity in which we can observe the intersection of certain traits (heroism, pomposity, self-consciousness, inquisitiveness, aggressivity) and the interaction of various social, political, sexual, and epistemological relationships or codes.[6] Finally, *The Boit Children* may be about four real-life girls who posed for Sargent's painting, but

whether Sargent meant it this way or not, his portrait of them is yet another
aesthetic depiction—a translation into color and form, later to be retrans-
lated by us—of specified traits (for example, obedience, passivity, docility,
inscrutability, and "object-ness") and relationships (female to female,
daughter to father, spectacle to spectator, representation to representation-
maker, object to subject). The traits and relationships that are aesthetically
embodied in *The Boit Children* are similar, even in some cases identical,
to those given form by *The Portrait of a Lady* and *The Agnew Clinic* during
the same period of American history.

In asserting that portraits make sense to us to the extent that they
expose what our education and experience teach us to perceive as universal
traits and relationships, and that this is accomplished by means of the
portrait's close observation of a single individual (or narrow group of individuals), I do not mean to suggest that we are interested in the portrayed
individual only insofar as we can abstract therefrom a set of universals. On
the contrary, if the portrait works, we are fascinated by the represented
figure and regard him or her as a quasi-alive, quasi-real individual interesting in himself or herself and to some degree representative of us. The
portrait-figure, if he or she has been constructed in such a way as to "come
alive," serves as a sort of screen upon which we can project our own
identification or antipathy or both.

Portraits fall somewhere between two extremes. At one extreme is the
portrait that gives such a fixed and rigid notion of its human subject that
the subject becomes a mere object: something to stare at, to scrutinize, to
pillage for an easily transportable meaning ("noble," "venal," "good,"
"evil"), and then quickly forget. At the other extreme is the portrait that
prevents us from treating the portrayed individual as an object of knowledge
that we can crack like a nut, flicking away the hard shell as we toss down
the plump morsel within; instead it compels us to recognize in others, and
in ourselves, a complexity of motive, of psychic flux and inner disorgani-
zation, that is ultimately beyond either our intellectual or our intuitive
comprehension.[7]

Mandates of artistic form—closure, internal consistency, logic of sequence—push the portraitist toward the first extreme while his or her deep-
ening experience of life, suffering, and human oddity pull toward the
second. Each of the three portraits we will be examining can be seen as
an attempted unification of these two opposed and irreconcilable poles.
Like so many portraits that lastingly command our attention, the three we
have before us are ones in which the portraitist's concern with artistic
formalism vies with his desire for psychological realism. Throughout the

three full-scale readings that follow, we shall encounter this crucial tension as it is played out in various oppositions: not only Art versus Life, but also Order versus Chaos, Discipline versus Freedom, and the quest for Science (knowledge) versus the acceptance of Nature (mystery). We shall also see that the portraitist's central problem of how to treat (and have us treat) his fictive characters is duplicated within the text by their problem of how to treat one another.

"From cradle to grave," notes Henry Adams in *The Education*, itself an intriguing work of portraiture, "this problem of running order through chaos, direction through space, discipline through freedom, unity through multiplicity, has always been, and must always be, the task of education, as it is the moral of religion, philosophy, science, art, politics, and economy."[8] So too is it the task of portraiture, which is a form of education, religion, philosophy, et al. Yet Adams finds it necessary to remind us of the awful dilemma involved; speaking of his own education as a child, he adds, "But a boy's will is his life, and he dies when it is broken, as the colt dies in harness, taking a new nature in becoming tame." So too can a portraitist, by trimming, pruning, fixing, and making consistent—in a word, by taming—a character's nature, also break it, depriving it of that disorder we call life. Elsewhere in *The Education* Adams observes, "Chaos often breeds life, when order breeds habit."[9] The portrait-maker must attempt to guide characterization between chaos and order, between life and mechanical habit. So too must the protagonists of our three portraits steer their way through that fictive world of theirs that closely resembles our own, and so too must we as readers carefully work out our interpretation such that it succumbs neither to the chaos lurking in the text, nor to the lifeless order that inevitably results from an overzealous critical repression of that chaos.

AMERICAN PORTRAITURE OF THE 1880s

Earlier, I suggested that a new sort of portraiture, more complex and ambitious, more concerted in its effort to depict and interpret character, began to develop during the 1880s in the work of such American artists as James, Eakins, and Sargent. To get some sense of why this should be so, we must investigate three separate but closely related levels of historical causation: the craft tradition of the artist, the dominant social forces of the era, and the artist's personal history.[10]

First, then, is the matter of craft tradition. It is important to recall that all three of our portraitists served artistic apprenticeships on the continent. James "studied" in Paris (1875–76) with Turgenev and Flaubert, both of whom had been self-consciously forging an aesthetic of literary portraiture for some years before James appeared on the scene. Although Eakins was an art student in the studio of the popular Parisian orientalist and history painter, Jean-Léon Gérôme, what seems to have made the deepest and most inspiring impression on him was the work of the seventeenth-century Dutch portraitists, particularly Rembrandt and Hals, and the masterpieces of the Spanish portraitist, Velázquez, with whom he was greatly taken on a trip to Madrid in 1869.[11] Sargent's experience a decade later was much the same: he was trained in Paris by the fashionable painter of portraits Carolus-Duran, but seems to have been far more profoundly "educated" by a trip to the Prado, where he too stood dazed before the dark, provocative masterworks of Velázquez.[12]

Without this direct, heady exposure to portrait theory and practice on the continent, neither James nor Eakins nor Sargent was so likely to have developed in the direction that they all did, for in America of the 1860s and early 1870s, there was not an ongoing tradition, in either writing or painting, of characterization in depth. Here I am referring specifically to the portrayal of individuals other than the artist. From Jonathan Edwards' *Personal Narrative* and John Smibert's picture of himself in *The Bermuda Group,* both from 1739, through to the poems of Emily Dickinson in the 1860s and 1870s, American self-portraiture seems consistently to have provided a density of psychological characterization rarely found in the artistic depiction of others. But self-portraiture is a genre unto itself; its techniques and operations are not readily transferable into the related, yet much different, activity I am calling *portraiture.* With the qualified exception of Hawthorne and Melville, what native literary portraitists—as opposed to fabulists, romancers, and satirists—were there for James to emulate? Where was the American equivalent to Benjamin Constant or Stendhal, first-rate technicians of literary psychology who established a tradition out of which the work of Flaubert and Turgenev evolved? Where for James was his American Jane Austen or George Eliot? The problem was similar for Eakins and Sargent; after the terrific outburst of creative portrait painting in colonial and early federal America—the work of Copley, Stuart, Charles Willson Peale, and others—portrait painting had stagnated as an artistic backwater in contrast to the turbulent eddy of such romantic allegorists as Allston and Cole, the clear reflective pool of genre narrativists Mount and Bingham, and the sweeping, onrushing stream of landscapists Bierstadt and Church. Even before the advent of the daguerreotype and the *carte de visite,* American portrait painting had become *rétardataire,* mired either in vacuous sentimentality, as in the work of Chester Harding and much of that

of Thomas Sully, Stuart's heir-apparent, or theatrical pomposity and stiff-
ness, as in most of the portraits of Samuel Morse and all too many of
G. P. A. Healey, a painter of great technical facility but little concern for
psychology. As with James, so too with Eakins and Sargent: no native
American tradition of forward-moving portraiture existed from which to
borrow, by which to be inspired, or against which to rebel.

Why not? Was there some artistic reason beyond merely arbitrary
personal idiosyncrasy that Healey, America's greatest portrait technician in
the decades prior to Sargent, had no interest in matters of psychology, of
character revelation through form and color? Why did the novels of James
Fenimore Cooper eschew individual psychology in favor of outdoor adventure, while at the same time, across the Atlantic, Honoré de Balzac went
so far as to make of individual psychology a sort of indoor adventure?[13]

The answer must surely have something to do with the typological
method of thinking that governed American artistic and critical efforts well
into the nineteenth century. Raised in a Puritan, or Puritan-derived, culture,
American writers and artists prior to the Civil War rarely thought of character as complex, ever shifting, and independent of conventional type.[14] As
Charles Feidelson has noted, "The crudity or conventionality of a great part
of American literature from 1620 through the third quarter of the nineteenth century may be attributed no more surely to frontier conditions,
provinciality, and industrialism than to inherited [Puritan] mental habits
which proscribed a functional artistic form."[15]

Hawthorne's Hester Prynne, with the scarlet letter of adultery affixed
to her breast, is in a sense the perfect literary paradigm for an America—
of the 1640s or the 1840s—that forced upon the individual an uncom-
fortable externalization of his or her inner self; an America in which the
dogged withdrawal from a community-sanctioned and strictly regulated
subjectivity was regarded almost as though it were a crime against the
public good. In many ways this state of things was in direct contrast to the
folkways of Europe. There the constrictions of both national borders and
social rank encouraged, even necessitated, closed, well-guarded behavior,
which led to a much closer scrutiny of both one's neighbor and oneself,
and of the many unwritten codes governing relationships between the two.[16]
In America, however, the social structure from the War of Independence
to the War Between the States was virtually tooled to combat introspection:
"Go West, young man" was Horace Greeley's advice, not "Go Within."[17]
Rare exceptions such as Hawthorne and Emerson, voyagers on the infre-
quently traveled path of subjective complexity marked out by Jonathan
Edwards, demonstrated that venturing "within" was not solipsistic but

profoundly social, for one could hardly investigate the self without also investigating one's many links to society. Yet for the most part, America's narrative or pictorial artists of those years, like Americans in general, seem to have tended toward externalization—a tendency evidenced on one level by westward expansion and the opening of trade routes to the Orient, on another by Transcendentalist optimism and utopian political reformism, and on a third by highly mediated codes of deportment that encouraged sentimentality, prudery, and theatricality.[18] This, certainly, was no climate conducive to searching explorations of the self.[19]

De Tocqueville observed in 1840 that "aristocracy links everybody, from peasant to king, in one long chain. Democracy breaks the chain and frees every link." Members of a democracy "form the habit of thinking of themselves in isolation and imagine that their whole destiny is in their hands." Therefore, "not only does democracy make men forget their ancestors, but [it] also clouds their view of their descendants and isolates them from their contemporaries. Each man is forever thrown back on himself alone and there is danger that he may be shut up in the solitude of his own heart."[20] Hawthorne's story "Egotism; or, the Bosom Serpent" (1843) allegorizes the danger of a man's being "shut up in the solitude of his own heart," but although the character Roderick Elliston illustrates the problem of neither seeing others nor being seen with complexity, understanding, and depth, he *as a character* is not individualized beyond that one level.

The atomistic nature of American social relations during this period, at least as both de Tocqueville and Hawthorne have described them, may have left Americans relatively unconcerned about the inner life of their neighbors, whereas the economic interdependence fostered by industrialization and urbanization once again linked them in a chain—with great anomie perhaps, but also with a need to be brought into contact with the subjectivity of their fellow links. By heightening the diversification, economic and functional, of the individuals within each social class, industrialization could be seen as having given rise to a particularizing, psychologically individuating portraiture not available in a previous era when intraclass distinctions were less necessary. By the final quarter of the nineteenth century, the individual, alienated from his fellows by the dual pressures of democracy (as de Tocqueville described it) and capitalism (as interpreted by Marx), but more than ever economically dependent on those fellows, found himself in a position where he needed, as never before, to know the other with whom he was paradoxically and anxiously involved. Thomas Haskell, in his account of proliferating interdependence in American life in the late nineteenth century, writes:

It is inconceivable that people could have lived through such a transformation of society without profound changes in their habits of mind, their modes of organizing experience, their very manner of perceiving human affairs. This was no ordinary transition from one generation to another, but a movement from one social universe to another governed by strikingly different conditions of action and explanation. To be born in one world and to have to live in the other—the typical fate of nineteenth-century men—was an intellectually wrenching experience, blinding to most but stimulating to a creative few.[21]

It was precisely this situation that provided a radically altered conceptual basis for the new, subjective style of American portraiture that arose during the generation following Hawthorne.

Of the American 1880s and 1890s, Neil Harris has observed:

The cultural life of this era was the product of social anxiety and general curiosity, of a restless, sometimes desperate desire to learn the habits, the thoughts, the working patterns, and dreams of others in the community. These decades witnessed the sudden discovery of pluralities—of class, age, nationality, condition—which made up the American community. The fiction, the newspapers, the amusements, and the education of a people reflected this desire to know more, to collect data and savor the experience of learning.[22]

Let us add psychological portraiture to Harris' list of cultural productions that were profoundly shaped by the desire—no, desire is too weak a word here: by the anxious *need*—of modern Americans to know what was going on beneath the masks of those strange others with whom they were bafflingly and yet inextricably bound. As we have already observed, portraiture, whether in paint or in prose, is more likely to provide a comforting illusion of insight, a reconfirmation of received truths about the world and the way various personality types fit within it, than to alter radically and lastingly conceptions about one's fellows, let alone one's relationship to them. Even at its best, portraiture is simply not capable of bringing together the alienated monads that we in our darker moments believe ourselves to be.

Certainly it is nothing but stale news that in the nineteenth century the rise of the mega-city and the concomitant predominance of impersonal machine technology created in people's lives a blistering sense of anomie, of social dislocation. The story has all too often been told of how old communal ties, in some cases ancient ones, were broken as workers from various social classes abandoned farms, villages, small towns, and other familial enclaves for urban centers that promised jobs, excitement, myriad possibilities, while, alas, delivering not only those things but an often numbing anonymity and loneliness as well. Usually linked with that tale has been the one about the worker run soulless by the soulless machine he was hired to run, or the captain of industry permanently lashed to the mast of his own monstrous ship. But to whatever extent such woeful narratives help us to see why at a certain point in history a relatively new and different mode of portraiture evolved in response to a relatively new, historically created sense of lack (a lack of personal closeness), they are anecdotal at best. Let us therefore extrapolate.

Many American freemen may have felt themselves bruised and abused by the mercantile economy of the antebellum years. But that was nothing compared to the postwar world in which, with the irreversible establishment of industrial entrepreneurialism and labor-intensive capitalism as the dominant economic mode, these Americans increasingly encountered a sense of powerlessness against cold, abstract forces far beyond their own or anyone else's personal control. Catastrophic nationwide depressions during the 1870s, 1880s, and 1890s, one after another, intensified many an individual's sense of impotence, regardless of how hard he or she tried to shove that sense out of sight and out of mind. Increasingly adults were forced to endure a very different view of themselves from that which they had entertained when their lives were less directly ruled by market exigencies.

Henry Adams observed firsthand the changes resulting from the postwar financial reclassification of the nation wherein North and South, East and West, all danced as best they could to the tune piped out by New York's Wall Street and Boston's State Street. "The world, after 1865," he writes, "became a bankers' world."[23] As to Adams' place in that financier's world: "He was for sale, in the open market. So were many of his friends. All the world knew it, and knew too that they were cheap; to be bought at the price of a mechanic. . . . The young man was required to impose himself, by the usual business methods, as a necessity on his elders, in order to compel them to buy him as an investment."[24] The supreme consciousness among artists and intellectuals of Adams' generation that the world treated all individuals as free-market commodities to be exploited (and self-exploited) must eventually have had its effect. Sargent came to consider himself unjustly and demeaningly used by his patrons ("No more Paughtraits!" he finally declared, years later), while other portraitists, such as Eakins, felt themselves inhumanely abused by critics, and still others, such as James, by a public that clamored only for more Daisy Millers. The term *exploitation* is not one they might have employed to describe their own situation, but the ugly feeling of helplessness, of being pulled about on someone else's string, of having to market oneself and one's art in this way or that, is a feeling they seem increasingly to have experienced, even as other classes in American society were experiencing it. This is not to say that earlier nineteenth-century creative artists on either side of the Atlantic had not found themselves similarly jangled and abused by the hostile realities of a market-dominated world; but by midway through the second half of the century, those market realities and the attitudes toward life they engendered had become institutionalized beyond the point of return. Regardless of how personally uninvolved James, Eakins, and Sargent were in the hardships of those who toiled in the sweatshops and coal mines of the seventies and eighties—indeed, regardless of how conservative their own political opinions or how disapproving their attitude toward militant "antisocial" behavior—we can sense in the many violent labor uprisings of the time, from the Great Railroad Strike of 1877 to the Haymarket Riot of 1886 to the Pullman Strike of 1894, and beyond, an external correlative to the violently rebellious but internally suppressed urges these artists unhappily and uneasily endured.

It is necessary to consider how, in a world not only supercharged with manifold forms of exploitation but also superconscious of it, artists of a certain nature were bound to gravitate toward an art such as portraiture, a mode of aesthetic performance that, by celebrating individual uniqueness and subjectivity, would enable them to redress damages done by society to that uniqueness and subjectivity. Whereas the painted portraits of seventeenth-century Holland or the American colonial period tend to celebrate the autonomy of the mercantile capitalist, the psychological portraits of the 1880s attempt instead to salvage what they can of individuals who are losing their autonomy.[25]

In what way does portraiture "celebrate" individuality and subjectivity? It does so, or at least *appears* to do so, by devoting attention to—by focusing the viewer/reader's attention on—traits, qualities, physical attributes, and patterns of characteristic behavior, as located in a single person. It treats its sitter (a fictional construct, remember, that, in paint or in prose, is based on one or several flesh-and-blood people) as someone who is worth looking at and thinking about, and as someone who has private feelings, cares, and concerns, to which we can intersubjectively respond. Regarded from the not unproblematic perspective of humanism, portraiture can instill in us the desire to stop and look at the unknown and previously uncared-for man in the street because of our having earlier been gratified by stopping and looking at portraits hanging on walls or stretching through novels.

Yet however much the portraitist may have deliberately, or only intuitively, attempted to recuperate the damaged and undermined subjectivity of his fellow Americans and confirm his own otherwise threatened subjectivity, we should recognize that the portraitist himself was constantly engaging in forms of exploitation. Sargent, done with his art studies and concerned with entering the Salon, used the four Boit girls as a means toward making his name known and admired. Similarly, Eakins used Dr. Agnew as a means of regaining a professional prestige that had slipped away from him. And again, James used his good friend and ally, Francis Boott, as a prototype for Gilbert Osmond, whose egotism and villainy provide *The Portrait of a Lady* with much of the gothic or melodramatic flavor that is responsible for its popular appeal. These are crude and rather literal examples of the portraitist-as-exploiter: real-life artists capitalizing on real-life people (who, in the two former cases, received in return relatively appealing depictions of themselves). But more subtle and more important, there is also the way in which the real-life portraitist exploited or manipulated his medium to develop his fictive construction ("The Boit Children," "Dr. Agnew," "Gilbert Osmond") and, simultaneously, manipulated the fictive construction as a means of challenging the medium.

Clearly these are two different levels of exploitation—one is of real people, the other of artistic categories and materials—but in both cases the portraitist advances his project by acts of reification. Thus, in the very process of defending human subjectivity, his own and others', the psychological portraitist betrays it; he strives to recreate consciousness, and finds himself forced to treat it as an elusive, slippery object: a mountain to be conquered or wild game to be bagged. Might it not be possible that even as certain artists of the 1880s delved into psychological portraiture as a means of withstanding the impersonal, antisubjective pressures of their time, they unknowingly helped transmit the very disease they sought to cure? This is a variation of the more familiar argument that those who rebel against a constituted authority tend involuntarily to internalize and make a part of themselves—"introject"—the authority against which they are in rebellion. In the Freudian view, even as the son is working out his oedipal conflict with the father, he is re-forming himself inside as a replication of the father. James with his incessant observation and analysis of human behavior, Eakins with his experiments in stop-action photography, Sargent with his astounding technical facility, were each a one-man artistic factory; an engineering expert who erected characterizations rather than bridges; a consummate professional who dealt in traits and qualities and shades and tones with the training and skill of an experienced lawyer reciting torts or a surgeon stitching together severed flesh. The professionalization of American art could hardly escape the reifying side effects felt not only in law and medicine, but in all the newly professionalized spheres of American life.[26]

With *The Portrait of a Lady*, James seems to evidence no more than a dim conscious perception of the paradox that a psychological portrait, by its very nature, needs to turn its subject into an aesthetic object, a *thing*, in order to convey the subjectivity of that thing, and that the portraitist, by imposing formal rules and order, cannot help but reify the individuality that his portraiture is an attempt to shield, express, and perpetuate.[27] The novel accentuates this built-in paradox to a degree that James may not have intended. In his later career, however, he seized more directly on this issue, so that by the time he wrote his fable "The Altar of the Dead" (1895), his narrator can say of the writer-surrogate protagonist who lights candles in commemoration of deceased acquaintances, "There were hours at which he almost caught himself wishing that certain of his friends would now die, that he might establish with them in this manner a connection more charming than, as it happened, it was possible to enjoy with them in life."[28] The wish to "aesthetify" a person contains within it the secret desire to still the life of that person. Thus the great pitfall of portraiture is its leanings toward death, fixation, reification—its restructuring of individuality in the name of form and convention, its smoothing out, not the surface warts and wrinkles that are the realist's badge of honor, but the internal inconsistencies and insolubles that make humans human but art inartistic. In 1842 Robert Browning demonstrated in "My Last Duchess" a perhaps prescient understanding of this socioartistic phenomenon wherein the aesthetic representation of an individual is often more satisfying than the individual himself, as well as how such representations can operate as denials of that individual's discomfortingly human reality.[29] Sargent and Eakins, men of the brush rather than the pen, left no verbal account of their having been conscious of psychological portraiture's inherent paradox, but as our separate analyses of *The Boit Children* and *The Agnew Clinic* will show, a deep ambivalence is present. Through a series of codes and filters, the artist-surrogate within the painting is figured as both exploited and exploiter, victim and master, puppet and puppeteer.

At the same time that exploitation in interpersonal relationships, as well as in business and artistic enterprises, was hardening into an inescapable aspect of American life, at various levels public and private life was becoming unavoidably centralized. Springing forth in America from the 1850s onward, a massive, manifold thrust toward national consolidation was drastically altering the material landscape to be sure, but also the internal one as well. This consolidation took form politically in the blood-stained triumph of federal power over states' rights, geographically in the laying of railroad track from coast to coast, arriving at a uniform track gauge, and standardizing time zones and transport timetables, financially in the establishment of corporate legality, and demographically in the magnetic attraction to the cities.[30] Henry Adams notes that the building of America's transcontinental railway system, which symbolized for virtually everyone the most benevolent and thrilling side of the centralization under way, was a task such as

to need the energies of a generation, for it required all the new machinery to be created—capital, banks, mines, furnaces, shops, power-houses, technical knowledge, mechanical populations, together with a steady remodelling of social and political habits, ideas and intuitions to fit the new scale and suit the new conditions. The generation between 1865 and 1895 was already mortgaged to the railways, and no one knew it better than the generation itself.[31]

Thus not only artists and intellectuals of the time but many others as well recognized that profound changes were occurring within. While some tried to ignore or deny these changes, others, such as James, Eakins, and Sargent, explored them. Psychological portraiture can be regarded as a means by which certain artists and certain of their audience were attempting to take stock (consciously or unconsciously) of this altered internal landscape. What is interesting but not surprising is that the portraits implicitly reflected the prevailing ideology by suggesting that each individual portrayed is a consolidation of traits, a centralization of perceptions (James's "central consciousness"). What is even more interesting is that certain portraits— the three we have before us—seem to rebel *within themselves* against this principle of central organization, putting forth in both form and content an opposing principle of multiplicity, divergence, and anticlosure, Henry Adams' "chaos [that] often breeds life."

Herein lies the true difference between the portraits we will be examining and other American portraits of the late nineteenth century: they concern themselves with—they are almost manifestly "about"—internal warfare. By this I mean not the interior conflicts of the personalities portrayed but rather the centralization-decentralization issue and the many important personal and artistic questions which devolve from it. In this one sense, then, these internally divided works of art can be seen as replays of the nation's own great internal division, the Civil War. ("The War Between the States" puts it even better.)

That this cataclysmic fratricidal upheaval had a profound effect on the minds and imaginations of American artists and intellectuals, whether they fought in the war or not, is beyond question. As Henry Adams, who was abroad for the duration, later observed of the war's start: "The storm burst and rolled several hundred thousand young men like Henry Adams into the surf of a wild ocean, all helpless like himself, to be beaten about for four years by the waves of war."[32] Such an experience (or "non-experience" for some) naturally had an incalculable effect on artistic sensibilities. Ambrose Bierce, for example, marched with Sherman, had his head "broken like a walnut" at Kenesaw Mountain, then hastened to fight again. The result, according to Edmund Wilson, was that Bierce became "constantly obsessed with death."[33]

For the generation of young artists who came of age during the war and spent the next decade or so serving their artistic apprenticeships, it was not until the late 1870s or early 1880s that they were prepared to register in their art the profoundly altered and chastened sense of humanity that the immense upheaval had bestowed upon them. The Civil War and its bitter aftermath taught many American painters and writers—the Ambrose Bierces, to be sure, but others as well—enough about the fragility of life, the dubiousness of high rhetoric, and the duality of human nature so that, after a suitable period of gestation, these lessons had a dominating, if subterranean, effect on their artistic choices of content and form. As the human spirit had proven to be precarious, internally divided, and all too easily deceived by institutionalized values, this spirit needed to be described anew and creatively reinterpreted in a character-centered art: portraiture. But why does relatively little of the American high-art portraiture of the late nineteenth century, psychological though it may be (for the various reasons we have been examining), concern itself with the sort of internal formal conflicts described above? Why, if the Civil War produced such an indisputable effect on the artists of a certain generation, whether they saw action or not, does not all American portraiture of the postwar period play out within itself the centralization/anticentralization, formalization/antiformalization, authority/antiauthority conflict that can be seen propelling such works as *The Portrait of a Lady, The Boit Children,* and *The Agnew Clinic?*

Whatever the answer, surely it is significant that the artists of these three works did not serve. They developed a wholly different set of attitudes toward authority from that of artists like the realist writer John W. De Forest or the realist painter Winslow Homer, who had been actively involved in the war (De Forest a fighting soldier, Homer a magazine illustrator at the front). As both Edmund Wilson and George Fredrickson emphasize, service in the military or the hospitals and firsthand observation of death and dying instilled in artists and intellectuals a deep, perhaps too deep, respect for the toughminded giving and taking of orders. "The men who had been soldiers in the war generation give the impression of speaking with certainty; yet what seems to be certainty is often mere rigidity," writes Wilson. According to Fredrickson, "The military experience, which had taught the young patrician intellectuals to take pride in a life of service and to emphasize professional skills and professional objectives, had destroyed whatever respect they might have had for anti-institutional thinking. . . ."[34] Wilson brilliantly analyzes the prose of combat-tested, war-traumatized writers such as Ambrose Bierce—a man whose scarred inner life reached "an impasse, a numbness, a void, as if some psychological short circuit had blown out an emotional fuse"—and finds, in Bierce's case: "His writing— with its purged vocabulary, the brevity of the units in which it works and its cramped emotional range—is an art that can hardly breathe."[35]

Of both Henry Adams and Henry James, "writers who had not taken part in the war, though they were old enough at the time to serve, but who had undergone the strain of the war years," Wilson asserts, again with subtle discernment, that "the effect of the war may be traced in the development of . . . [certain] qualities—ambiguity, prolixity, irony—that reflect a kind of self-confidence, a diffidence and a mechanism of self-defense." Fredrickson likewise suggests that "the emphasis on an extremely heightened 'sensibility' in James' writing, the willingness to make much of what in conventional terms would seem to be a pitifully small amount of human experience, was encouraged by what he called 'my "relation to" the war.' " That relation, according to James, consisted of "seeing, sharing, envying, applauding, pitying, all from too far-off."[36]

Non-servers James, Eakins, and the decade-younger Sargent, each by the late 1870s undistractibly (some would say overly) dedicated to his self-perceived life's work of making art, seem to have found in this dedication an alternative to the obedient adherence to pragmatic orders that service had turned into the mainstay of their contemporaries' lives. Yet theirs was not simply a case of taking orders from art in lieu of orders from the army. Unlike the figures described by the passages above, they had not been hardened and hard-bitten into a "cramped emotional range," instilled with rigidity, or had the anti-institutionalism forever drilled out of them.

This is important, for what it means is that James, Eakins, and Sargent, unlike so many of the American male creative artists of their time, were "deprived" of the opportunity to confirm and define their "manhood" through the ritual of war. James appears to have been embarrassed by this, even ashamed: for the rest of his life, he felt compelled to attribute his not having served to an undocumented "obscure hurt" that he suffered at some time near the start of the war. As for Eakins, his biographer Gordon Hendricks states simply, "Why he did not [volunteer] is not known; perhaps he was just afraid of getting killed." Of course Sargent, born of a New England/Philadelphia family in Florence in 1856 and raised entirely in Europe, obviously was both too young and too distant from the American scene ever to have faced for himself the question of service during the war. But this was not the case with his father, FitzWilliam Sargent, who, having at the insistence of Mrs. Sargent forsaken a promising medical career in Philadelphia for an idle, nomadic life in Europe, was nonetheless, according to his son's biographer C. M. Mount, "a patriot in a very true sense, watching the fortunes of his country with a wistfulness one could not but notice, viewing the agony of the Civil War from afar, not without qualms of conscience. . . . Undoubtedly he felt some call of duty, all of it centered in the hope, indeed the plan, that one day his son would be the man he was not, to take his place." Yet it was all too soon clear that John was headed for neither of the two manly professions his father wished for him— medicine or the navy—but was instead destined for the "foreign mores and frills" of the art career his mother proposed.[37]

In this regard, then, these three portraitists, as well as the other two most interesting American portraitists of the time, Adams, who was an attaché in England during the war, and Howells, who was the American consul in Venice, differed from others of their generation in not having been *visibly* tested, initiated, made to show their mettle, or otherwise "masculinized" by military training—or even by civilian proximity to the action.[38] In a psychological sense they were unclean outsiders, gentiles uncircumcised by the war, to be excluded from full participation in the purportedly hale and hearty male universe that held sway in the postwar decades.[39]

In effect, certain male portraitists in the postwar era were partial— not by any means total, but partial—strangers to what has generally been characterized as the "male sphere," or the socially constituted and steadfastly exclusionary realm of rationalism, instrumentalism, pragmatism. To the extent that they were outsiders to this sphere, these male artists, by default, were members of the antithetically posed "female sphere": inasmuch as they were different from the "manly," they were classed with the "womanly." In Simone de Beauvoir's formulation, woman is "defined and differentiated with reference to man and not he with reference to her; she is the incidental, the inessential as opposed to the essential. He is the Subject, he is the Absolute—she is the Other."[40] It was this de facto participation in Otherliness, I believe, this having skipped over, or, in Sargent's case, been skipped over by, participation in a male-defining war and the male world view produced by it, that gave these portraitists a special vantage point not only on the modern character, but also on what is involved artistically in reproducing it. It may be helpful to embark on a speculation—

not having any firsthand reports, it can be no more than that—about the sexuality of the artists we are considering, but let us first refer to the most prominent and pressing sociosexual issue of their era: the so-called Woman Question. Insofar as Eakins, James, and Sargent each seem to have searched out and scrutinized in his portraiture the "modern woman" at a level of complexity and depth far beyond that attempted by other late nineteenth-century male American artists, the Woman Question is certainly relevant, but it becomes all the more so when we consider how it may have held up to these men a reflection of privately pressing questions they were forced to put to themselves.

"The Woman Question," according to Barbara Ehrenreich and Deirdre English, "was nothing less than the question of how women would survive, and what would become of them, in the modern world"—a world, that is, in which industrialism, urbanization, and feminism had thrown into disarray for many middle-class women of America and Northern Europe their time-honored sense of themselves and their place in the scheme of things. Of course not only women but also men were baffled by the new (post–Civil War) disruption of the traditional notion of womanhood. "At the same time that it arose as a subjective dilemma among women," write Ehrenreich and English, "the Woman Question entered the realm of public life as an 'issue' subject to the deliberations of scholars, statesmen and scientists."[41] Not only scholars, statesmen, and scientists sought out the meaning of "being a woman," but artists, portraitists foremost among them, did so as well.

Some artists reacted defensively, even hostilely, to "the new woman," as James himself did with his scathing antifeminist caricaturing in *The Bostonians* (1885), while others offered archly sentimental views of femininity and motherhood that perhaps the majority of American women found flattering, an ideal of which to be worthy.[42] Still other artists, including James at various notable points in his career, such as during the writing of *The Portrait,* and Eakins and Sargent on and off in their careers, made a concerted (though less than successful) effort to abolish the stereotypes and investigate what it was that caused women to be different from men, and individual women to be different from one another. By means of their art, these portraitists, whether male or female, sought some sense of what it was that women desired, and what it was they suffered.

There was reason now, as there had not been previously, to come to terms with feminine consciousness, feminine subjectivity—in short, with the female as subject. Here for some was important, even urgent, new territory to cover. In European fiction and painting, a tradition existed wherein portraiture centered upon exactly that territory, the internal feminine landscape, but for the American portraitist there was, during the course of the century, nothing native to back him or her up save for occasional efforts by a Hawthorne (*The Scarlet Letter*) or a Stuart (*Mrs. Richard Yates*). The success of James, Eakins, and Sargent in the "new" endeavor of exploring the feminine consciousness through portraiture is certainly debatable, but what does seem clear is that each of these three, whatever his personal and aesthetic motives may have been, devoted to this endeavor a major portion of his best energy and creative intelligence.

"Whatever his personal motives may have been. . . ." Repeatedly in our look at the social and historical factors leading to the psychological portraiture of the 1880s, we have caught glimpses of private, personal factors as well. Until now, though, we have pushed the personal to the side. The time has come to make it central. Since we are especially concerned with portraits that revolve around matters of sexual difference and feminine subjectivity, we shall focus our look at the artists' personal histories with the question of how they related to women both in general and in particular, and how they responded to the feminine within themselves.

One is struck by several common biographical elements in the lives of these artists, despite the many conspicuous differences.[43] All three men appear to have been emotionally devoted to their mothers and yet guiltily eager to become free, if not of them in particular, then of later substitute matriarchal figures such as aging unmarried sisters who were "difficult," society matrons who supported their artistic careers but not without incessant demands, and doting spinster friends who could at times be accused of lavishing unwanted affection. All three artists experienced close but probably nonsexual companionships with women to whom they were neither married nor, so far as we can ascertain, romantically involved. All three spent large portions of their adulthood living and working in female-dominated households or society. Finally, they all seem to have sought out the companionship of men at least in part as an antidote to their frequent and ongoing social, familial, and professional relationships with women. Stated thus, these similarities may seem too general to reveal anything of significance about the emotional histories of the three artists either as a group or as individuals. But inasmuch as no intimate diaries or written confessions of feeling have survived from them, we can do little more than glean what we can from salient biographical details, read between lines, and make guesses that we may choose to call educated or intuitive but which, in either case, are only guesses.[44]

My own guess, derived from reading between the lines of the biographies and the artworks, too, is that James, Eakins, and Sargent all repressed homoerotic tendencies that brought about in each an unusually close identification with women and, at the same time, a negative reaction to them. I do not mean to suggest that these three men were closet homosexuals or closet misogynists; what I am trying to say is that their personal lives were filled with a deep-seated, deeply hidden sexual ambivalence brought into relief by their lack of participation in the war and in the efficiently businesslike, often self-congratulatory, male culture that followed in its wake. It was this ambivalence out of which much of their art sprang and by which much of it is informed. The creation of the male and female character studies embodied in their portraiture may, it seems to me, be regarded as an unconscious device that enabled the artist to represent, and thus in a way experience and investigate, those physical, behavioral, emotional, and intellectual characteristics that attracted and repelled him in each sex. Portraiture was a testing out, an acting out in sublimated form of the artist's own sexuality. It was a means of declaring the otherwise indeclarable, a method of externalizing and temporarily reconciling that highly unstable, even volatile, sexual difference that was felt within but not understood.

How typical, how common to post–Civil War American artists—indeed, to post–Civil War American males in general—was this unarticulated sexual ambivalence? No one can say for sure. Yet one wonders if it was not at least present in vast numbers of men whose "masculinity" (despite appearances to the contrary) was less stable, less self-assured, than that of their fathers and grandfathers, thanks to the emotional atrocities and guilts of war, the insecurity of the Social Darwinist open market, the crisis in the authority of religion, and the ever-darkening cloud of feminism, which even at that point was threatening to burst stormily forth upon the home that had been a "haven in the heartless world."[45] However much Eakins', Sargent's, and James's psychosexual histories differed from one another and from those of other American men, what does seem clear is that at no prior time in the nation's history had males so much cause to worry about whether or not they were being male. One way to make sense of the new portraiture that arose in America at this time is to view it as a response to that worry. In portraits from all the periods in American history preceding as well as including the late nineteenth century, we can discern attempts by the artist to posit sexual nature as though by fiat: "Here is a man, here is a woman; this behavior is womanly, this trait manly"—hence the male subject who grasps a wooden staff, a telescope, or a quill pen, and the female subject who sits overlooking the garden with a bowl of ripe fruit on the table before her. Psychological portraiture this may sometimes have been, but in its determination to be neatly clear-cut and logical, to be efficient, orderly, authoritative, to treat its human subject as a well-defined *type,* this is a portraiture very different from that which we will be examining. In the works to be discussed, what comes across finally is not a fixed position on sexual nature but a sort of bottomless doubt.

James, Sargent, and Eakins gave over large portions of their artistic careers to the portrayal of women: women in general as well as in particular. What *The Portrait of a Lady, The Boit Children,* and *The Agnew Clinic* have in common historically is that each portrait marks its artist's first fully formed attempt to treat what he afterward treated, almost obsessively, over and over again: feminine subjectivity, sexual identity, the struggle of that which is male to know and possess that which is female, and, finally, relatedly, the problem of whether portraiture is an act of reproduction or, instead, of destruction.

READING PORTRAITS

There are two concepts or underlying organizational principles central to the "reading-work" that we are about to undertake. One is *duration,* and the other *relation.* Let us take stock of these.

Duration

Duration suggests time, chronological sequence. It has to do with the diachronic ordering of both *story,* that which involves the various internal elements of a portrait (such as character and event) and *discourse,* or the narrative means by which those elements are conveyed. Narrative theorists have made, accordingly, the distinction between the duration of story and that of its discourse.[46] The former is the amount of "real-world time" that would have been needed, were the story not fictional, for all its explicit and implicit occurrences to have transpired. The latter is the sequence by which the events of the story are narrated. A novel's characters, we might say, experience the story, while the reader experiences the discourse about that story. In the story of *Oedipus Rex,* parents are warned by an oracle, they attempt to rid themselves of their son, the son grows up, he kills his father, marries his mother, learns his identity, and ends the story by putting out his own eyes, in that order. In the discourse of *Oedipus Rex,* however, the order is different: a protagonist learns in one day of various events that occurred years earlier—and then ends by putting out his own eyes. Clearly there are two different types of duration here, which we shall call *story time* and *discourse time*. To these we might also add *reading time,* the duration of one's act of reading (or viewing) a portrait, and *writing time,* or the duration of the portraitist's original act of fabricating the portrait.[47] Writing time is not of great interest to us in the present context, but the other three types of duration are. The story time of *The Portrait of a Lady* is approximately fifteen years, for the actual story begins at the moment that Madame Merle bears Gilbert Osmond their illegitimate child, Pansy. The novel's discourse time, despite frequent ellipses (in which months at a time are eliminated), is approximately six years, for about that much time occurs between Isabel's first appearance at Gardencourt and her final return to Rome. The reading time of the book is six hundred pages or however long it takes to read those pages.

These related forms of duration exist, though much less apparently, with painted portraits as much as they do with those that are written. The discourse time of *The Agnew Clinic* or of *The Boit Children* may perhaps be no longer than a split second in the lives—the story time—of the protagonists, but the reading time of both paintings is a great deal longer than that. It is in fact a great deal more than can be experienced in a single viewing. Contrary to what many viewers wending their way through the lengthy corridors of a major art museum tend to believe, a painting is like a novel in demanding and deserving an extended, noninstantaneous reading. A painted portrait has an internal set of cues that provides, when attended to by the viewer, an aesthetic experience that moves through time and is therefore durative.

The discourse time of a classic realist novel is imparted in a straight-forward manner. The reader is expected to read page two after page one, page three after page two, and so on until arriving at the conclusion of the discourse. The painting's discourse is far less mechanically ordered. It does not inexorably force us to view one and only one shape or color combi-nation after the shape or color combination preceding. This is not to say that a painting's discourse is random: every painting has a sequential order, and thus duration, through which it "discourses" itself. But without a close phenomenological analysis it is impossible for us to be consciously aware of this order, so rapidly, in comparison to verbalization, does it transpire. From culture to culture, individual viewer to individual viewer, and viewing context to viewing context, the painting's discourse—its way of telling or announcing what it has to say—will vary, but what remains constant is that it does have a discourse, and that this discourse is durative: it is not instantaneous, but requires from the reader/viewer a span of time, a so-called reading time.[48]

In effect what this means is that the form of a representational painting is such as to call the implied viewer's attention first to one part of the canvas, then to another and another until finally it permits the release of that attention either by directing it away from the canvas (by means, for example, of a small open window or doorway painted into an upper corner, or by a secondary figure's off-canvas glance) or by allowing it to run down its energy (for example, by causing the viewer's attention to traverse the same areas of the canvas by the same visual routes over and over). Thus, though such is rarely realized, the reading of a painting, any painting, like the reading of a realist novel, requires a step-by-step cognitive or quasi-cognitive action on the part of the viewer. Furthermore, as with the novel, the order of those steps is preestablished. Again, this is not to claim that a painting dictates the sequence in which it is to be read with anything even approaching the sequential totalitarianism of the novel. But certain grooves or channels, certain directional cues and signals, certain "Go ahead" and "Do not pass" traffic markers are a part of every painted image and have the necessary task of moving the viewer's eye—attention, that is—accordingly. Though these signals are unable to push the reader's attention in only one "forward" direction, as is the tendency of the narrative in a novel, they do have the ability to guide that attention; and indeed, the stronger the painting's formal elements, the more irresistible is this guidance.[49]

It is relatively easy for us to think in words about a novel's discourse because it is uttered in words. The currency of exchange, as it were, remains basically the same. But to think in words about a painting's visually uttered discourse first requires that we cash in those images for a coinage acceptable to the verbally based intellect. This is a transaction I attempt to perform in chapters 2 and 3. I have made the effort to recreate retrospectively and in descriptive, analytic, *verbal* terms, the path of my eye as it read or saw or listened to the discourse of *The Agnew Clinic* and *The Boit Children*. These verbal treatments are heuristic models: they are not and never could be identical, one-to-one reproductions of the act of viewing, which is too swift, amorphous, and averbal to be translated and recreated without a portion of its original content being lost. But they can give us a worthwhile indication of how, internally and for the most part unknowingly, we do translate images and combinations of images into ideas whose words we may not know we are hearing but that have their profound influence on us nevertheless.[50]

Relation

Psychologists of visual perception such as Rudolf Arnheim and E. H. Gombrich have done much to show us how our "eye" (the term is a euphemism, a sort of anthropomorphism, a figure of speech) moves from one part of a painted or photographed image to another. Quite literally, they have mapped trails that the eye is likely to follow in certain basic visual configurations, regardless of whether these configurations occur in abstract or representational images.[51] Likewise, early cinematic theoreticians such as Sergei Eisenstein and V. I. Pudovkin have alerted us to ways in which two separate images, when placed side by side (that is, when attended to in sequence), produce within the viewer a third entity, an idea.[52]

By combining the perceptual psychologists' insights with those of the montage theorists, we become aware that the eye and mind edit the internal elements of any single image in much the same way that, jointly, they edit two separate images spliced together in a film. That is, they turn from one selected or focused-upon element within the image to another also within that image, and produce meaning along the way. Thus, looking at a painting is like watching a preedited movie: by relating disparate elements, we arrive at various conclusions about ourselves, society, and the physical world. These are conclusions that largely remain submerged and unacknowledged, but they can be decisive in the way we go about leading our lives. The conclusions at which we arrive are determined by those relationships to which we attended, and these are in turn decreed to a great extent by the image's internal editing cues, themselves determined by the cultural encoding of visual form—an encoding upon which any given society's permutations have had their formative effect. The circularity of this argument mirrors the circularity of life imitating art imitating life.[53]

To give the fullest possible reading of a painting, we must try to tease out all the signifying relationships we can discover between the image's various constituent elements. This means covering the entire field of the painting with a quick eye, sewing together spatially disparate parts with the thread of our vision; it means mentally juxtaposing the square shape in the upper left-hand corner against the bright orange patch that seems to float toward the center, and then relate the cumulative effect of these newly paired entities to the effect created by a red line's proximity to one that is white. It is only upon having proceeded to scrutinize the work in such a manner—that is, in terms of its formal relationships—that the critic is properly prepared to move outward from there toward a study of the social and cultural relationships initiated and designated by the text. It is only at that point that the critic achieves the opportunity to become, as Bryan Wolf has put it, "a storyteller, a translator if you will, whose role is complementary to that of the historian and whose work begins where the latter's traditionally leaves off." It is then that the critic is qualified to fulfill "his task, perhaps his vocation, to trace through the labyrinthine turnings of the texts he investigates that narrative thread which binds the writer to his culture and the reader to both."⁵⁴

Reading a novel is also relational in terms of the reader's having to juxtapose disparate elements within memory and consciousness, only in this case the elements (characters, settings, events) to be juxtaposed are, in their initial presentation in the text, separated temporally, not spatially. Just as it is the traditional novelist's role to reveal his protagonist by placing her in a variety of contexts and situations and against a variety of secondary characters, but always in a forward-moving chronological sequence, it is the reader's responsibility to reshuffle the deck, holding up an early situation to a late one, or measuring together two characters who never share the same narrative space, or cross-examining one narrational description of the protagonist with another. Not only is it the reader's responsibility to relate disparate story-level elements to each other, but also to relate those elements to various discourse-level elements such as the narrative's structure, the narrator's diction, the manner in which direct quotation is rendered, and so forth.⁵⁵

This is akin to the sense of relation that is necessary for an effective reading of a painting. Chapter 4 is an attempt to read James's *Portrait* with a "relationality" similar to that applied in chapters 2 and 3 to the two painted portraits. A major difference is, however, that with the paintings I have emphasized the durative, sequential aspect of their discourse, while with the novel I have so de-emphasized duration of discourse that to a large extent I treat it as synchronic, occurring all at once, as is usually considered to be the case with paintings but not with novels.

Yet over and against this attempted methodological consistency, I have read each portrait as individually, as idiosyncratically, as the work demanded—on its own terms, rather than in terms carried over from the reading of the other portraits. To the extent that a portrait is a testament to individuality, it succeeds best when showing how its protagonist is unique. It does this by following the peculiar twists and turns of character and appearance, delineating that which distinguishes the protagonist from that which does not. Such a portrait pinpoints particularity and difference amid the intersection of general types. The readings that follow are efforts to particularize these portraits even as they particularize their subjects. Thus each chapter constitutes a critical portrait of a portrait. Although all three readings have much in common, they cannot and should not be expected to resemble each other any more closely than *The Portrait of a Lady* resembles *The Agnew Clinic* or than *The Agnew Clinic* resembles *The Boit Children*.

Returning to America after a six-year absence, Henry James wrote in his notebook of a need to reimmerse himself in his family and the "sense of consequences that these relations entail. Such relations, such consequences, are a part of one's life, and the best life, the most complete, is the one that takes full account of such things."[56] So too is the strongest artistic portraiture that which takes into full account all the relationships by which its subject can be conveyed. And so too is the strongest critical reading of a portrait that which takes the fullest possible account not only of the formal and thematic relationships within, but also those relationships that tie the portrait to the portraitist, to his time and place, and ultimately to our own.

CHAPTER TWO

The Agnew Clinic

T HE AGNEW CLINIC (fig. 1) today hangs high on a wall in the foyer of the University of Pennsylvania Medical School. The painting cannot be taken in all at once; approximately six feet high by eleven feet long, it is exceptionally large. What first attracts the eye is the white-clad figure standing in isolation in the foreground, left of center. This is Dr. D. Hayes Agnew, for whom the painting was named and of whose surgical clinic it purports to be a record.

If Agnew comes first to our attention, it is because of the compositional and coloristic isolation in which he is poised. His figure is a white column set off against the dark background of seated individuals clustered together and somberly dressed. Agnew, particularly his gleaming brow, seems to be lit by an overhead spotlight, not shown, which singles him out all the more from the shadowed figures behind. Moreover, his form and features are rendered with sharp focus, while theirs are not.

In addition to these reasons, there are several others why our eye is immediately pulled his way. The sequence in which I name these reasons is not, however, meant to suggest their order of priority or any sort of temporal order of occurrence to the viewer, because, even if we only become cognizant of them one by one, they all contribute simultaneously to a single effect: the initial directing of our visual apparatus to the linear and coloristic form—or, more accurately, configuration of forms—designated as "Dr. Agnew." The railed wooden frame of the operating pit swoops around

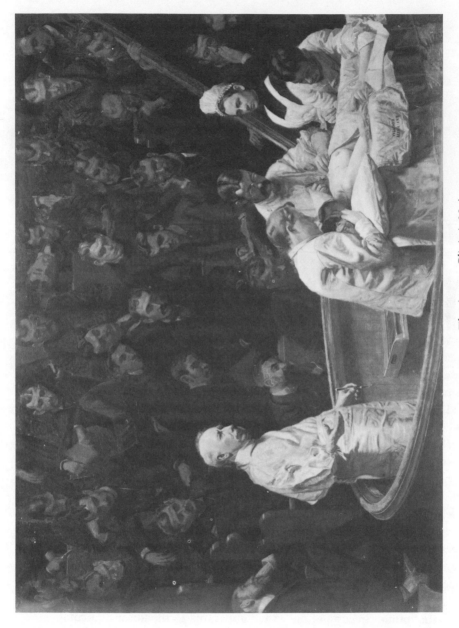

1. THOMAS EAKINS, *The Agnew Clinic* (1889).

behind and then in front of him, redoubling his isolation from the crowd, as well as corralling our attention back onto him before it can begin to stray. In this regard, the curving wooden structure behaves in a similar fashion to the convex, open-paged tome that serves as a *répoussoir* for the teacher holding forth in Rembrandt's well-known *Anatomy Lesson of Dr. Tulp* (1632; fig. 2). From the upper left corner of *The Agnew Clinic*, parallel diagonals thrust at the surgeon. The bottom diagonal is created by the polished and gleaming surfaces of the two ornate benchposts. The fleur-de-lis shape of these benchposts, the apparent light upon them, and their smooth, tactile surface attracts, yet at the same time pushes us along rapidly toward that first visual stopping point: the doctor. The other parallel diagonal is suggested by three heads, a collar, a cuff, and one or two hands that, like the descending benchposts, exert upon our eye a downward pressure. Whereas the line implied by the benchposts stretches visually across Agnew's elbow and along his forearm to his open, extended hand, the second diagonal, itself formed by a series of heads, culminates abruptly in Agnew's head. In fact, this sight line can be traced diagonally downward from the starched collar of the man in the top left corner, through the heel of his hand, down the part in the next man's hair, along the upper ridge of the nose belonging to the man below him, and then directly into the gaping ear cavity of Agnew, as though this, more than anything else, were the focal point of our gaze.

The postures of the bodies immediately behind Agnew make them appear to be exploding away from each other, as if the doctor were some sort of projectile ripping upward into their space—a rocket cleaving the heavens, a vessel parting the waves, a phallic object penetrating a region dark and womblike. But more about that later.

Our eye leaps in Agnew's direction also because of his odd posture—a sort of backing off, backing away, that invites us to come fill the space he vacates—and because of the open hand, which almost seems to seek ours, as though to take hold of us and draw us in (lest we be reluctant?). The scalpel, held delicately in his other hand, seems cold and sharp. A potentially dangerous instrument, even lethal, it serves visually and psychologically as a lightning rod, attracting a portion of our gaze and conducting it, like so much electricity, into Agnew. Or does the reverse occur: do the sight lines that thrust at the man, the index finger of his extended right hand, and the slope of his upper body all converge so as to direct us down into that narrow rigid instrument of manifold suggestiveness? Agnew's operating apron and his surgeon's smock, both replete with deep, engulfing folds, help draw our eye to his form, as does the smattering of red that

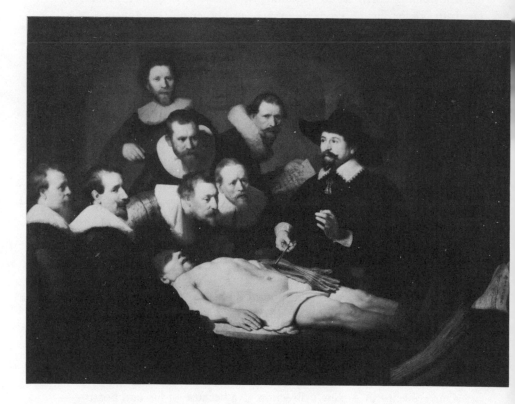

2. REMBRANDT VAN RIJN, *The Anatomy Lesson of Dr. Tulp* (1632).

stands out upon the white. The contrast beckons the eye even before the mind realizes that what it is seeing is (a representation of) human blood.

Composition, lighting, focus, texture, color, posture, gesture, costume, and prop are thus all reasons that the viewer of *The Agnew Clinic* looks initially at Dr. Agnew. If one accepts Arnheim's contention that viewers generally focus on the left portion of a canvas before the right, then a further reason is provided for our focusing first upon Agnew.[1] There is a nonvisual reason as well: for the viewer who possesses prior knowledge that this painting was intended as the portrait of a particular individual, the initial activity in looking at the work will be to locate that privileged person among all those others who serve as, to use James's term, appurtenances. Yet despite these various coercives, the look elicited from us does not linger. The pull to the other half of the canvas is too strong, too coercive in its own right. In speaking of "the other half," by the way, I am being precise. Longitudinally, the composition is bisected by a line that, if drawn, would shoot straight down from the left ear of the man seated top center, split the *v* in the vest of the individual two rows below, and catch the bottom hem of the white jacket of the surgeon whose back is to Agnew.

The mass of human forms rising in a pyramid from the right-hand base of the painting tears our eye away from Agnew toward this half of the composition. Whereas before the eye was attracted by the isolation of the single figure, now it is drawn by what at first appears to be a cluttered, inchoate mass of figures, the very opposite of Agnew's distinguished solitude. While initially the eye was brought to Agnew because of his manifest difference, now it is drawn away by clutter, confusion, entanglement: by the challenge or need to sort things out, dispelling the visual dissonance, selectively categorizing and marking difference here where it is less immediately evident.

There are numerous other reasons for our eye to be pulled toward this grouping. There is the matter of weight: this cluster of forms, because of its density, unequaled by any other region of the composition, exerts what amounts to a visual force of gravity. Agnew is simply outweighed. The overhead lighting, its source not in view, is as strong on these figures as on Agnew, and the focus as sharp. Therefore, while the lighting may have helped draw our eye to him initially, an instant later it has ceased to cede him privilege. The white dome of his head is counterbalanced by the nurse's smooth oval face and her cap, which rises upward like an oven-baked muffin. Her white starched apron, set off against a severe black gown, equals in visual interest his arresting garb, which makes him vaguely reminiscent of a village butcher (the apron), a seventeenth-century swashbuckler (the billowing sleeve), a clergyman (the collar), and an Athenian philosopher or Hebrew lawgiver (the classical drapery).

From the upper right corner, the wooden handrail thrusts downward in a compositional echo of the parallel diagonals on the opposite side. This diagonal is explicit; the others were only suggested by a sort of visual syncopation. Whereas the lower diagonal on the left culminated in Agnew's crooked arm, and the upper in the cavity of his ear, the right side diagonal transects the crooked arm of one of the assisting doctors and points through it directly into what can eventually be deduced as a cavity bored in the chest of an anesthetized patient.

While Agnew's reared-back posture and his extended right hand helped to draw us into the left half, his half, of the picture, the effect is now duplicated by two compositional elements in the right half. Four figures enclose the patient in an open curve that visually invites us to come within. On the picture plane, the four figures comprise a compositional triangle that possesses a base but lacks an apex. There is an individual, an onlooker, who might have supplied the top to this triangle, but he is prevented from doing so because he is seated too high, dressed too darkly, and tilted too much to the side. There are therefore only two ways by which we can fill this visual ellipsis—and our scopic compulsions are such that fill it we must. Either we mentally move Agnew over and up so that his head fills the space, which is not inappropriate given his professional preeminence, or we eradicate the absence with our quick, penetrating stare. Probably both: unconscious of what we are doing, we "complete" the triangle with a mental transfer of Agnew from left to right (propelling him there with the assistance of that slingshot-like, paraboloid wooden dock in which he is slung), and since that in itself is not sufficient, we attempt to plug up the troublesome void with our own—some would say phallic—gaze.

Sooner or later the eye is able to discern who it is that these people are operating upon. It is a naked woman horizontally reclined and covered toe to breast by a hospital sheet (fig. 3). Her breast is the first part of her anatomy to define itself for us and, in so doing, to alert us that a human body is laid out here, and a female one at that. There are several reasons why the breast, especially the nipple, now commands our gaze. One's eye is invariably attracted to any pinpoint of color, density, or texture that appears to reside upon a smooth neutral field, as is the case here. Also, the instant we recognize this as a female breast, interest is intensified. Regardless of our gender, we cannot but experience shock or excitement upon perceiving this intimate part of anatomy so unabashedly revealed, and in front of so many raptly attentive, fully clothed men.

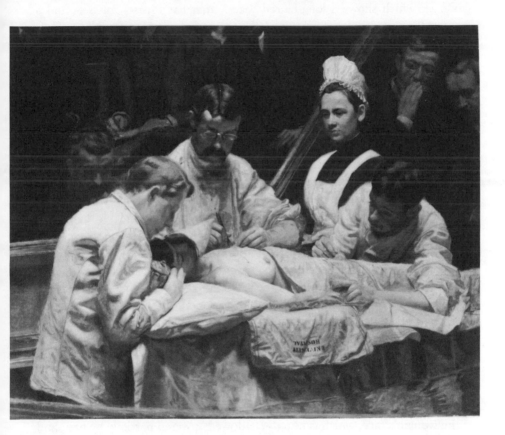

3. *The Agnew Clinic* (detail).

A pair of female breasts looks like a pair of eyes. The metaphor suggests itself naturally, given the geometric similarities: dark rounded forms concentrated in the center of substantially lighter rounded forms.[2] For a picture worth a thousand words, see René Magritte's illustration *The Rape* (1934; fig. 4), which shows a long-haired "face" that has breasts for eyes and a vulva for a mouth. In *The Agnew Clinic,* the single breast resembles a single eye particularly because of the eyelid-like folds formed by the top edge of the patient's arm, the hem of the sheet, and the contours of the bosom itself. Thus, if this woman's breast resembles an eye, it is an eye turned back at us. Were it to look any more like an eye, our gaze might be repelled rather than attracted. As is so often the case for most of us, our uninvited stare ricochets away the instant it is met by the eyes at which we had surreptitiously been gazing. Here, however, the breast is enough of an eye to increase our interest without reprimanding or warding off our attention.

Not only does this bosom suggest a human eye, but also a bull's-eye—the term used to denote the center of a target. The nipple occupies the exact center of the semicircle or open curve described earlier; it is the nodule in the midst of the gap that our gaze has sought to penetrate. If we were to drop a line from the nipple to the bottom edge of the canvas and use this as a radius with which to trace a circle on the picture plane, its arcs would travel close to or through the crown of each attending physician but just beneath the eye of the woman who looks on, linking her not with the doctors but with the observers in the gallery. Thus the nipple is a bull's-eye not only for the "target area" that recedes into the picture plane, but also for the one that stretches across part of its surface. The gaze—our visual shaft—is attracted accordingly.

Other elements here also attract. The eye observes the vivid splatter of blood on the upper chest. It tries, and fails, to take an accurate reading of the woman's face, which is heavily shadowed, covered partially by hair, and tilted away from us. The surgeon in the middle uses a steel tool to probe, tweeze, or rake, and this intrigues or appalls us even more than Agnew's cold sharp scalpel, because whereas that instrument was suspended in mid-air, this one tears into human flesh. In a sense, this physician is Agnew's double, for not only does he wield a visually similar instrument held at almost the same angle, but he too wears a chin-high smock similarly stained with blood, is of the same height, and displays an almost identical walrus-style moustache, different only in its color.

Now, if not sooner, the eye departs from this sector of the painting. It begins to scan the background, the figure-packed region which falls straight down behind the physicians like a painted theater curtain or an illusionistic

4. RENÉ MAGRITTE, *The Rape* (1934).

opera scrim. Probably the initial focal point of this human backdrop is the individual who occupies the center of the entire composition. Let us call him Medical Student A (fig. 5). From the title of the painting as well as from its immediately legible iconography, we discern at once that these young men are medical students or interns or perhaps, in the instance of the older-appearing spectators, full-fledged doctors who have come to the clinic for further instruction.

The reason we focus on A is not simply that he is seated in the center. His is the only fully frontal depiction contained within this large group portrait; his brow is highlighted; his hands are inserted into his pockets in a casual, almost insouciant manner—a gesture that provides vivid contrast to the studious intensity of the other figures. Two further reasons can be advanced to account for his visual appeal. One is that there is a clearing around his figure. A similar situation obtains around Agnew, but while in the doctor's case the bodies twist away, in A's they twist inward. It is as though Agnew were bracketed by a sort of open parenthesis, and A by one that is closed:)Agnew(versus (A).

The second reason has to do with the moustache worn by A. It droops downward around his mouth in a manner exactly like the other two moustaches we have already noted, and, aside from these, is decidedly unlike any of the other combinations of facial hair shown in the painting.

The eye passes from A to the others around him in the fraction of a moment. We scan the backdrop of which he is a part in an effort to make sense of it. Probably at no point does the viewer actually quantify this large grouping, so let us do so now. The men are seated in five tiers. Though the backdrop itself appears to be flat, the benches seem to curve around with the rail of the operating pit below. Four figures, one behind the other, are crouched in a right-hand aisle, squeezing themselves in, presumably because all the seats in the amphitheater have been taken. On the right, the wooden handrail separates these spectators from a wedge of space within which two other men are located. To the left are the two ornate benchposts, and seated on the far side of them is a single figure, his elbow at rest on a raised knee and his back squared off against the edge of the painting. In the top tier are five or six spectators, discernible by their hands or waists only, except for one whose face is visible because he is resting it on someone else's knee as though to acquire a better view of the proceedings below. Stretched out horizontally, this figure resonates with—or perhaps playfully mocks—the horizontal and helpless figure of the patient.

There are two men in the bottom row. (I am not counting the fellow across the aisle, behind Agnew's back, because he is apart from the back-

5. *The Agnew Clinic* (detail).

drop.) The next row contains five figures, the third of whom is Medical Student A, with whose lower legs Eakins has played an illusionistic trick: they appear to be draped over the seat-back of the row in front, and yet the appearance of depth necessary for that to occur realistically has not been granted. By this and similar hidden devices, Eakins produces the effect of flatness for the human backdrop without letting on that he is doing so. This trick was performed to achieve the formal goal of a flat, rhythmic surface; to achieve the realist goal of verism, it had to be kept a secret.

The next level up contains eight individuals, and the one above that nine, if we include the horizontal student, even though his face is aligned with the faces a level down. Thus, in ascending order, the groupings in this central seating area are, numerically, two, five, eight, and nine: a sort of inverse pyramid that lacks a point. The same, we recall, was the case with the "pyramid" of surgeons and nurse. The two truncated pyramids interlock on the planar surface of the painting, with the one that is smaller and rightside up superimposed over the larger, inverted one. In purely formal (that is, nonprogrammatic) terms, this overlapping of one form by its inverse reduction cements the front of the scene with the back. The bond is strongest at the point at which the observer lowest down and farthest forward edges his chin into the space vacated by the bent-forward neck of the physician in front of him. His visible arm and shoulder, incidentally, are curved in almost perfect harmony with the spine and shoulder of the physician, further strengthening the formal bond. A programmatic interpretation of this inversion of forms would perhaps find here a sign of these two groups being reversed in function and yet being, at the same time, inextricably bound to each other, a relationship similar to that of passive audience and active performer; of reader and writer; of viewer and artist.

In the gallery, then (I am not counting those two observers at the extreme right, beneath the handrail, but am including the lone figure who is seated off to the left), there are precisely twenty-five male spectators whose faces can be discerned, plus hands, legs, or arms belonging to an additional five or six. Collectively, these twenty-five to thirty individuals are a compendium of poses and postures for the clothed and seated male form. There is the diversity here and the delight in observation that one finds in the pages of Leonardo's notebooks, or in other paintings such as Eakins' own *Swimming Hole* (1883), Thomas Anshutz's *Ironworkers— Noontime* (1880/81) and, a generation later, George Bellows' *Riverfront, No. 1* (1915), as well as the motion photographs of both Eakins and his contemporary, Eadweard Muybridge.[3] Wholly apart from whatever programmatic content or realist intentions this curtain of men may suggest, the curtain itself affords the eye a particular type of visual pleasure.

This pleasure results from what amounts to a frolic for the eye through or across the multiformity of postures and positions, which is the plastic equivalent of the seemingly inexhaustible melodic invention of baroque music. Heads lean this way and that, shoulders tilt forward or back, spines are curved or rigid, hands are up or down (one hand, in the act of inscribing initials into the back of an upper row bench, clasps a penknife in a witty echo, even a parody, of Agnew with his scalpel), knees are pressed together or spread apart, hair is thick or thin, and faces bearded, mustachioed, or clean shaven, all in varying combinations. I count four pair of eyeglasses in this curtain of men, thirty-four ears, twenty-seven earlobes, forty-eight eye sockets, twenty hands, a mere five wrists, about seven knees, and a full two dozen starched collars. Although the viewer's eye does not literally count these items as I have just done, it does, I contend, flicker about at high speeds from one figure to the next, even one body part to the next, mildly intoxicated by the repetition, variation, and superabundance of cadenced form.

Yet it is not this rhythmic multiformity alone that endows the backdrop with its visual appeal. The multiformity is particularly fascinating to us because it plays off, in a sort of visual counterpoint, against a specific uniformity, one that is engendered by the monochromatic dark hue and monotonous styling of the men's suits, the sameness of their flesh tones, the brownish red of the benches seen behind and between them, their arithmetically ordered division into rows, the flattening effect of the hierarchical composition, and the everywhere downward cast of their eyes. Thus the comparison to baroque music is all the more apt: in both cases, local variation is played off in rhythmic fashion against universal or generic similarity.[4]

We have now described in some detail the three initial fields of visual interest in this composition. These are Dr. Agnew to the left, the operating frieze to the right, and the curtain of spectators behind. This leaves four areas about which nothing has yet been said. Three of these we can characterize as unoccupied space: (1) the lower left foreground; (2) the base of the operating table at the right; and (3) the midground space between Agnew and the physician who is huddled over the head of the patient. Space 1 is bounded by the concentric arcs of the lowest bench seat and railing of the operating pit. A single hand is inserted at the edge of this space. Space 2, flat in appearance, is rendered with gestural, painterly brushstrokes, and is labeled by two words that, within the fiction of the painting, are block-lettered onto the institutional linen draped over the operating table and appear upside down. Were the painting to be inverted, the words would clearly read "UNIVERSITY HOSPITAL." Space 3 is bounded above and below by the railing, to the left by Agnew's apron, and to the right by the rear edge of the attending physician's operating jacket. Dr. Agnew's scalpel-wielding left hand dips into this space. A wooden tray arrayed with medical instruments projects into the space laterally.

The fourth area is that pie wedge formed by the handrail of the am-phitheater and the right edge of the canvas. It is occupied by two figures, one partially covered by the nurse before him. The other individual is half in the picture and half out; his full-frontal torso is sliced down the middle by the edge of the canvas, as is the back half of his swiveled head. Those familiar with Thomas Eakins' appearance in middle age will recognize him in this figure. According to Lloyd Goodrich it was painted by the artist's wife, Susan MacDowell Eakins, herself an accomplished painter.[5] At this point, let us avoid referring to him as "Eakins" or "the artist," in order to maintain a distinction between what we see on the canvas and what we know about it by way of exterior information. Thus, the man with the spectacles is whispering to the man who is visually bisected. Although this second man appears to be hearing the words of the first, he lacks visible ears. There is only one other figure in this entire painting, one other out of the two and a half dozen depicted, who has not been painted with at least one ear. This is the woman on the operating table—the patient who has been sliced down the middle not only visually, but, by her doctor's surgical blade, also literally.

During the course of our phenomenological description of *The Agnew Clinic,* we have remarked upon color only in passing. Likewise, our dis-cussion of the appearance of depth in the work has been unsystematic. Now, however, having exhaustively detailed the compositional elements in terms of their linearity, mass, deployment, and iconography, we must con-clude this descriptive tour with attention to both color and depth. These two elements are inseparable here; perhaps they are in any oil painting. As is richly demonstrated by the paintings of Eakins' contemporary, Paul Cé-zanne, depth can be suggested as much by the juxtaposition of color planes as by perspectival composition. In this painting, where the perspective sig-nals are minimal—the sight lines and rhythm cues lead the eye up, down, and across the picture plane much more than "within"—it is the color values that indicate the viewer's hypothetical proximity to the figures por-trayed.

The dark forms seem to recede while the brighter ones stand forth. These latter figures are clothed in brilliant, eye-catching white, their flesh is pink and fair, and the spotlighting endows each of them with radiant luminescence. The dark figures of the medical observers are drably dressed, obscurely lit, and cramped together upon wooden benches whose warm reddish glow is more prominent visually than are the observers themselves.

What appears to be the nearest spot to us, the viewer, is the section of railing that transects the bottom edge of the canvas before disappearing from sight. With this as our starting point, we can reconstruct the path of the eye as it moves into the composition. That path seems to take us from the near doctor in the foreground across the body of the patient to the doctor bent over her legs, then continues in a zigzag to the surgeon, the nurse, the observers in the front row of the spectators' gallery, and from there to the seemingly flat human curtain. Dr. Agnew and the patient appear to be parallel, spatially centered within their arcs of the operating pit, and they both offer to our eye equal amounts of brightly lit, pinkish flesh: his atop his head, hers along her body.

Although the human curtain appears to be flat, the curved benches make us feel that the gallery is sweeping around the operating pit in a circular or semicircular fashion. This gives us the sense that we, also spectators of the scene, are seated in the gallery on a curving bench. We are the continuation of these observers; thanks to the depiction of curvature, we find ourselves included in the painting. Through a visual metonymy, we are inscribed within it. The technique of making us feel the immediacy of a scene by means of curving structures that sweep toward us was employed with great success by Eakins' teacher, Jean-Léon Gérôme, in his *Thumbs Down! (Pollice Verso)* (c. 1859; fig. 6), and other works similarly aimed at pulling the viewer into the scene—or pulling the scene toward the viewer.

If we are located in the gallery overlooking this medical event, precisely where are we "seated"? Judging from the horizontal and vertical angles accorded us, we are located in the second row, directly across from Medical Student A, the young man with his hands in his pockets. In a sense he is a mirror image, *our* mirror image: what we see when looking directly at a smooth highly polished flat surface, which in this case happens to be dark. "Through a glass darkly," we are perhaps looking at ourselves when we look at him.

In the same way as we perceive the backdrop across from us to be alternately flat or curved, depending upon the manner in which we read it, we can also feel ourselves to be below the painting (which, given the location of the artifact as it is hung today, is literally the case) and yet still

6. JEAN-LÉON GÉRÔME, *Thumbs Down! (Pollice Verso)* (c. 1859).

experience a sense of being on its level. Thus, our eyes may seem to us to be directly across from A's eyes. We might therefore suspect that his eyes are positioned at the center of the work. This, however, is not true. Instead they are situated above the center of the composition. So is the spot where his heart would be located. So is the pit of his stomach. Surprisingly, dead center of the painting is a spot immediately above the joining together of his two pocketed hands, at about the likely location of the tip of an upright and fully extended penis. This covered-over male reproductive organ, the magic wand of male desire, is firmly, fixedly, positioned at the literal center, the very heart of the artistic reproduction/representation known as *The Agnew Clinic*.

* * *

In my description of the painting I have moved spatially, first through the left half of the image, then the right, then onto the inverted pyramid, and, finally, into miscellaneous patches in the foreground and midground. My descriptive analysis produced a narrative precinct by precinct; "chapter by chapter" in literary terms. We might instead have scanned the image as a television screen is beamed electronically, or as a page of print is read: left to right, line after line in a downward sequence from top to bottom. We could have worked from the bottom of the composition to the top, or started at the far right and traversed in a series of vertical strokes to the left. A spiral out from the center would have been possible, or we might have chosen first to classify the painting's horizontals, then its verticals, then its diagonals. We might have begun by referring to the oval shapes on the canvas, then the full circles, then the squares. Less geometrically inclined, we might have classified the painting first by distinguishing between animate and inanimate objects represented, and then within each of these categories have made further classifications by dividing the animate figures by their apparent age, sex, or facial direction, while dividing the inanimate forms by their size, density, and dramatic function. This is only a sampling of many conceivable types of classification we could have undertaken. Any one of these alternatives would have resulted in our noting data otherwise missed and missing data otherwise noted. Consequently the conclusions we would have drawn in regard to the work as a whole would in some fashion, large or small, have differed from the conclusions we are about to draw, even though the chosen method of classification (a sequential read-through attempting to reconstruct the eye's initial journey) is neither more nor less neutral than any of the modes of classification mentioned above.

To divide the composition into sectors that we allege are looked upon one at a time is, in a sense, to transform the painting into a motion picture. In our lengthy phenomenological description we have edited the painting so that we see, first, a shot of Dr. Agnew, then a shot (from the same camera angle) of the operating group, followed by a loose, wandering pan through the gallery of spectators going back to shots of Agnew and the operating group interlaced with detail shots of the hand in the lower left corner, the instrument tray, the inverted words UNIVERSITY HOSPITAL, the two men under the handrail, and so forth. Binding together the medium shot of Agnew with the "five-shot" of the operating group are various inserts: close-ups of Agnew's face; of his hands; of the patient's breast; of the nurse's head. We might therefore speak of the one global image, *The Agnew Clinic,* as having its own internal montage, a "cutting within the frame."

The ideological power of montage is that it communicates ideas through a visual dialectic, a predetermined juxtaposition of discrete images that persuasively presents an argument to the viewer without the viewer being fully aware of it. To subvert ideology, the critic of film seeks to make the viewer conscious of how montage, during any particular sequence, urges its point. The critic must describe the montage (always unsatisfactorily, given the intrinsic differences between written language and cinema) and its ideological effect on the spectator. Having claimed that *The Agnew Clinic* guides the eye in a manner analogous to filmic montage, I shall proceed to trace the various ideas or significations that this montage engenders.

*   *   *

A literal, material description of *The Agnew Clinic* might go something like this: "*The Agnew Clinic* is stretched and gessoed canvas, x inches wide, y inches long, upon which various pigments of oil paint have been applied and now are dry." Such a description, though, is of scant value apart from making a warehouse inventory. Another literal but perhaps more helpful description might assert: "*The Agnew Clinic* is an oil painting, nearly twice as long as it is high, in which an off-white vertical on the left rises up from the bottom edge two-thirds of the way to the top, and is counterbalanced on the right by a pyramidal (though truncated) white, pink, and gray mass that also appears to rise up from the bottom edge. Behind these foreground shapes is a background that joins one side of the canvas to the other, and upon which darkly painted (red, brown, gray) forms are rhythmically deployed."

This second description, although in one regard literal, may nevertheless seem abstract, like the description of an abstract expressionist painting. Here, then, is a third literal description:

Dressed in white surgical costume, like his assistants, and holding his scalpel in his left hand (he was ambidextrous), Dr. Agnew is talking to the class about the operation he has just performed, for cancer of the breast, while his assistant Dr. Joseph White . . . applies a dressing to the wound, Dr. Joseph Leidy II holds a sponge to wipe the blood, and the anaesthetist, Dr. Ellwood R. Kirby, stands at the patient's head. In the entrance to the amphitheater, at the extreme right, appears the artist himself (painted by Mrs. Eakins); Dr. Fred H. Milliken is whispering to him. The students, dressed in dark street clothes, are all portraits.[6]

This is from Lloyd Goodrich's 1933 catalogue raisonné of Eakins' works. Whereas the first brief description above was literal in terms of the material object, and the second brief description was literal in terms of the form and color rendered upon its surface, Goodrich's description concerns itself exclusively with the painting's mimetic content—its alleged one-to-one correspondence with particular individuals who had a real-life historical existence.[7] We thus can see that there are several ways in which *The Agnew Clinic* can be read literally.

To read it figuratively, however, there are virtually endless possibilities. To read the work "figuratively" is to read it—whether at the level of visual form or at the level of representation, or combining the two—as a complex of tropes and metaphors that, depending upon how they are mentally assembled by the viewer, can have a variety of significations. By noting how the constituent formal and representational elements of this painting relate to one another, we will begin to discern thematic coherencies, and incoherencies, emerging from the whole.

* * *

On the first or most apparent figurative level we see before us an aged physician stepping back from a medical dissection in order to lecture on some fine point of surgery or anatomy, perhaps even to launch from there into a philosophical rumination on the healing profession and its relation to life, death, and the human condition (fig. 7). He might even postulate, in the phrase of a well-known twentieth-century medical writer, "the exact location of the soul."[8]

More likely, though, he speaks of nothing so potentially rousing, for

7. *The Agnew Clinic* (detail).

there is a curious detachment here. The assistants are intent upon performing their job, the students are either observing the operation or are lost in thought, and Agnew, his gaze sliding down the sloped ridge of his nose to and beyond his hands and then finally slipping below the picture plane, is so disconnected from all the others that the words he utters can only be addressed to the past, or to posterity, or to himself. (Unless his gaze is connected by means of symmetry to the gaze of the nurse, his opposite number compositionally.) Indeed, there is no trace of speech. This cannot be attributed to a failing of the medium; over on the far right the gentleman with the upraised hand is clearly whispering to the man without ears who leans his head to the side as though carefully listening. There, we *hear* the rustle of words, probably words of explanation or translation, because we see indication of their delivery and reception. Yet in the "shot" of Dr. Agnew no provision is made for the sound of speech; his lips are not parted, the muscles of his neck are hidden, and the posture of his upper body does not reveal any rapid intake or expulsion of the oxygen physically necessary in order to speak.

A viewer conversant with the career of Thomas Eakins will surely recognize here one more attempt by the painter to catch or fix or transfix a physical action at its apex: the point that is neither start nor finish but is instead precisely balanced between the two. Notable Eakins works of this nature include *John Biglin in a Single Scull* (1874) where Biglin is primed at the instant of energy release, *The Swimming Hole,* with its diver midway between earth and water, and *Salutat* (1898). In *Salutat,* the figure to the right of the wrestler is applauding: at the beginning of any one clap in a sequence the hands are pressed together, and at the end of it they are again pressed together, ready to begin anew, but here they are separated at the distal point of the cycle. Looking over some watercolors of Eakins', his mentor Gérôme advised: "There is in all prolonged gestures, such as rowing, an infinity of rapid phases. . . . There are two moments to choose for us painters—the two extreme phases of action. . . . You have taken an intermediary moment and from that comes immobility."[9]

It was probably this very immobility that fascinated Eakins, and did so for decades after his teacher cautioned him to avoid it. Such scholars as Sylvan Schendler have regarded this "immobility" as one of the glories of Eakins' painting, since it seems to show the intersection of the finite and the infinite, the "now" and the "forever." Referring particularly to the rowing pictures, Schendler writes, "What caught Eakins' eye were the faces and postures of men seen in landscapes simultaneously fixed and changing. He saw character in time."[10]

In motion-picture photography, slow motion is achieved by running film through the camera at faster speeds than normal; the more frames per second with which the action is photographed, the slower—more inactive—it appears to be. Similarly with still photography: the faster the shutter speed, the less blurred and thus less indicative of motion is the action depicted. We have seen, for example, hummingbirds photographed at such high speed that their wings appear as motionless as marble; sports magazines, on the other hand, often provide pictures of racing events photographed at a slow shutter speed to convey that impression of high speed experienced by on-the-spot spectators.

The impressionist painters sought to demonstrate the fleetingness of time, the ephemerality of the moment, the rapidity of human existence, when they produced works such as Renoir's *Dance at Bougival* (1883), in which the blurred dancers in the background seem to be all in a whirl, Degas' *Dancers Adjusting Their Slippers* (1883), and Pissarro's *Boulevard Montmartre* (1897). In terms of camera technique, they may be said to have employed a slow shutter in order to convey the impression of speed. Eakins, on the contrary, painted with a fast shutter to put across the opposite effect: time transfixed, time held still. In this regard his frozen-action paintings can be compared to such post-impressionist works as Seurat's *Sunday Afternoon on the Island of La Grande Jatte* (1886) and Cézanne's *Cardplayers* (1890–92) which, like Eakins' *Chess Players* (1876), creates the impression of motion slowed down to such an extreme that the instant portrayed looks as though it will last an eternity.

Of all modes of rendition of the human form, none seems more suggestive of eternal permanence than sculpture. Thus it is not surprising that painters such as Cézanne and Eakins, both of whom were interested in depicting the intersection of the ephemeral and the eternal, the mortal and the immortal, painted their figures to resemble statues. This tendency to "carve" figures, making them appear to be made more out of stone than either flesh or paint, can be discerned in Eakins' works as varied as the frieze-like *Mending the Net* (1881), the Praxitelean *Salutat,* the *Portrait of Amelia Van Buren* (1891), with its deployment of limbs in space reminiscent of early Rodin, and *The Agnew Clinic,* where the doctor, ensconced within the wooden oval of the operating pit, looks as solid and three-dimensional as a marble monument permanently placed in the center of a city square.

Returning now to that painting, we see that Agnew's lack of visible speech, like his gesture, form, and placement within the horizontal niche, serves to monumentalize him, for if there is any one characteristic common to statues, it is that they refuse to speak. One might argue that statues cannot "refuse" to speak, for given the nature of their medium, they have no choice in the matter. This overlooks, however, the more important point that a statue or public monument is a symbol of the eternal, the ever-with-us, and that nothing can be less eternal, less ever-with-us, than the spoken word as it flies in vibration from lip to ear. The apotheosized hero had therefore better not talk, for when he does he immediately dispels the illusion of his transcendence. Eliza Doolittle appears to be a queen among women until she opens her mouth; Miss Churm in Henry James's "The Real Thing" (1893) could easily pass (in one of the narrator's magazine illustrations) for the noblest of aristocrats even though, in truth, she is without "an ounce of respect, especially for the 'h.' "[11] This is not to suggest that the real Dr. Agnew spoke a sort of Philadelphia cockney, or that what he had to say when lecturing would in any way demean him. But Eakins knew or sensed that to monumentalize his man—clearly the purpose of the commission—required depriving him of that most common, most temporal, and sometimes most trivial of human activities, speech.[12]

We know Dr. Agnew vehemently insisted that the painter remove the blood he had painted onto the surgeon's scalpel-wielding hand. The anecdote is often recounted to show what that determined realist Eakins was up against in trying to ply his trade honestly in genteel Philadelphia, where the depiction of blood was stodgily believed to have no more place in portraiture than did frontal male nudity in life-study classes for women. Such a point is no doubt well taken even if it is used in today's art history lectures for a purpose every bit as moralistic in its own way as those nineteenth-century strictures of taste to which the present-day teller of the tale implies we are superior.

The fact of the matter is, a man with blood on his hand *does* bear resemblance to a butcher—the very connection, apparently, that Agnew wished to avoid. At a time when vivisection was still deemed a tainted activity in many corners of society, tantamount even to "murder in the name of science," Agnew could hardly be blamed for timidity on this point.[13] His demurral is even more understandable given the public and critical outcry against *The Gross Clinic* (1875; fig. 8), painted by this same artist in the same city fourteen years earlier.[14] As the reviewer for the *Philadelphia North American* noted in shocked terms when discussing the portrait of Agnew's celebrated colleague Dr. Samuel Gross, "There is an especially objectional finger and thumb, which will go far to cause the

8. THOMAS EAKINS, *The Gross Clinic* (1875).

corner in which this grisly picture is hung to be severely left alone during the duration of this exhibition."[15] Another reviewer of the earlier *Clinic* referred to the "bloody lancet in bloody fingers, [which] gives the finishing touch to the sickening scene."[16] The female observer in the painting, who recoils in horror or disgust from the scene before her, prophetically embodies Philadelphia's reaction to the work.

Matters of taste and *scandale* aside, Agnew's demand that the blood be removed was not in the least out of step with the work's heroicizing and monumentalizing project, for exposed red blood, like speech, is a sign of mortality rather than immortality, of ephemerality, vulnerability, and prodigal expenditure: spilled blood, like spoken words, can never be repossessed. Certainly no one looking at the painting would have thought, after a moment's reflection, that blood had emerged from Agnew (instead of from his patient), but what about in that instant before reflection? *Visually* it might appear that the doctor had cut himself. Blood emitted from a god? It would be unthinkable, as unthinkable as blood issuing from Lincoln seated in his monument. In effect, then, Dr. Agnew was insisting that an aesthetic consistency be maintained in this painted representation that was to immortalize him as a figure of transcendent status.

Agnew's name, it is worth noting, comes close to the French term *agneau*, lamb, which derives from the Latin *agnus*, as in Agnus Dei, Lamb of God. Depending on how we interpret Agnew in this painting, he is, if not a medical and professorial god, then a lamb (sweet, gentle man with fleecy white hair) or a slaughterer of lambs (a butcher). If we do read him as a god, then it is she, the patient laid out upon the operating table (altar to science?), who is the true Agnus Dei.

We spoke earlier of Agnew's apparent disengagement from the spectators behind him, the human tableau before him, and the audience that waits at this side of the picture plane: us. He is indeed in complete isolation, one that is imposed as much by his own silence and downcast gaze as by the compositional and coloristic devices that we noted at the start of our detailed description. This isolation, besides endowing Agnew with the privilege, the honor, of being the first form singled out by our eye, also feeds, by way of literary association, our immediate response to him as a superior being. Clad in a loose-flowing garb redolent of antiquity, he is a Socrates whose lips are sealed, or a Biblical scribe whose right hand, a fleshly lightning rod, draws in the word of God while his left hand, poised with a penlike instrument, scrawls the air as though it were a parchment.[17] Fourteen years earlier, Eakins had posed Dr. Gross as a stern medical Moses clothed in, but not disguised by, present-day costume; the physician was elevated hierarchically as though his feet were planted upon the base of Mount Sinai. In the present work, Agnew's position is more lowly within the picture plane, more down-to-earth—but not by much.

Dr. Gross may have towered over his assistants, yet because he was in their midst, he seemed bound to them, whereas Agnew almost haughtily stands apart. Horizontal rather than vertical displacement is simply an alternative means of paying homage to the subject of the portrait. It visually demonstrates his superiority; it puts him in a class of his own. This compositional device represents Agnew as a leader and teacher who stands back from the embroilment of human interaction and mortality instead of, like Gross, emerging from the thick of it, hands sticky and stained.

Almost invariably, people who write or speak about portraits attempt to assess, verbally, in characterological terms, the "meaning" of the subject's face as painted. Such attempts, however imaginative or poetically interesting, are in every case fallacious, as they are wholly unverifiable. Suppose we lived back in 1889 and, after looking closely at Agnew's face in this portrait, we received an impression of what kind of man he was, either in general or during the particular moment Eakins had depicted. How would we go about verifying our impression? We could ask the painter, and his words might more or less concur with what we had decided after looking at the representation, but there is no guarantee that those words would mean the same to us as to him, or that they would adequately convey his impression of the doctor, an impression he probably formulated in his mind imagistically rather than verbally. Nor could we be sure that Eakins' sense of Agnew would be the same that we would receive if we met the physician ourselves. Nor would the impression received from a single meeting with Agnew, or even a lengthy series of meetings, necessarily correspond with the impression that would emerge if we knew Agnew over a period of years. Moreover, of the people who knew him well—his wife, his children, his colleagues, friends, employers, students—overall impressions would certainly be varied depending upon such factors as the age, sex, profession, status, and social background of the interpreter, not to mention the psychological needs and outlook that would strongly filter any impression. No two individuals who knew Agnew, even those who knew him intimately, could have seen precisely the same side of him. Agnew himself was most likely unaware of just how illusory and contradiction-denying is that mirage of singleness that one trustingly and habitually, by a naturalized figure of speech, refers to as "myself." Along these lines, a character in Pirandello's *Six Characters in Search of an Author* observes:

The drama lies all in this—in the conscience [*coscienza*—consciousness of self] that I have, that each one of us has. We believe this conscience to be a single thing but it is many-sided. There is one for this person, another for that. Diverse consciences. So we have this illusion of being one person for all, of having a personality that is unique in all our acts. But it isn't true.[18]

Even if we were somehow able to read Agnew's mind and probe into the recesses of his psyche (note how this and the following phrase imply that there is a depth and core to personality) to arrive at his most private sense of himself, and then on the basis of that revise our interpretation of his face as painted, we would be unable to verify the validity of what we see, for it is impossible not to attribute to the image meanings that we already consciously or unconsciously have in mind.[19] Agnew's face can be read in as many ways as there are viewers to read it, and indeed a single reader can justly supply several readings. While some of these readings will seem more plausible than most others, their truth value in terms of correspondence to a confirmed reality is logically impossible to determine, either by corroboration or falsification.

It is possible to show that a single interpretation of Agnew's face is consistent with the interpretation made of other elements of the painting (his stance, his mass, his compositional relationship to other figures) but what of it? A painting or novel that helps push us off in the direction of several contradictory interpretations all at the same time is more intriguing than a portrait with an interpretation so symmetrical and internally consistent that it bears nothing but the most superficial relation to the mystery, strife, and indefinability of any single human consciousness. ("*Chaos often breeds life, when order breeds habit.*") This is not to lay down over consciousness a cloak of romantic mystification and thus avert a scientific, ideological investigation of it, but it is, if not to celebrate, at least to tolerate heterogeneity, indeterminability, and the stubborn, cagey resistance of mental phenomena to attempted formalization.

Goodrich looks at Agnew and writes, "His face, a striking likeness, is concentrated, showing in its frown and in the firm lines around the mouth the marks of a life lived at high pressure; but calm, with a steely steadiness."[20] Schendler looks and finds "a consciousness of intellectual power and of human dignity in the extraordinary living figure, in the study of intelligence and professional competence joined vitally to feeling and to compassion. In the sculpted nobility of that head there is the best of civilization in late nineteenth-century America."[21] What a lot that is to find in a single face, a single head! All the more so when we remember that the face, frozen in expression, is deprived of the mobility in space and time that allows living individuals to express themselves by a nod or a shake, a wink, a slow grin, or a stringing together of looks and gestures, transforming these from static, isolated, iconic "words" of bodily expression into a far more communicative "sentence."

But it is not only because of the frozen, discontinuous quality of Agnew's expression that one is skeptical of Goodrich's and Schendler's, or anyone's, attempts to verbalize its meaning. Faces lie; one need not be a professional actor to marshal the facial muscles into a pattern socially encoded to indicate feelings very different from what one subjectively perceives the self to be feeling. Even when no deception is intended by the person being looked at, a second person may egregiously miscalculate, seeing in the first person's expression the feelings that he either experiences himself or expects the other to be experiencing. Goodrich and Schendler project onto the face and head of Agnew precisely those modern-anxious or humanitarian-noble qualities and feelings that years of literary conditioning led them, and might lead any of us, to expect.[22]

In the early 1920s, two Soviet filmmakers, Lev Kuleshov and V. I. Pudovkin, to demonstrate the problem of interpreting facial images, constructed an audience-response test that has come to be known as "the Kuleshov experiment." Pudovkin writes:

We took from some film or other several close-ups of the well-known Russian actor Mosjukhin. We chose close-ups which were static and which did not express any feeling at all—quiet close-ups. We joined these bits of film in three different combinations. In the first combination the close-up of Mosjukhin was immediately followed by a shot of a plate of soup. . . . It was obvious and certain that Mosjukhin was looking at this soup. In the second combination the face of Mosjukhin was joined to shots showing a coffin in which lay a dead woman. In the third the close-up was followed by a shot of a little girl playing with a funny toy bear. When we showed the three combinations to an audience which had not been let into the secret the result was terrific. The public raved about the acting of the artist. They pointed out the heavy pensiveness of his mood over the forgotten soup, were touched and moved by the deep sorrow with which he looked on the dead woman, and admired the light, happy smile with which he surveyed the girl at play. But we knew that in all three cases the face was exactly the same.[23]

Depending upon how we process the visual information, we can look at Agnew and regard him as talking to his students or not talking to them. The former is more likely to be the case because, unthinkingly, we leap to this conclusion. If he is not talking to his students, what else can he be doing? In the same way that we know a mime is "talking" when we watch him assume the conventional postures for it even though there are no audible words, we know that Agnew is engaged in the act of speech. His body language, we might say, tells us so. Experts in kinesics, the science of body communication, have noted that in our culture a person who is speaking tends to lower his head and his hand, as well as his pitch, at the conclusion of a statement. Intuitively, perhaps, we perceive this to be the case with Dr. Agnew, and thereby assume that he has at this very instant concluded not his lecture but rather a particular assertion or statement of fact in that lecture.

Yet while there is a part of us that intuitively ascribes speech to Dr. Agnew, there is another part that intuitively denies it. Perhaps this is what occurs: our ears inform us he is not speaking, but our familiarity with the conventions of painting quickly discounts that information, and our eye responds accordingly. It emphasizes those gestural signals that look like speech if our susceptibility to these artistic conventions has overridden the evidence of the ear; or, if those conventions have less hold, it emphasizes instead the posture and muscle tone that look like absence of speech. We can glance at Agnew and see him talking, then just as easily gaze and see him silent, a phenomenon that is similar to what takes place when we examine a "trick" illustration (as if there were some illustrations that were not tricks) that switches from a beautiful young woman to a hag and back again with no change in the drawing or in our position while viewing it. This point has broad ramifications for our interpretation of the painting: the viewer looking at Agnew can see him both as a teacher engaged in the act of teaching and as the symbol of a teacher. On the one hand he is an individual existentially active in the here and now of the painting's narrative, and on the other a flesh-colored statue, a monument that symbolizes a single teacher in particular and the Teacher Ideal in general. In the former instance, Agnew's gesture and posture seem convincingly idiosyncratic, and we attribute to him speech, and thus human individuality. In the latter instance, his gesture and posture appear as formal and abstract as that of a bronze orator perched upon by pigeons; he seems in this mode too inhuman, too divine, for words. The portrait of the doctor is like a two-faced coin, with "becoming" depicted on one side and "being" illustrated on the other. The difference between the portrait and a coin, however, is that the coin has two discrete images with which to convey the two ideas, while the portrait has but one.

In fact, as we are about to discover, the image of Agnew in this portrait has not merely two values, but is multivalent: in addition to the presentation of the man as "teacher" and "Teacher," he is presented in numerous other roles as well. Just as a word might have a single denotation but endless connotations, so with the visual image, once we have construed it literally, we find beckoning to us on the horizon a practically infinite number of figurative constructions. However many finite literal or a priori (denotative) meanings the image conveys, its figurative, a posteriori (connotative) meanings are unlimited. Gombrich speaks of "the figure in the clouds" and Leonardo made a practice of finding sources for his drawings by reading human faces and anatomies into the notches and cracks of crumbling walls. The meanings are there in the image as long as someone, anyone, is in a position to see (deposit) them there. I will describe, in the following paragraphs, other meanings that the image of Agnew suggests to me, and if I succeed in making my reader see them, then they exist in the image for her or him as well. This is not simply an exercise in fancy. Each newly construed meaning for Agnew can be tested, not for its intrinsic truth value, but for its consistent or inconsistent relation to the meanings we ascribe to various other elements of the painting. The more relationships we can discern between these varied and sometimes contradictory meanings, the more greatly enriched is our appreciation of the portrait as a whole, and the more multidimensional is the resulting characterization of Agnew.

The portrait of Dr. Agnew is never finished. Every time someone discovers a new relationship or meaning, *The Agnew Clinic* has been altered, revised, recreated. A painter at work on a painting makes myriad changes in it, as does an author writing and rewriting text. But years, even centuries, after the painter has laid down the brush, or the author the pen, the creative work of revision continues as long as there are viewers to gaze at the image or read the text. The viewer/reader may not shift around the actual physical materials of the artwork as the artist once did, but within this later consciousness, or perhaps unconsciousness, an editing of the work occurs nevertheless. As a material object, a literal object, *The Agnew Clinic* has a static, permanent, unchanging existence (aside from the hazards of decay and vandalism), but as a figurative object, a psychologically invested object of perception, it is never the same from one moment to the next, let alone from one viewer to the next.

In addition, then, to seeing Agnew as a practicing surgeon and a real, as well as ideal, educator and scientist, we might also see him figured as artist. The artist metaphor is suggested by Agnew's pose; he leans back from the tableau before him as though it were a painted composition he had just rendered. His loose-fitting operating cloak, tied about by an apron, reminds us of the traditional artist's smock. The lancet in the doctor's left hand might be the artist's brush, while his extended right hand, palm and thumb upraised, is perfectly positioned for wielding a palette. In fact, in this capacity Agnew resembles no one so much as Eakins' own artistic hero, Diego Velázquez, as self-portrayed in *Las Meninas* (1656; fig. 9), which Eakins had admired at the Prado during his visit to Madrid two decades before. ("Now I have seen what I always thought ought to have been done. . . . O, what a satisfaction it gave me to see the good Spanish work. . . . I will never forget it. . . ."[24]) In *Las Meninas* Velázquez leans back precisely the same way Eakins has Agnew lean two and a quarter centuries later; he is similarly belted at the waist; his sleeves are similarly puffy; and his hands are in nearly identical positions, except that the Spaniard holds a paintbrush in his right hand and a palette in his left, which is the reverse of Agnew. The color of their outfits is also reversed, but obviously Eakins felt he had to draw the line somewhere in his recasting of Agnew as the Spanish artist; black would not do for a realistic portrayal of a surgeon in the post–*Gross Clinic* era of surgical hygiene. Both these attitudes are echoed by the showman-like, even shamanistic, gesture used by Charles Willson Peale, a Philadelphian of several generations earlier, as he pulls back the curtain in his self-portrait, *The Artist in His Museum* (1822; fig. 10).

The other major difference between Velázquez's Velázquez and Eakins' Agnew-as-Velázquez is that, although both figures address a tableau, in the Spaniard's case this means that he is also facing us, unlike Agnew. It is as though Velázquez shows the artist relating directly and openly to his audience, with nothing to hide—a sign of his trust and self-confidence—whereas Eakins' surrogate artist appears to have defensively turned sideward. Velázquez looks us in the eye, while Agnew casts down his eyes like someone slightly afraid of us, lacking self-confidence, too timid to confront our authority. Originally we imagined Agnew's extended right hand held out to us as an offer, an invitation, a steadying guide, but now it seems ready to ward us off, a tool potentially defensive, like the pointed blade in the left hand. In other words, when we regard Agnew not as surgeon or teacher but rather as artist, his gesture and posture radically change their meaning. Velázquez reveals himself as a court painter assured of continuing royal patronage, while Eakins, recently removed from his post at the Pennsylvania Academy, having no assurance whatsoever of either aristocratic or public patronage, presents an artist whose relationship to the viewer appears troubled and insecure.[25] If we notice that Eakins himself is pictured in the painting, there is all the more reason to perceive professional malaise, for in effect the artist has been divided (or multiplied) into two selves, one at the left of the canvas and the other at the right; in addition, the "real" artist—the one on the right—has been visually torn in half. The implied double fragmentation speaks ill for the condition of the artist in modern

9. DIEGO VELÁZQUEZ, Las Meninas (1656).

10. CHARLES WILLSON PEALE, *The Artist in His Museum* (1822).

society, at least to the extent that the artist is Thomas Eakins. Indeed, it now seems particularly significant that Eakins had himself filled in by his wife, as if in a spirit of impotence and dejection, unable to posit a solid, present, nonoscillating identity for himself, he turned over to her his paintbrush and whatever phallic potency it carried.

If Agnew can be seen as artist, he can also be seen as the reverse of the artist, the critic. Inasmuch as he is expounding upon the performance taking place before him, he is fulfilling a role similar to that any of us takes when we stand before a painting, lean back, and deliver commentary upon it. The scalpel in the doctor's hand can now be interpreted as a symbol of critical instrumentality: like the analytic intelligence of a capable critic, it can be used to sever, probe, and slice minute particles of (human or artistic) matter, and like the critic's choice of words, it can be a factor of some importance in bringing about the life or death of the subject, painting, or text operated upon.[26]

When he explicates, a critic is a teacher, but to the extent that he is a creative synthesizer, he is also an artist. Therefore, to see in Agnew the depiction of a critic is not incompatible with interpretations of him as teacher and artist. Although the three professions are commonly considered discrete, here is a particular instance in which, as metaphors for a man who belongs to yet a fourth profession, they can be conflated. Eakins' Agnew, like any of us in real life, according to that passage from Pirandello, is the locus for multiple meanings, each one of which has an existence *within the painting* (or within the real-life individual) independent of the other meanings, although all of them intricately interrelate. We are attempting not only to peel away these superimposed meanings one by one, but also to observe how they come together. This process is the basis of reading a portrait, whether it is written or painted.[27]

We have spoken of Eakins' highly insecure relationship with the public that viewed—or neglected to view—his paintings, and have seen in the depiction of Agnew-as-artist a trace of this insecurity. Agnew's furrowed brow and downward drawn face seemed to bespeak a man deeply troubled, either by the perplexities of the artistic labor before him or by the anxiety built into his professional situation. But when we look again, this time seeing not Agnew-as-artist but instead Agnew-as-critic, and knowing as we do the treatment Eakins received at contemporary critics' hands, the furrowed brow seems to suggest bombast, the extended hand didacticism, the posture smugness, and the instrument held between fingers a scribbler's pen used in pompous fashion to besmirch the honest work of the artist, who in the painting's spatial terms is about as far away from the critic as can be. If Eakins seems severed in half, that pointed instrument in the "critic's" hand—his pen (or penknife), his sharp tongue—appears responsible. There is much controversy these days over whether or not the critic deserves to rival or even replace the artist as our center of interest, but while that debate may be new, the usurpation certainly is not, at least from a disgruntled artist's point of view. If we look at this painting with the interpretation of Agnew-as-critic, it appears that he has stolen the spotlight for himself and literally pushed the artist out of the picture.

To regard Agnew-as-critic is therefore to see a degree of aggression and hostility not at all present in our various benign interpretations of him as humanitarian, rescuer of life, philosophical seeker of truth, teacher of the young. As that aggression and hostility come into focus, the doctor may now seem like some sort of medical Jack the Ripper, his knife in hand, his mutilated prey stretched naked before him.[28] Or, if our bent is more mythological, Agnew bears a remote correspondence to St. George: the long slaying lance has shrunk to a surgical lancet and the writhing serpentine dragon become a catatonically supine female whom "St. George" pierces by a sort of remote control.[29] St. George, of course, lances not the damsel in distress but rather her tormentor—unless we choose to regard that slithery, untamed creature as an objective correlative for the dark, dangerous, and unwanted side of the female whom the male champion allegedly wishes to save.

It ought to be apparent at this point that how we interpret Agnew is greatly affected by how we interpret that naked patient. If we read her as dead, he seems in some way her killer. If we read her as rescued from disease and death, he is her savior. If she is a work of art, he appears to be the artist (it could be a sculptor's chisel in his hand as well as a paintbrush, and those around her the master's artisans gathered to perform tasks mundane). If she is Galatea soon to be roused, he is Pygmalion; if she is some sort of "bride of Frankenstein," he is the mad scientist; were she a white whale, he would be harpoon-bearing Ahab. If she is a Christ-figure deposed from the cross, he is St. Peter clasping in his hand the key to eternity. (See, for example, Botticelli's *Pietà* [c. 1496; fig. 11].) If she is a symbol of the astonishing beauty of human life and female form, he is Keats's Balboa standing in awe before the Pacific. If she is human sacrifice laid out upon the altar of modern science, he is the presiding high priest, cold, stern, perhaps even pharisaical—or then again, maybe he is a tenderhearted patriarch, a Father Abraham whose precious child, Isaac, has been demanded

11. SANDRO BOTTICELLI, *Pietà* (c. 1496).

by a hungry modern Jehovah as offering.[30] Each reading we give to Agnew depends upon how we interpret other elements of the painting—in this case, the patient.

Before moving on to Agnew's relationship with various other figures, we need to take note of one more way in which his figure relates to that of the patient, and that is erotically. The eroticism comes from the fact that the woman lies naked upon her back while he towers over her, a phallic instrument held lightly in his fingers only inches from the joining of his legs. One is reminded of Picasso's etchings of old men, satyrs, and apes gazing longingly at naked young beauties recumbent and in slumber. Agnew observes this woman from a distance; if he penetrates her at all, it is only by way of his surrogate, the young surgeon, Dr. White, who probes her with a lancet that visually echoes Agnew's. To this extent, Agnew is voyeur, and what his downcast gaze reveals is a man for whom the erotic image before him is subsidiary to what his memory projects on the inner edge of his eyelids. He is a study in the mediation by which all erotic objects are invested, determined, made into fetishes. Looking away from the actual body, he might be seeing, either by memory or imagination, a form idealized and internalized. In this context, his fingering of the downward pointing phallus is not precoital, but postmasturbatory. Had Agnew permitted Eakins to leave a smear of blood upon those fingers, we could interpret it, at this point, as signifier of self-spilled sperm, the color white, as in "Dr. White," displaced to red.

One might object that while this interpretation of Agnew-as-masturbator corresponds neatly to the interpretation of Agnew-as-critic (criticism being often regarded as an act of masturbating to someone else's endeavor), it fails to mesh with the interpretation of Agnew-as-artist. But such an objection is based on one or both of the following groundless assumptions: (1) that the activity of art-making is too active and other-involved to be correctly deemed masturbatory; (2) that masturbation is too passive and self-involved to be considered artistic. As for the first assumption, Eakins himself, closeted from society at large and detached from the mainstream art world, fits neatly into the category of solipsistic, masturbatory romantic artist, a category in which he is joined by such other eminently alienated painters as Allston, Blakelock, Ryder, and various Abstract Expressionists. Of course Eakins' artistic enterprise, at least at this point in his career, seems far more directed to an external social world than was the enterprise of the earlier romantics or later expressionists, and in that way he needs to be distinguished from them. But as with late James, so with much of late

Eakins (*Agnew* and beyond): the artist's hermetic and solipsistic tendencies, always latent, become pronounced. As for the second assumption, masturbators from Jean-Jacques Rousseau to Philip Roth's Portnoy have demonstrated that the onanistic activity is anything but passive, and, in its intensification of recollected or imagined experience, can indeed be considered artistic. See in this regard Thomas Hovenden's bawdily suggestive self-portrait of the artist "fiddling" with himself, *Self-Portrait of the Artist in His Studio* (1875; fig. 12).

A moment ago I spoke of Dr. White as the older man's surrogate. A scenario from the pages of de Sade is conjured: *le patron,* the devil incarnate, issues commands as his grooms and lackeys, his demons, hover with torturous intent over the body of the helpless victim. The tableau that had once seemed benign—a pietà—now appears horrific, a sort of late nineteenth-century version of Fuseli's *Nightmare* (1781; fig. 13), with doctors taking the place of horses and incubi, and the setting not a gloomy bedchamber but a well-lit amphitheater. The gang-rape aspect of the tableau is augmented by the way one doctor leans over the patient's lips, another over her crotch, and a third over her breast; by the way the nurse, whom Schendler found so humanely compassionate,[31] suddenly appears to be observing these proceedings quite frigidly, like a cruel, black-clad *maîtresse;* by the way one man covers his mouth, either to whisper titillation or to gasp in horror; and by the way thirty adult men, fully clothed, sit back with varying degrees of interest ranging from rapt, almost mesmerized attention to near boredom. Even the operating room's decor makes a visual contribution to the rapelike aspect of the scene, with the diagonal of the wooden handrail thrusting down into the victim's chest, calling to mind once again the medieval depictions of St. George spearing the dragon, or Homer's account of the blinding of Cyclops, the one-eyed giant. Note how the man in the aisle three rows up has his hand and cheek upon the railing, thus reinforcing its look of being thrust. One can read into both of those myths, as well as into this painting, a psychosexual subtext in which male phallic penetration subdues a threateningly bizarre creature—a dragon, a one-eyed giant, a naked female.

I do not wish to claim that what this painting is *really* about is the ravishing of woman by man. Certainly that was not in the realm of conscious intention. Yet the depiction of masculinity subjugating femininity does seem an essential component of this work; to ignore it or fail to be aware of it is to prevent ourselves from fully appreciating the energy and tension the painting embodies. Recent writers have come to regard the rationalism and positivism of nineteenth- and twentieth-century science as

12. THOMAS HOVENDEN, *Self-Portrait of the Artist in His Studio* (1875).

13. HENRY FUSELI, *The Nightmare* (1781).

a sort of male imperialism exerted over the mystery of feminine ("Mother") nature. For example, "The relationship between scientific ideas and social ideology has rarely been more obvious," writes Sarah Stage, "than in the way [nineteenth-century] doctors used disease as a sanction to enforce traditional behavioral norms." To this she adds, "Advances in medical knowledge only furthered the mystification of the female body."³² A present-day physician, Robert S. Mendelsohn, writes,

As far back as Hippocrates' day, during the fifth and fourth centuries B.C., doctors believed that the female reproductive system was a source of hysteria and even insanity. For more than two thousand years, if a woman stepped out of the expected pattern of subservience and humility, her ovaries and uterus were blamed. The term *hysterectomy,* in fact, derives from the Greek word for hysteria (*hysterikos*), which means *suffering in the uterus.*

Mendelsohn continues, "Nineteenth-century medical literature is replete with references to the frailty and hysteria of women. If a woman . . . failed to maintain an appropriately subservient and retiring family or social role, her reproductive organs were assumed to be the cause and castration the cure." Finally, he quotes a Dr. David Gilliam who, in 1896, concurred with noted colleagues "that [female] castration pays; that patients are improved, some of them cured; that the moral sense of the patient is elevated, that she becomes *tractable,* orderly, industrious, and cleanly."³³

Here in *The Agnew Clinic,* an operation for breast cancer is being performed. Ellen Frankfort writes of such operations, which are little different now than they were a century ago: "Because women are rarely given a choice, the only way they know how much has been removed is by clutching their chests when they are awake from surgery. All decisions of how much to cut are made while the woman is asleep on the operating table." Frankfort goes on to cite numerous studies that call into question the health advantage for the patient of radical, as opposed to simple, mastectomies, although the radical, which was developed in Philadelphia's neighboring city Baltimore in the 1880s by William Stewart Halsted, is commonly the surgeon's preferred procedure: the more one slices off, the more certainty one gains, or so seems to be the logic.

Nowhere is an absolutist way of thinking more pervasive than in medicine [Frankfort concludes]. This is a great irony, since little in biology is absolute. . . . But rarely is the behavior of doctors borderline or tentative or hesitant. Few doctors admit that they don't know the answers or that there may be no answers. Because of their mystique, doctors feel impelled to behave as if they have all the answers.³⁴

Schendler's remark that in *The Agnew Clinic* "the teacher is the inspired vessel of the meaning discovered in the woman upon the table,"³⁵ demonstrates all too well the traditional conception of woman-as-enigma, as bothersome feminine mystery, that logical, reasonable man must attempt to disburden himself of by means of an analytic, if not actually corporeal, dissection.

Later we shall question, on the basis of the visual evidence of the painting, where Eakins stood vis-à-vis this alleged colonization of the feminine. But for now I wish to concentrate on Dr. Agnew and his relationship to other figures on the canvas, namely, Dr. White, Medical Student A, and the nurse. I have already indicated that White seems to me a sort of visual double for Agnew much as, in *The Portrait of a Lady,* Ralph Touchett and Gilbert Osmond are doubles. They are not precise, literal doubles (as, for example, William Wilson doubles the narrator of the Poe story by that name, or as "the secret sharer" doubles the narrator of the Conrad tale), but they echo each other in various ways, and, in so doing, implicitly comment upon one another.

As pictured here, White's upper body forms a triangle: his forearms are the base, his shoulders and upper arms (one of which, hidden, may be imagined) the sides, and his head the apex. Were Agnew to swivel around toward us without changing his posture, his upper body would be a similar triangle on the picture plane. That fact, together with their identical garb, their surgical instruments, their downturned moustaches above clean-shaven chins, and their parallel placement within the painting's foreground all work together to provide visual doubling. It is as though on the left we have the doctor in old age reflecting upon the days of his early maturity as a physician, while the tableau on the right is his imagined recreation of those long-ago days, with Dr. White playing the part of the young Agnew. If this were a comic strip illustration, the tableau on the right would be contained in a cloud connected to Agnew's brow by a series of smaller, dotlike clouds. If it were a Hollywood production of the forties, we would have a watery dissolve from a close-up of Agnew to the image of his recollected youth and then, with another dissolve, a return to the present-time close-up.

There is sufficient physical correlation between Agnew and White to permit us to translate their displacement in space as a displacement in time; the synchronic image proves itself adaptable to the diachrony of narrative. Although we first read the image as the representation of multiple but related occurrences in a single place during a single instant, there are grounds for making a second reading in which these multiple occurrences take place at different instants of time. Prior to the Renaissance, painters had no qualms about depicting several temporally disconnected moments within one overall image. There are single canvases showing Adam and Eve both before and after expulsion from paradise, and others showing Christ both on and off the cross.[36]

Again an objection: "What about the eyeglasses? If Agnew-in-the-present is not shown wearing a pair, then Agnew-in-the-past probably had no need for them, so therefore it is wrong to regard White as a younger version of Agnew." But this is being too literal; with metaphors, one object is perceived as being *like* another but not, of course, point by point the same. Gilbert Osmond is sufficiently like Ralph Touchett and different from other characters to encourage us to see him as in some sense (but not in every sense) Ralph's double. The same holds true for Agnew and White: they are sufficiently like one another in visual terms and different from all other figures except A, whom we will discuss momentarily, that it is valid to regard them as doubles and make of it what we will.

White holds his surgical instrument in his right hand, whereas Agnew uses his left. Dr. Agnew was in reality ambidextrous, but this is information not provided by the painting. The viewer therefore might well assume that White grasps his instrument for actual use, and Agnew does not. Whether or not the young doctor stands for Agnew as a young man, he clearly is engaged in labor with his tool while the elderly doctor holds his suspended in midair.

Now let us observe Medical Student A. The young man's upper body forms a triangle remarkably similar to White's (and to Agnew's, were Agnew turned toward us). Like both doctors, and unlike everyone else in the painting, he is clean shaven but for his downturned moustache. On the painting's horizontal axis, he is situated precisely halfway between the two doctors. Yet whereas both their pairs of hands are visible, neither one of his hands can be seen. Putting all this together, we can find in the one global image a sort of triple portrait in which Dr. Agnew is depicted not only in the present (1889), but also in two previous stages of his life: as an approximately forty-year-old surgeon and, before that, as a young medical student. Thanks to A, we thus have a visual conceit for three ages of man, the man in question being Dr. D. Hayes Agnew. Agnew-as-student is thin, almost gaunt; Agnew-at-his-prime is solid, filled out; Agnew-as-grandee is stout and jowly. Likewise, Agnew-as-student and Agnew-at-his-prime have nearly the same hairstyle, hair color, and hairline, while the hair of Agnew-at-present is sparse and white. The placement of hands fits with this interpretation: the young man, not yet a doctor, must keep his hands withdrawn, while the man in early middle age makes active use of his, and the elderly man, retired or about to retire from the practice of surgery, uses his hands not in actual work but, instead, for rhetorical flourish. One Agnew listens, one works, and one talks.

A not uncommon pastime of young would-be surgeons is to tie and untie knots in small cords concealed within their pockets; later that same dexterity will be needed for knots obscured by bones, organs, and blood. Surgery students sometimes practice, from within their pockets, the one-handed manipulation of a Halsted hemostatic clamp, an instrument used to compress bleeding arteries and veins. The "Halsted hemostat" was designed by William Stewart Halsted, the aforementioned Baltimore physician who pioneered the radical mastectomy. A Salon painting by Eakins' French contemporary Henri Gervex shows a beautiful, anesthetized female patient with flowing tresses and exposed breasts hovered over by a group of whiskered medical gentlemen, nearly all of whom seem less interested in her than in the doctor who gestures to them, Agnew-like, with one open hand while he fingers lightly with the other an upraised hemostatic clamp. See *Before the Operation: Dr. Péan Explaining the Use of Hemostatic Clamps* (c. 1887; fig. 14).[37]

Another way to make sense of the old man's relationship to these two other figures, these alter egos, is to see them as expressing different sides of his nature. We will observe in chapter 4 how Isabel Archer is "expressed" on one side by Henrietta Stackpole and on the other by cousin Ralph; a similar approach might be taken here, with Medical Student A representing the passive, reflective, philosophical side of Agnew, and Dr. White representing his active, decisive, behavioral side. (This tension between passive and active modes of being and behaving also plays itself out at length in both *The Boit Children* and *The Portrait of a Lady,* as well as in numerous other individual works of the portraitists with whom we are concerned, leading us to wonder if this tension can legitimately be regarded as the master key that might unlock for us the particularity of this era, as distinct from the historical-cultural eras that come before.[38]) To choose which interpretive route we prefer—taking the two men as representing different sides of Agnew's character or as illustrating stages of his past—is to choose whether we wish to regard *The Agnew Clinic* as the visualization of the doctor's present qualities or of his past history. Both procedures, however, one primarily synchronic, the other diachronic, are operative (ahem!) within the painting, and both contribute to a more specific individualizing definition of the portrait's subject, Dr. Agnew.

The one way in which (besides apparel) Medical Student A most differs from Agnew and White is that he, unlike them, does not hold a small, stiff, probing instrument in his hands. Or does he? Are his hands not plunged

14. HENRI GERVEX, *Before the Operation: Dr. Péan Explaining the Use of Hemostatic Clamps* (1887).

deep into his pockets, coming together at the joining of his legs? Like Isabel Archer's cousin Ralph, whose hands are always buried in his pockets, making a ribald pun on his last name, "Touchett," Medical Student A appears to be sitting out his life passively, dreamily, masturbatorily.[39] Using our eye cinematically, cutting (the term is appropriately surgical as well) back and forth between one-shots of the student and the naked woman lying upon her back, we create for ourselves a Kuleshovian montage in which A's lust for her appears indisputable. Referring to his 1954 film *Rear Window,* Alfred Hitchcock once described a similar effect: "Let's take a close-up of [James] Stewart looking out of the window at a little dog that's being lowered in a basket. Back to Stewart, who has a kindly smile. But if in the place of the little dog you show a half-naked girl exercising in front of her open window, and you go back to a smiling Stewart again, this time he's seen as a dirty old man."[40]

Our own experience of life might tell us that there is something preposterous about my interpretation: the woman is being surgically dissected, by God, and everyone around her is completely deadpan—to detect dirty thoughts within this antiseptically clean setting is not only preposterous, it is perverse![41] Maybe so, and yet we must try to divest ourselves of preconceptions as to how things are *supposed* to be. It is not out of perversity, a penchant for parlor tricks, or a desire to outrage that such interpretive possibilities are proposed, but because the best way to read a portrait is to coax from it as many viable interpretations as it will yield; then, instead of choosing one and disposing of the rest, we must make a serious effort to discover the bearing that all of them have upon one another. Treating the portrait as a palimpsest of codes and meanings, a juncture of ideologies, an irruption of social contradictions otherwise repressed beneath a smooth surface of moral, artistic, and hermeneutic conventions, we make visible the invisible, audible the inaudible, indigestible the predigested—and thus better comprehend how social phenomena that are cultural and arbitrary attempt to pass themselves off as natural and inevitable. For example, by "perversely" attempting to "peep" at the dirty underside of *The Agnew Clinic,* this seemingly factual report of scientific, institutional hygiene, we come to realize that at a deeper level the true story of the painting is the manner in which society's superstructure (Law/Art/Medicine) masks its own devices, its repressing/sublimating/sterilizing of erotic, irrational, antijuridical, antiformal, and anti-antiseptic desire.

I repeat, therefore, my contention that a cinematic scanning back and forth between Medical Student A and the naked woman leads us to wonder, is it not lust aglow beneath his half-closed eyes? and could that therefore be a covered but erect penis touched lightly, lingeringly, by his pocketed hands?[42] True, the angle of his downward gaze appears to be away from the woman; he no more looks directly at her than does Agnew. Yet that helps support the earlier thesis that the young man/student and the old man/teacher are at stages in life when they are only indirectly involved in the activity before them, while the doctor who is in the prime of his career is directly involved. His gaze, significantly, is locked fast upon the woman.

Interestingly enough, a line drawn down the ridge of A's nose to reveal where he might be looking comes to a halt at the lancet in Agnew's left (passive) hand. If it is agreed that the lancet is phallic, then Medical Student A can indeed be seen as having sex on his mind—and sex in his hands. Moreover, if it is agreed that Agnew's handling of the lancet can be deemed autoerotic, then not only is the relationship between Agnew and A further established, but those qualities of passive spectatorship and active imagination are also more clearly expressed.

Now we have the basis for perceiving a narrative of male sexuality to go along with the narrative concerning the three stages in Dr. Agnew's professional career (student, active practitioner, grand old man). The three newly perceived stages are these: mentally looking forward to penetration of the female; actual penetration; and mentally looking back at prior penetration. These three stages, anticipation, action, and recollection, not only describe a male's biosexual history over the course of his life, but also his psychosexual history every time he has sex: without anticipation, there is no erection, and without the act itself, nothing to recollect. The three stages also happen to be necessary in reading any work of art. When one listens to a symphony, for example, pleasure is derived from (1) anticipation of how a particular theme will be varied, (2) hearing the actual variation when it occurs, and (3) recalling it immediately after. A similar process takes place when one reads a novel or looks at a painting.

This brings us around to the topic of our own inscription in *The Agnew Clinic*. As previously noted, we are placed directly opposite Medical Student A, who is in a sense our mirror image. He is our double, our surrogate: the difference between us is that his eyes are downcast while ours gaze straight ahead, but all the same, we, like him, are passive spectators, our hands literally or figuratively thrust into our pockets in accord with the universal admonition to art viewers, "Look but DO NOT TOUCH!" Thanks to this positional, behavioral, and symbolic equivalence between A and us, we are linked to the other points of the triangle, Drs. Agnew and White, and are in that sense accomplices to the penetrative act that one of them performs and the other recollects/recounts. But we are more than mere accomplices, for if the unseen tip of A's erect penis occupies the exact center of this composition, then, once again by equivalence, the unseen tip of our symbolically implied penis is also dead center. The composition and iconography of *The Agnew Clinic* provide the viewer, whether male or female, with a perspective that is phallocentric; regardless of gender, the viewer is *constructed* as masculine. The painting depicts an almost exclusively masculine universe whose Cartesian center is male desire, focused and pinpointed. *The Agnew Clinic* permits—in fact, encourages—the spectator to take a "penis-eye view" of the world. Those lines of spectatorial gaze that at the beginning of the chapter we found converging upon Agnew's blade can here be seen as helping to draw together into an amalgamation—penis / scalpel / instrumentalism / reason / control / analysis / penetration / phallicism—various aspects of a profoundly masculine worldview.

*   *   *

Making a few minor mental adjustments, regard this painting as though it were the depiction of a magic show performed for an all-male audience. Dr. Agnew is a white-robed wizard clasping an abbreviated magic wand in his hand, the nurse is his specially costumed female assistant, and the patient is a woman upon whom the wizard is practicing the art of levitation. Note how stiff, even cadaverous, she is in this role; mentally eliminate both the pillow and the cloth-covered table beneath her, and she appears suspended above the ground as though floating. The trick is marvelous, no? One audience member covers his mouth in astonishment, while three observers who have been brought forward and assigned special cloaks scrutinize every inch of the levitating body in a futile search for some clue that would give the game away. One of them peers down into her impassive face, one pushes against her heart, and the third looks for an invisible string or cord attached to her waist; yet nothing is to be found, there is no trick, the master magician has this woman completely, unequivocally, under his spell. This is an image of absolute control.[43]

It is also an image of theater, and a special kind of theater at that. It is a live sex show with an all-male audience, a male superstud, and a dainty damsel, helpless, supine, and bared at the bosom for the male spectator's delectation. She, the damsel, does not turn her eye to us, but that does not mean we are deprived of the sexual excitation traditionally achieved in erotica by the naked female's return of the viewer's gaze, for, as noted above, her bosom is suggestive of an eye. Indeed, more than an eye is suggested; the creases of the sheet and folds of flesh join together to form an open, vagina-like pocket that invites the viewer to send forth "his" phallic visual shaft. The centripetal shape of the amphitheater, culminating in the tight ring of the operating pit, similarly works as an inducement to the viewer to plunge inside.[44]

The literary conceit by which a gaze is likened to an arrow or other aggressive instrument goes back at least as far as Shakespeare: eyes, says Phoebe in *As You Like It,* "Should be called tyrants, butchers, murderers," and adds, "if mine eyes can wound, now let them kill thee."[45] Centuries later, Ortega y Gasset described the look that has erotic intention as having "the straight-line accuracy of a bullet."[46] The connections between the lover's look, the connoisseur's gaze, a painting's sight lines, an archer's (or Archer's) arrow, an ejaculation, a portraitist's selective insights into his subject, modern rationalistic society's progressive instrumentalism, and the erect penis of an aroused male are connections that it is important to explore.

A scene in Edith Wharton's *House of Mirth* (1905) has some bearing on this topic of erotic looking and its reifying effect. Lily Bart, the protagonist, is a guest at a country estate where, for the evening festivities, the women stage a series of tableaux vivants—scenes from well-known paintings "brought to life." Lawrence Selden, a young man who loves Lily Bart but has not the means to offer her marriage, is in attendance that evening. Wharton relates: "Each evanescent picture touched the vision-building faculty in Selden, leading him so far down the vistas of fancy that even Gerty Farish's running commentary—'Oh, how lovely Lulu Melson looks!' or: 'That must be Kate Corby, to the right there, in purple'—did not break the spell of the illusion."[47] In other words, Selden so willingly suspends his disbelief and partakes of the illusion fostered by the tableaux that he temporarily forgets that these are women he knows on a day-to-day basis, not imaginary characters come to life. His "vision-building faculty," or what Wharton a page earlier describes as "a corresponding adjustment of the mental vision," enables Selden to stare at these women with an unabashed directness that propriety permits one to bestow upon old master paintings, yes, but not upon human beings whom society deems worthy of respect.

When Lily's turn arrives, however, she creates a stir: "Even the least imaginative of the audience must have felt a thrill of contrast when the curtain suddenly parted on a picture which was simply and undisguisedly the portrait of Miss Bart." Whereas the other young women had used artifice to allow the men in the audience to look them over under the guise of art appreciation, Lily dispenses with such pretense and allows herself, quite brazenly, to be looked at as nothing other than herself. Observing her unadorned physical beauty, Selden promptly sublimates it, as Ralph Touchett would be inclined to do, into a much more acceptable spiritual beauty—"The noble buoyancy of her attitude, its suggestion of soaring grace, revealed the touch of poetry"—thus allowing him to catch "a note of that eternal harmony of which her beauty was a part."

Selden abstracts and objectifies Lily no less than he had the women who appeared previously. He has continued to make use of his vision-building faculty, the difference being that whereas earlier he was free to look over the female body by willingly submitting to the illusion that he was perusing great art, now that there is no illusion of great art—since Lily has stripped away that convenient fiction in order to display her own physical self as a desirable commodity—Selden is forced to tell himself he is admiring her particularization of "eternal harmony."

This may seem a uniquely nineteenth-century sort of stratagem, this need to ennoble corporeality and to dress the particular in the robes of the ideal. It is the sort of thing Isabel Archer was prone to do, as for instance with her initial impressions of Gilbert Osmond and Madame Merle. But of course it is a twentieth-century stratagem as well, and nowhere more evident than in the way those who write on Thomas Eakins' portraiture insist upon reading noble and profound meanings into the flesh and blood bodies and faces—the oil pigment shapes and forms—that he depicts.

This practice, simplistic, reductive, and ultimately body-hating, is only a step or two removed from the Philadelphian attitude that broke Eakins over the course of years. He suffered first for the body unennobled with *The Gross Clinic,* and then suffered again, a decade later, for the body unclad in a so-called life-study class. Probably the only reason he never had to pay a similarly brutal price for the two female nudes he painted at the opposite ends of his career is that he was savvy enough to give them exactly the right sort of artistic-mythic rationale, entitling both works *William Rush Carving His Allegorical Figure of the Schuylkill River.* Eakins dared on only one other occasion to paint a female nude, this time clothing her body not with a double layer of art and allegory, but instead with medical good intentions and an opaque sheet upon which was lettered (invertedly) those sanction-bestowing words "UNIVERSITY HOSPITAL."

In the Wharton novel, no sooner has Selden been transported to a sense of eternal harmony than his aesthetic bliss falls victim to crude muttering from the cad beside him, a notorious "connoisseur" of "the female outline." Yet however different the intentions or the sensations of the two men when they gaze at Lily on display, both have in some sense pinned her, fixed her, nailed her with their gaze. Their gaze traps, implicitly denying life and individuality. Selden's aesthetic rationalizing aside, the impetus of male desire is present in both instances. To stare a person down, as the expression goes, is to demonstrate control over that person; it is to assert self as master of other. This is one desire, the desire to dominate, that both men attempt to gratify by staring at Lily—even if only to fulfill it ritual-istically, detached from reality. The other desire fulfilled is a related type of sexual desire, the desire for arousal. When a male is aroused, he feels himself to be potent, capable of penetrating reality, of thrusting himself into the thick of it. By staring, therefore, at Lily-as-Lily (as distinct from Lily-as-Mrs. Lloyd), both of her male admirers, however different they are from one another, achieve a sensation of double potency, for tightly focusing upon her allows them to dominate her visually and to experience arousal.

The stare can thus be seen as an aggressive act, an act of appropriation, domination, objectification. Lily is possessed by the men who make up her audience. In much the same way, the men in *The Agnew Clinic*, and that includes us, male or female, to the extent that we are inscribed within it, possess the woman stretched out upon the table. The point of Dr. Agnew's scalpel is not nearly so sharp nor precise as the look by which we attempt to penetrate her. Here again sfumato comes into play: the shadows upon the patient's face make us stare at her that much harder, more piercingly, more forcefully.

Portraiture, whether it occurs in a novel or in a painting, provides the spectator with the opportunity to stare at a character, real or imagined, to penetrate beneath that character's surface, and in so doing to experience both an arousal and a feeling of mastery—for we, the spectator, gain insight into the character that he or she does not gain from us. Peter Brooks pertinently addresses this topic:

The act of knowing which underlies the composition of a portrait is insisted upon in [Crébillon's *Les Egarements*] by the repeated use of verbs *pénétrer* and *fixer*, and the noun *pénétration*. To "penetrate" someone is to find him out, to lay bare his true motives and sentiments. . . . To fix someone—in the sense of arresting his movement and attaching him with permanence—it is necessary to have penetrated him, caught and held him in definitions. . . . To let oneself be fixed is to sacrifice prestige and freedom of movement. . . . To reduce someone to the categories, ab-stractions, and judgments of the portrait . . . is to be in a position to control that person.[48]

In short, according to Brooks, "to bring someone to the metaphorical arrest of the portrait implies and in fact proves social superiority and dom-ination." These observations about portraiture as a means of achieving real or imagined superiority call to mind Michel Foucault's discussion of the "Panopticon"—the hypothetical prison designed by Jeremy Bentham, in which all prisoners' cells were open to the scrutinizing view of the centrally located prison-keeper. "Each individual . . . is seen," notes Foucault, "but he does not see; he is the object of information, never a subject in communication." The individual is fixed, trapped, dehumanized by panoptic surveillance just as he himself has the prerogative to fix the helpless, inanimate subject of a portrait (even though people sometimes feel that it is the stuffy old picture of Uncle Alphonse hanging above the mantelpiece that keeps a surveillant, guilt-inducing eye on them, rather than the other way around).[49]

If portraits are able to offer the viewer a modicum, a sensation, of dominance and control, this has traditionally been even more true of nude figure studies. In *Ways of Seeing*, John Berger remarks upon the proprietary implications of such works:

The nude in European oil painting is usually presented as an admirable expression of the European humanist spirit. This spirit was inseparable from individualism. . . . Yet the tradition contained a contradiction which it could not itself resolve. . . . The contradiction can be stated simply. On the one hand the individualism of the artist, the thinker, the patron, the owner: on the other hand, the person who is the object of their activities—the woman—treated as a thing or an abstraction.[50]

While one man, in gazing at Lily Bart, regards her as a thing, and the other views her as an abstraction, both, it follows from Berger's remarks, are typical of the way that oil painting in the humanist tradition has encouraged its viewers to treat the female nude. This leads us, then, to ask if in *The Agnew Clinic* Thomas Eakins, like those humanist painters and patrons Berger refers to, exploits the naked female form by treating it as "meat or myth" but not as a woman, or if instead the painting formulates a protest against just such dehumanization and exploitation.

This is a question to which there is no simple answer. It seems to me that the formalist in Eakins, the logician and symbolist, artistically makes use of categories and divisions that parallel the treatment of this female as an object laid out for male delectation. Zealous in his attempts to be realistic, even verist, in his art of fixing the passing moment, Eakins studied anatomy, experimented with stop-action photography, and invested much time and energy in perspective drawing. Linear perspective, to use the apt phrase of William Ivins, Jr., is "the rationalization of sight." Ivins further defines perspective as "a practical means for securing a rigorous two-way, or reciprocal, metrical relationship between the shapes of objects as definitely located in space and their pictorial representations."[51] Albrecht Dürer

(1471–1528) and other artists of his time went so far as to set up rectangular grids through which they measured the subject from a fixed point of
view, incrementally copying down what they saw on a sheet of paper. Berger
shows Dürer's well-known woodcut depiction of this act of art-measure-
ment (c. 1525; fig. 15) and writes, "Dürer believed that the ideal nude
ought to be constructed by taking the face of one body, the breasts of
another, the legs of a third, the shoulders of a fourth. . . . The result would
glorify Man. But the exercise presumed a remarkable indifference to who
any one person really was."[52] Berger's critique, inspired by Walter Benjamin's "Work of Art in the Age of Mechanical Reproduction," associates
the rationalist, perspectivist, mechanist endeavors of Renaissance humanism
with the reifying processes of bourgeois capitalism. Benjamin had quoted
in his essay the fascist aesthetics of Marinetti: "War is beautiful because it
initiates the dreamt-of metalization of the human body."[53] If we place the
Dürer image side by side with *The Agnew Clinic*, we will see not only a
striking similarity between the two men (artist and doctor) and the two
women (model and patient) but we will also recognize a perhaps heretofore
unsuspected connection between rationalized vision (perspective), modern
science (medicine), and modernity's "metalization" of the body (that which
is "natural" or "feminine").[54]

But there is another Eakins, a feminine Eakins, who visually identifies
himself with this particular woman and, because her face is veiled, with
women in general. This second Eakins is the disenfranchised, disempow-
ered artist that he surely felt himself to be at the extremely low stage of
his career when he painted *The Agnew Clinic*. Like the vulnerable, helpless
patient, and like the nurse, the Eakins figure, shoved off to the corner of
the work, is depicted without hands, those appendages that in Eakins'
iconography stand for power and instrumentality. Also like the patient, he
is without ears—appendages that over and over in Eakins' oeuvre appear
larger than life, as though they held some special significance for him. With
Eakins the outer ear is sometimes depicted in such a way as to resemble
the female sex organ, and seems to symbolize for the painter human fe-
cundity, creativity, aliveness. An absence of ears, therefore, might indicate
a denatured and feckless state of existence. In this painting neither the
patient nor the artist-figure behind her is fully human or alive; both of them
have been visually sliced in half.

Who has done this slicing? Within the fiction of the painting, the
woman has been dissected by the surgeon (Agnew and company), while in
the reality of the painting as an artistic creation, the Eakins-figure has been
dissected by the painting's creator (Eakins and company). Consequently the

15. ALBRECHT DÜRER, *Man Drawing Reclining Woman* (c. 1525).

painting provides us with multiple levels of identification. On one level the artist appears to be identifying himself with the woman who is passively laid out on the table, seeing himself, like her, as the victim or object of the dominant male, who within the picture is Agnew-as-vivisector/scientist, Agnew-as-artist, and Agnew-as-critic, and who outside the picture is Eakins himself. Certain tales by Poe, Hawthorne, and James such as "William Wilson," "The Artist of the Beautiful," and "The Jolly Corner" give literary expression to what I see here as the troubled artist's bifurcation of himself into victim and oppressor, one part of him driving and dominating the other at enormous psychic cost.

At the same time that Eakins seems to identify himself with the woman, he of course also identifies himself with the doctor, for reasons previously given. Yet there is finally a third level, a mediating identification that balances Eakins the doctor and painter with Eakins the patient and painter. That mediator is Medical Student A. Like the Eakins-figure and the woman on the table, A is depicted without hands, signifying him to be inactive and powerless, yet he also bears formal resemblances to Agnew. By means of these visual similarities to A, Agnew is feminized and drawn into a closer relationship with the patient being operated upon and the painter being painted than is implied by his spatial distance from them.

And what of the nurse? What is her role in all of this? It is ambiguous, to say the least. In her institutional garb, her postural rigidity, and her compositional balancing of Dr. Agnew, she could be thought of as yet another signifier of antiseptic social pressure hovering oppressively, surveillantly, over the vulnerable individual subject whose memory and desire are being anaesthetized.[55] Such an interpretation is further supported by her seeming to obstruct "Eakins' " line of sight to the patient. But she too lacks hands (instrumentality, power); the arc that passes through the crown of each attending physician passes instead through her lower face, where organs of expression and feeling are located; and, perhaps most important, her downcast gaze is a symmetrical reversal or countering of Agnew's gaze (thus effecting, in cinematic terms, a shot/reverse-shot). These points all lead to a viable interpretation of her as an antagonist, however overpowered, of patriarchal phallocentrism. She at least, unlike the patient, is upright and conscious; she is sentient, capable of experiencing pain and remembrance. She possesses a necessary ingredient for rebellion.[56]

By now *The Agnew Clinic* may seem more laden with transferred identity than a Shakespearean comedy. What is truly confusing is not that there are so many layers of identification or meaning here, but that they are so tightly fused together—so "con-fused." We have been trying to peel the various layers apart in order to take them one by one, but the problem is that each individual layer, like an Eakins brushstroke, is colored by the layers on either side of it. To look at any one layer in isolation from the others is to see it differently from when it is camouflaged by its context.

The great strength of *The Agnew Clinic* is that it can give impetus to so many distinct but densely knotted-together interpretations. The painting is a master key that readily opens numerous locked doors, each one leading into a space different from but intersected by the various spaces lying outside the other doors. Our job has been to turn this single key in as many locks as possible, to open as many doors, and to sketch out, however rudimentarily, a map that charts the intersections of the spaces that lie beyond.

*   *   *

We shall never know the Dr. Agnew of real life in any full sense, or Eakins either. But in the one man's artistic rendering of the other man and of the world that, however uneasily, they both shared, we find clues and mysteries and stimuli at least as suggestive as those cracks in walls by which Leonardo prompted his own imagination. If Dr. Agnew himself—or if not he, then his painted image—emerges from this chapter hero and villain, philosopher and fiend, Old Testament prophet and modern bourgeois, it is not necessarily because he was such an extraordinary man (though he may have been), nor because Eakins' portrait of him is so extraordinary (though it certainly is), nor even because we as readers of the portrait are so full of fancy, but rather because, to paraphrase Montaigne, what any one of us is capable of being or doing, all of us are capable of being and doing—and seeing. If something is human, then it is a part of us. Proust writes, "I was not one man only, but the steady advance hour after hour of an army in close formation, in which there appeared, according to the moment, impassioned men, indifferent men, jealous men—jealous men no two of whom were jealous of the same woman."[57]

There is this about great portraits: the better we understand them, the better we understand that from within any one of us, the portrait's subject, artist, or viewer, there surges forth a veritable army, difficult to discipline and ever on the verge of mutiny.

CHAPTER THREE

The Boit Children

W HEN WE LOOK AT *The Boit Children* (fig. 16), we see four attractive, healthy, fair-skinned girls posed variously in a sumptuous and elegant interior uncluttered by Victorian bric-a-brac, unpapered, and uncarpeted save for a patterned blue-gray rug on the floor. These girls are clean-scrubbed, well-bred, well-groomed, well-fed. They are true offspring, it appears, of the haute bourgeoisie. A family resemblance between them is plausible, though certainly not remarkable; our knowledge that they are actual sisters rather than, say, co-boarders at an expensive girls' school, derives from either of the painting's titles, *The Boit Children* or *The Daughters of Edward Boit*.

Is it possible for us to know them as individuals, each one's personality or character in some way distinguishable from that of the others, or are they relatively indistinct in terms of personality? In other words, can we legitimately believe that we see in one child evidence of a particular outlook on life or way of responding to it that is different from that which could be attributed to her sisters? Just as when reading a novel we applaud the author's skill at individualizing the main characters and keeping them distinct from one another, so in looking at a group portrait we expect the figures depicted to "tell" us something about themselves, and in such a way that they do not seem interchangeable.

The characters in a novel may impress themselves upon us by what they do and say and by what is said about them by other characters and

[83]

16. JOHN SINGER SARGENT, *The Boit Children* (1882–83).

the narrator. Their physical appearance, verbally transmitted, is of course a contributing element in their characterization, but a relatively minor one considering how little text is normally allotted to any one character's bodily description. The setting in which a character is placed—her immediate physical environment as described by the narrator—tends to be more germane to characterization, if only because more words are used in the narrative to talk about the room or house or city that situates the character than to talk about the actual body that she occupies. Barring disfiguration or substantial aging, a character's appearance, once described, will remain constant from scene to scene, whereas each new setting she enters merits a new description. As René Wellek and Robert Penn Warren observe in their *Theory of Literature,* "Setting is environment; and environments, especially domestic interiors, may be viewed as metonymic, or metaphoric, expressions of character. A man's house is an extension of himself. Describe it and you have described him."[1] In 1875, Henry James stated approvingly of Balzac, "The place in which an event occurred was in his view of equal moment with the event itself; it was part of the action; it was not a thing to take or to leave, or to be vaguely and gracefully indicated; it imposed itself; it had a part to play; it needed to be made as definite as anything else."[2]

A realist portrait such as *The Boit Children* must of course rely entirely on description—painted, rather then written—to characterize; here, obviously, there can be no such aids to the artist as dialogue, interior monologue, continuous action, or direct authorial exposition and analysis. All that the painter has to work with is the visible appearance of the body, the manner in which it is clothed, and its arrangement in a space defined by lighting and locale, in this instance a pair of furnished rooms. Therefore, inasmuch as these four girls resemble one another physically, are dressed much alike, and are shown together in the same setting, can we possibly read them as four separate individuals, having four distinctly different identities?

The answer, as we shall see, is yes. Attuned to principles of metonymy and metaphor, much as Wellek and Warren's readers of the novel are asked to be, we, the viewers of this painting, can obtain clear notions of who each girl is by what she is wearing, how she wears it, and where she is located in relation to the surrounding decor, the furnishings, the other figures, and the three prime axes of the image itself: left-right, up-down, and near-far.

First, however, we should give individual names to the girls, as this is not done by either of the portrait's two titles. A bit of research would provide us with that information, but since it is not disclosed by the image, we shall for the present have to find some alternative way of referring to them, one that derives only from what the work makes manifest. I propose to call each girl by a different letter of the alphabet. The little girl on the rug we will refer to as *J* because of the upright torso from which the lower leg curves off to the left with a slight hook at the ankle. Her sister who stands full front, with her thin legs apart and her arms bent elbow high behind her waist, can be likened to an uppercase *A*. The sister who leans back against the Oriental vase, because of the hollowing out of her profiled upper body by the oblong black slot representing her arm, bears some similarity to the letter *R*. Finally, the sister who stands straight with her arms pressed close to her sides will be called *I*.

Begin with J (fig. 17). She is seated while the other girls are standing. This may signify privilege. She appears to be considered special: she sits enthroned. The apparent cost of the rug beneath her suggests a costliness to her as well, an abundance and plenitude which is perhaps less an expression of her own character (hardly to be set in place at such a young age) than of the value that doting parents ascribe to her. She must be viewed as a part of that rug, its condensation and culmination perhaps, but a part of it nonetheless. Thus, unlike her sisters, she is characterized by whatever it is that the rug suggests.

But what exactly does this particular rug suggest? Protective layering perhaps—it guards the floor from one's feet, while at the same time saving the feet from the hardness of the floor. J herself, fleshy and layered in children's clothes, but also padded by the very young child's ignorance of life's hardships, can be characterized by protective layering.

The doll that rests at length between J's legs and is flanked by her inwardly curled feet forms a sort of buffer zone that obstructs both the head-on gaze of the viewer and the direct approach of light from the painting's lower left corner. What this buffer zone protectively blocks from our gaze and from the revealing light is J's pudendum, as though to disclaim it, deny it, forswear its existence. J may thus, as was the case with middle-class children prior to Freud's study of infantile sexuality, be characterized as thoroughly presexual and wholly unavailable to sexual investigation, whether scientific, artistic, or prurient. Nevertheless, that she protects her genital zone reflects how deeply sexualized she is, or how effective an act of repression this painting (like *The Agnew Clinic*) must achieve in order to abide by an ideology of sexual innocence. Any assertion such as the one I have just now made—"that she protects her genital zone reflects how deeply sexualized she is"—can also be read as saying that she appears to

17. *The Boit Children* (detail).

be or can be seen by a present-day viewer to be protecting her genitals reflects how deeply sexualized is our present-day habit of viewing. The second assertion is very different from the first but by no means incompatible with it. The fact that J is placed lower in the image than any of her sisters works as a geographic confirmation of the easy-to-make assumption that she is also the lowest in age. But paradoxically it suggests as well that despite the privilege accorded her by her centrality and by her being seated while the others stand, she is lowest in the children's hierarchy of power; her sisters are, quite literally, above her. As for her appearing to be nearest to us in space, what is implied is that she is personally the most accessible, the child most nearly within our reach—within our grasp, we might also say, as in "able to be grasped," or made sense of. To the extent that the viewer of this painting is placed in the role of the parents who commissioned the work, such an interpretation seems likely: J is still at an age when a child is unambiguously dependent upon, and therefore especially close, both spatially and emotionally, to her parents. J can be seen as both the star of this family and its most powerless member. In this sense she is a paradigm for the Victorian child and, indeed, for the Victorian woman: on a pedestal but unempowered.

Although the light entering from the left is lavished upon J, one portion of her body, the upper half of the head, is metonymically linked to the back room, superimposed upon its threshold. This threshold consists of a wedge of graded shadow. J's face, from her nose to the tip of her head, fits neatly within it. If we think of light as suggesting (as by convention it does suggest in literature, painting, and film) the presence of reason, mental clarity, safety, openness, moderation, and sunny disposition, and, again according to convention, take darkness to suggest mystery, obscurity, irrationality, potential danger, and moodiness, then there is an indication here that for all J's apparent "sunniness," there is already, "in the back of her head," an admixture of qualities prepared to negate it.

J's sister A (fig. 18) is also washed in light. She too is allotted a face of enormous sweetness. Of the four sisters, she is perhaps the most generously swathed in brushstrokes fructuous with texture, color, and vibrance. Her lips, the color of raspberries, are a truer, redder red than anything else on the canvas, even the scarlet screen commanding the opposite side of the picture. All this molding, depth, and color in A's face makes her appear not only sweet in disposition, but also vivid and ripe and full of vibrant, energetic life. Though she stands posed obediently before us, it is with a certain Huck Finn sort of independence: feet oblique (unlike J, whose feet close ranks as another sign of her huddled insulation), one

18. *The Boit Children* (detail).

leg tentatively forward, arms clasped behind in an independent, self-pos-
sessed manner, her long hair curly, almost tousled, and her eyes pointed
politely in our direction but focused somewhere beyond us to our left. Thus
A seems to inhabit her portion of the world with unselfconscious presence.
But then, as ever, the image lends itself to a diametrically opposite reading:
far from being an independent figure, an outsider comfortable to remain
just that, A has a pose that can be seen as not her own, but rather as a
position she takes self-consciously, eager to please the viewer by modeling
independence while at the same time silently querying, "Am I doing it
right?"

Aside from frontality, all I (fig. 19) has in common with A (as opposed
to the other two sisters) is the ruffled collar around her neck. Yet even here
there is a major difference, for while A's collar flairs outward expressively,
I's collar is narrow, restrained, almost inward-folding, a suggestion that she
is a restrained young woman, narrow and withdrawn. This is reiterated by
her appearing to stand away from the viewer, backing off into the shadows,
thus playing out an encoding of modesty or shyness. The unruffled smooth-
ness of I's white smock, when contrasted to the drama and turbulence of
R's smock adjoining, suggests placidity: her hands dropped at her sides
designate her as passive, noninstrumental (unlike A, who uses her hands,
even if only to hide them from view). I has about her a quality of waiting:
her lips are parted as though she was caught at a moment of incompletion.
Her open lips form an oval, an O, an ingestive hole, a pocket, cavity,
wound. Though her face is directed toward us, her eyes deflect away, avoid-
ing us at the last instant. Her eyebrows are paper-thin, her face narrow,
her hair unvoluptuous.

R offers the least in the way of readable, translatable information. Not
only is she alone seen in profile, but her face is heavily shadowed. All that
her face seems to reveal is that she would prefer it not to be revealed. (A
reminder: we are attempting to decipher the "personalities" of fictive entities here, characters constructed by the artistic manipulation of plastic materials and sociocultural codes. The actual, real-life personalities of the Boit
girls are irrelevant to this discussion, as well as impossible to salvage from
history.) R appears to be the stoutest of the sisters and also the tallest; we
might assume because of this that she is the oldest. Yet slouching back
against the large Oriental vase, she is not depicted as the dominant child,
at least not by the conventional means of being placed stage center, given
a corner of the foreground, or made to tower over the others. On the
contrary, it would seem that R has renounced or lost in the female hierarchy
any position of privilege that might have been accorded her by her pre-

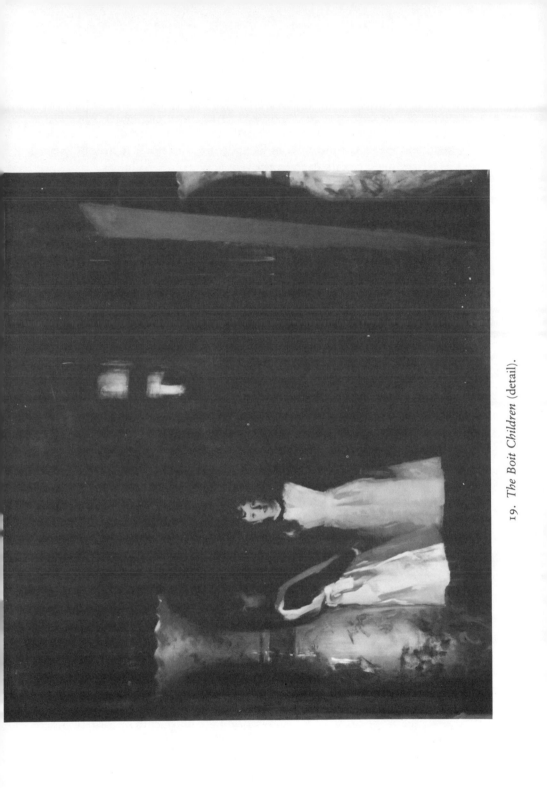

19. *The Boit Children* (detail).

sumptive seniority. But perhaps these particular signifiers of hierarchical upper status have been abandoned in favor of an alternative wherein the superior individual maintains a relaxed posture in the presence of others rigid and erect. On the basis of her posture, therefore, R may be viewed as possessing a certain degree of sovereignty over her siblings.

Her relationship to her sisters is shown ambiguously, but not so her relationship to the viewer. As a fictive character presented to us by the painted portrait, she is characterized as moody or defiant, but in either case remote: turned away from us, she has lowered her head, retreated under the veil of deep shadow, and, most defiantly of all within the universe of Sargent's portraiture, has completely disavowed the viewer's gaze. There is not even a hint of that gaze being returned. While the other sisters might, by a minute shift, turn their eyes in our direction, with R this appears impossible. Such is rarely the case in Sargent's portraiture. Another exception occurred infamously with *Madame Pierre Gautreau* (1884; fig. 20), painted a year or so later. Can R, in her youthful, almost ungainly way, be regarded as a prototype for that svelte woman of the world? Gautreau's profile taunts and provokes, and thus is palpably addressed to us, as is the rest of her body, a commodity for window-display; look but do not touch.[3] Altogether differently, not at all in a teasing manner, R's profile wholly dismisses us. Unlike her sisters, R waits neither for us nor upon us. She is indifferent, oblivious to our presence. Her dark, murky, enshrouded existence denies our own.

*   *   *

I have attempted to distinguish the "personalities" of the four female representations wholly on the basis of the painting's available information. Of course, people have personalities, and representations do not. It must continually be remembered, therefore, that we are talking about the *suggestion* of human personality—the representation of it, as well as of the body— and not the thing itself.

We will now cease individualizing the sisters and instead conflate them into a single symbolic being, the Female Child. The painting offers not one but several texts on the nature and social reality of this particular Female Child, the pre-adult female of a particular class (upper), race (white), place (refined Europe or America), and period (late nineteenth or early twentieth century).[4]

The most obvious and thus the most naive text goes something like this: a young woman (infant, adolescent, maiden) is sweet, adorable, obe-

20. JOHN SINGER SARGENT, *Madame Pierre Gautreau* (1884).

dient, passive, an article of beauty put on this earth for no immediate purpose other than our privileged adult enjoyment. Such is what a glib and hasty reading announces. Pursuing the matter further, though, causes a less blithe interpretation: a young woman is depicted by the *male artist* as a costly aesthetic object, like the gleaming Oriental vase; a pearl to be displayed, like A in her fixed position within the open jewel box formation of the panel and the floor; a plaything or puppet, like the doll J rests in her lap; something to be trodden upon, like the rug; something that is ultimately blank or empty, like the rectangular fireplace directly behind I.[5] The major difference between the second level of interpretation and the first is that (a) attention has shifted from *what* is being presented to *how, by whom,* and *for whom* it is being presented, and (b) indignation has crept in, a sense on the viewer's part that the depiction insults its subject by metaphorizing it (the Female Child) as trivial, ornamental, wholly predicated upon someone else's enjoyment and delectation.

The first interpretation reads the image as if it were reading the world itself and at the same time reads the world unthinkingly, as though it existed unproblematically according to tenets of received wisdom such as "girls will be girls" or "boys will be boys." This interpretation sees in the painting a nice, simple confirmation of what is taken to be nature, reality, the way things are. The second interpretation regards the image as someone's ideologically-loaded *impression* of the world, a world that is by no means set, but is open to ideological contest. This interpretation would decry the painting as implicitly sexist and authoritarian, a smug, proprietarial likening (as in the tableaux vivants scene from *The House of Mirth*) of young woman to aesthetic object, fragile, beautiful, and useless.

The first reading leads the interpreter to gush, "How nice, how true" and then be on "his" way. The second reading leads the interpreter to cry, "How wrong, how degrading" and then be on "her" way. In either case, the interpretive act is short-circuited: the viewer ceases to view, and the possibilities to achieve deeper, more complex meaning are closed. Such a short-circuiting should be avoided, for further examination shows *The Boit Children* to be anything but a pretty and soothing confirmation or idealization of the patriarchal world.

The work's scale gives us our first hint that something else is going on here. One Sargent scholar, referring to the Oriental vases, writes, "The huge scale of these vases, and of the room itself, in relation to the diminutive figures, has an almost Surrealist touch."[6] It is true; the children, it begins to seem, are eerily dwarfed. Either the vases are huge or the girls miniature. One's sense of size and proportion is confounded; relativity runs amok.

Here are four variants of Lewis Carroll's Alice appearing as though they, like Alice, had just stepped through a looking glass, such as the one flanked by the two smaller vases on the mantel in the back room, and been shrunk accordingly. Like Ibsen's Nora, these girls are stranded within a doll's house, a world of property and propriety that truly overwhelms them. Such literary allusions subvert both a naive, unquestioning acceptance of Sargent's painting and a blanket condemnation of it, by connecting the work intertextually to satire, as in *Alice in Wonderland, Through The Looking Glass,* and *Gulliver's Travels,* and moral censure, as in Ibsen. When Gulliver, for example, is miniature in the land of the giant Brobdingnagians, he is petted and cooed over in a most disgusting manner, indicating, as *The Boit Children* could also be seen to indicate, criticism of self-centered adult disregard of the little person's integrity. For little person we might say Other—the member of a lower or alien sexual, racial, or economic class—and muse upon how that disregard is a form of resistance by the empowered and authorized toward the as-yet unempowered and unauthorized.

Regardless of whether Sargent had the Carroll novels or the Ibsen drama in mind when he conceived this work, both Alice and Nora are part of the cultural landscape determining our present-day interpretive horizons. Likewise, whether or not Sargent was consciously making use of discrepancies of scale to achieve Carrollian satire or Ibsenian censure, our ability to recognize within the work a possible opposition to or subversion of patriarchal norms is sufficient for that opposition to be contained "in" or generated "by" the text. After all, opposition lies not in an inert piece of painted canvas, nor in the visible forms upon it, but rather in the mind, the will, of the spectator. When we say that a work is politically subversive, what we are really saying is that it readily allows—makes itself available to—an oppositional reading.

Miniaturizing the girls it depicts, *The Boit Children* can be seen as exaggerating the notion of woman as diminutive person (female as diminutive male; a person lacking male size and potency) as a way of mocking it. Thus begins a third level of interpretation. The painting's gross reduction of the female to the size and status of ornamental object encourages a critical, oppositional, perspective toward the social formation signified. The painting mocks that patronizing view of the female that the first interpretation blissfully upholds ("Oh, these pretty little things, aren't they sweet") and that the second accuses the painting itself of putting forth ("Sentimental sexist claptrap").

Are we placing undue emphasis on the question of scale? There is, after all, such a thing as an oversized vase, against which children may indeed appear diminutive.[7] Certainly if this were all we had to go on to arrive at the proposed third level of interpretation, our case would be weak. Yet the issue of scale is only the starting point.

The "dollhouse" the girls inhabit is presented as one large box centrally partitioned. Oddly, though, of the six sides of the cube, only one—the bottom (the floor)—is visible. The front wall is transparent (like the so-called "transparent wall" of late nineteenth-century theatrical realism), the rear wall indeterminate, and the top and side walls cropped from view. How, then, with one wall clearly defined and another only vaguely, even confusingly, suggested, are we given such a distinct impression that it is indeed a box that these doll-like creatures inhabit?

The answer has to do with Sargent's eccentric choice of a square-shaped canvas. In describing "this large canvas," William H. Gerdts notes that Sargent "has hollowed out the composition, distributing the solid forms around the edges of a dark central void; indeed, the picture was condemned by some as 'four corners and a void.' The *Revue des Deux Mondes* spoke of the work as composed according to some new rules, the rules of 'the four-corners game.' "[8] The effect of this "four-corners game," however bizarre the critics of Sargent's time may have found it, is to stamp the image with an absolute and perfect regularity, one that determines the way we see and think about what is contained within. By its simplicity, its uniqueness, and its visual equilibrium, the square shape disposes of the need for walls by superimposing onto the room its own incontrovertible structure. Consequently what appears is a square stretched out in depth: in other words, a box.

In English, "box" is defined as "a rigid typically rectangular receptacle often with a cover; something having a flat bottom and four upright sides."[9] *The Boit Children* unquestionably offers a rigid rectangular receptacle as the location wherein the four doll-like girls are placed. Moreover, this quality of "boxiness" is reiterated within the image itself by the rigid, rectangular panel behind A, the black receptacle of the fireplace behind I, and the glimmering, windowlike looking glass above its mantel.

The Boit Children, this so-called "four corners and a void," was painted by Sargent in Paris, where the Boit family lived and where he himself was resident. Though English was Sargent's mother tongue, he had known French intimately for years. One wonders, therefore, if the artist did not, consciously or unconsciously, make the simple linguistic slide back and forth between "Boit," the name of the painting's patron, and *boîte,* the French term for "box." ("Patron," by the way—this will be of value later—

has both in English and in French several meanings significant to our discussion.) A French dictionary defines *boîte* (pronounced bwat) as "récipient de matière rigide" (a receptacle made of rigid material) and as "cavité, organe creux qui protège et contient un organe, un mécanisme" (cavity, hollow organ which protects and contains an organ or mechanism, as in *boîte crânienne,* the part of the skull that encloses the brain, or *boîte de vitesses,* a gearbox.)[10] Intended as such or otherwise, *The Boit Children* makes a visual-verbal pun by translating into *Les Enfants de (la) Boît(e):* the children of Boit and the children of the box.

B-O-I-T: four letters; four girls; four vases; four sides; four corners. "Four corners and a void": how aptly the phrase describes the image, but also, with a minor adjustment, the family name: "four letters and a void"— the void, of course, being the absent *e* needed to transform "Boit" into Boîte, which is both the painting as it appears (boxlike) and that literal object composed of four corners and a void, an empty box.

Charles Bigot, reviewing the Salon of 1883 for the *Gazette des Beaux-Arts,* described this painting as "these pretty little girls grouped by Mr. Sargent in a space that is a little too large and at times rather empty."[11] The largeness of the box surrounding the children, its relative emptiness, its central void, apparently had a disturbing effect upon contemporary critics. It bespoke absence, whether formal or, perhaps less obviously, psychological. In a palpable way, it signified lack.

But what is absent? Where is the lack? Absent in many more senses than one is the body—the conspicuous, corporeal presence—of him who pervades the image in spirit: the father. It is their father upon whom these pretty little girls attend, *jolies fillettes* waiting for their Godot. By "father," I refer first of course to Edward Darley Boit, the American expatriate artist who was the girls' *pater* and Sargent's *patron,* both on this occasion and for the later, Halsian portrait *Mrs. Edward D. Boit* (1888; fig. 21).[12] But also they seem to await fathers—creators—of another sort: God in the metaphysical sense (as annunciated by the Holy-Spirit-like bird in flight glazed into the vase) and, at a different level, John Singer Sargent, who is the father creator of this painting as a physical, material object. These various senses of the term *father* do not compete with one another, do not cancel each other out, but instead condense around the word so that by tugging at any of these lines of meaning, we tug at them all.

Like Gilbert Osmond's Pansy and Dr. Agnew's patient, Edward Boit's daughter ("the Female Child") awaits patient-ly the presence of the father, his wisdom, his initiating action, his grand seignorial behest. And like all of James's personages in *The Portrait of a Lady* and all Eakins' in *The*

21. JOHN SINGER SARGENT, *Mrs. Edward D. Boit* (1886).

Agnew Clinic, the four here in *The Boit Children* are from now through eternity frozen into an artistically complete but existentially suspended being. Isabel is forever and always on the verge of returning to Osmond, Agnew on the verge of uttering his next word, the girls on the verge of growing older. The real-life creator (father/progenitor) of the portrait in question is fused with the fictive father/progenitor who is manifested within it or, as is the case here, is conspicuously left offstage. Thus may we link John Singer Sargent (the author of the portrait), Edward Darley Boit (the author of the real-life girls),[13] and the titular *Edward Boit,* who is both a paternal presence, present not only in title but in spirit—the spirit of the architectural formality enclosing the girls—and a paternal absence, for he is corporeally absent; his figure, his bodily form, is excluded from the portrait.

The portrait's title, it should be recalled, is officially registered as *The Daughters of Edward Boit.*[14] The use of the preposition indicates possession; these girls are his daughters, they are his "dolls," his playthings, his pleasure-providers boxed within the (mostly) hidden walls or constraints of his home, his name. Now, in a resolution of mystery that is more mysterious than the mystery itself, we return to the portrait's overriding visual-verbal pun and discover that the single letter that separates patron (Boit) from painting (*Boîte*), the letter *e,* is the first letter of the patron's given name, Edward. From *Daughters of Edward Boit* to *Daughters of E. Boit* to *Daughters of Boît(E)* is a progression that now seems stunningly direct, though hardly simple. It far oversteps the bounds of credibility to think that Sargent had any of this in mind before, during, or after he painted the painting. But need we be surprised if somehow a psychic transfer or transmutation occurs between the verbal part of the creative mind that comprehends both English and French and the visual part that thinks in terms of pictorial form? Linguistic chains have a determining effect on the way images are conceived, just as images, in turn, influence our reception of language. *The Boit Children*'s visual image united with its verbal text (its title) constitutes a nexus of meaning wherein those inversely-linked issues with which we are concerned intersect: artistic formalism and psychological realism, symmetry and asymmetry, eros and anti-eros, image and language, past and present, male and female, daughter and father, activity and passivity, absence and presence.[15]

Perhaps the prototypical work of portraiture that incorporates an absence into the portrayal so that what is revealed is predicated *by* that absence is Velázquez's *Las Meninas*—a work of enormous importance for Sargent, as it was for Eakins. Of *The Boit Children,* Richard Ormond writes, "The most obvious source for its pictorial idea is Velasquez' *Las Meninas*, which Sargent had copied in Spain in 1879." As Ormond points out, "the relation of the figures to a large and totally encompassing space is very similar."[16] Some years ago Michel Foucault analyzed the way in which the royal couple who commissioned this painting from Velázquez were made to be at once bodily absent while both bodily and metaphorically present at the scene, thanks to the framed mirror that hangs in what is perceived as the far region, the deep space, of the image. The mirror reflects and encapsulates them, positions them above the rest of the family, and at the same time designates them as central to that family.[17] Here too in *The Boit Children* a mirror glimmers in the background, but unlike the one in *Las Meninas*, this mirror is empty, devoid of human content. Velázquez's mirror surely gratified the patrons of the family portrait by affording them a cleverly discreet enactment of their own narcissism—a view of themselves, and not only that, but one that privileges them hierarchically in terms of pictorial space, for though their reflection is positioned in the rear of that space, what is implied is that they themselves are in the forefront. Because Sargent's empty mirror does not permit this gratification of the patron/ parent (and his surrogate, us the present-day viewers), but is instead set askew, making any reflection of us or of the girls impossible, might we not legitimately wonder if once again, as in our earlier comparison of Velázquez and Eakins, discrepancies between the two paintings can rewardingly exemplify certain variations between the two cultural and historical eras?[18]

The differences between the Sargent and the Velázquez suggest, though they certainly do not confirm, several major cultural dissimilarities between the two eras of family history represented.[19] First, the 1656 family, an extended family, is woven together in such a way that, save for the two unseen parents who are positioned nearby but set apart from the others, each individual touches or overlaps, as in connective tissue, the next person in line; in the 1882 family, not an extended but rather a nuclear family, again minus the visible presence of the parents, the children are spaced wholly or partially apart. Second, the patron/viewer of the 1656 family, as already noted, is included *within* that family (and, by being situated spatially at opposite ends of the near-far axis, also encloses or enfolds it, like brackets or bookends), while the 1882 patron/viewer, by not being materially manifested within—by not appearing in the mirror—seems more estranged from that family, separate and dissociated, as the children themselves appear to be. Third, in the 1656 image, there is a clear-cut distinction between patron (the couple located in the mirror) and painter (positioned between the canvas in front of him and those several that are behind[20]), while in the 1882 image patron and painter (and parent) are conflated; there is now expressed the sense that raising a proper family is an artistic, aesthetic achievement, like painting a major painting. Or at least that these three variant modes of power, of social contract—painter, parent, and patron—have merged.

The point to be noted concerning this last difference is that by the late nineteenth century, parents positioned above the working and artisan classes had come to regard child-rearing as an art, and not simply something one did by instinct or tradition.[21] As the system of capital increasingly stole from individuals of the upper classes their opportunity to enter into direct creative contact with the material world, changing them from producers into consumers, it also heightened the need of the individual to find an alternative means of expressing subjectivity and, directly or indirectly, experiencing creativity.[22] One way of meeting this need was through avid art spectatorship; hence in the decades after the Civil War the founding of America's major art museums and symphony orchestras, the flourishing of publishing houses and magazines specializing in fiction, and the proliferation of scholarly and journalistic criticism of the arts. Another way of meeting it was to "mold" one's children, to "make masterpieces" of them, to "cultivate" each of them into "a work of art."[23]

Let us explore further some of the important differences in family life suggested by these two paintings. If the image from Madrid, 1656, depicts family members, friends, and servants loosely and comfortably knit together, each individual occupying a position well-defined in relation to each of the other individuals, it is because these are people who know where they stand in terms of themselves and the world they inhabit.[24] They are securely anchored (though perhaps not happily so) in a prefigured hierarchy, a thoroughly well-established social order. Imagine an axis running from the mirror-reflected royal couple as they are ensconced in the back to where, presumably, they preside from the front: each individual depicted is, in effect, a coordinate on or near that axis, his or her rank signified accordingly. *Las Meninas* is a paradigmatic image of the traditional patriarchal family order that prevailed in Western society until the birth of the modern age: Father, with Mother by his side, rules, defines, encompasses, orders. (Think of "rules" in both senses: as reigning with commanding authority, and as measuring against, or holding up to, predetermined standards.) What Bernard Bailyn writes of Western families in general during this period applies particularly to the royal family of Philip IV of Spain as painted by Velázquez:

Families were not merely the basic social institution; they were considered the archetype of all social order, public as well as private. In this micro-community, it was believed, all order germinated, all patterns of inferiority and superiority took shape. The political commonwealth was but an enlargement of the family. Rulers were conceived of as patriarchs whose dominance as heads of commonwealths was justified by God the Father of all.[25]

According to Philippe Ariès, the uniqueness of the family of the seventeenth century lies in the fact that within its functions and operations, be they the ideological ones Bailyn addresses, or the interpersonal ones that Ariès has in mind, the private and the public spheres intersect—"modern family: it was distinguished from [the traditional family] by the enormous mass of sociability which it retained. Where the family existed, that is to say in the big houses, it was a centre of social relations, the capital of a little complex and graduated society under the command of the paterfamilias."[26]

After the transitional seventeenth century, however, the family came increasingly to be seen as the domain of privacy, from which all that was public was necessarily to be excluded. It was now regarded as the place, the psychic locality, in which one could escape, if only temporarily, the pressures and corruptions of the social, outside, alien world. As such, the family now became romanticized, a fetish emotionally invested with redemptive and recuperative powers. The role of the father continued to be embodied in the rule of the father, but now the child, his innate and magical goodness propagandized by the likes of Rousseau, took on a significance in daily life heretofore unknown. For all that the mother was sentimentalized, her function was clearly secondary: to provide an animating warmth to the refuge that the father structured by his decision-making logic, and that the child made worthwhile by his innocence—his serving as a blank screen for the projection of parental fantasy, and his appearing to recapitulate within himself those personal characteristics to which each parent was narcissistically attached.[27] Thus *Las Meninas* of the mid-seventeenth century has it all, so to speak: family members intermingled with servants and friends; a father whose power and rule is decisively connoted and whose wife cleaves to his side; and, finally, the golden, radiant centrality of the child.

The Boit Children, however, reflects a different world. Not an entirely different world, of course, for to say that the seventeenth century was transitional is to say that many important characteristics of the modern era were already in place. Philippe Ariès remarks that in the seventeenth century a balance was established between "centrifugal or social forces" and "centripetal or family forces."[28] *The Boit Children* retains the centripetal without the centrifugal. It sucks inward not only visually but antisocially, for there is no outside or social world here, as was signaled in *Las Meninas* both by the human figures arranged close to each other like beads on a string, and by the open, light-filled doorway to the wide world beyond. The father and mother have been displaced entirely. The child here, unlike in the Velázquez, is shown not only in total isolation from the outside, and not only in isolation from the mother and father, but even in isolation from its siblings. Thus the nuclear family is revealed here, however inadvertently, in terms of the troubling paradox that Victorian ideology tried so hard to conceal: the family cannot successfully close itself off from the outer world without, as an unexpected result, the various family members sealing themselves off from each other. "The nuclear family is a state of mind rather than a particular kind of structure or set of household arrangements," writes family historian Edward Shorter. "Its members feel that they have much more in common with one another than they do with anyone else on the outside—that they enjoy a privileged emotional climate they must protect from outside intrusion, through privacy and isolation."[29] However true this may be, what Shorter neglects to delineate is precisely the paradox that *The Boit Children* calls to mind: the retreat toward familial interiority tends to nurture rather than diminish one's underlying sense of alienation. To put this in a time frame, the more interpersonal affections came, during a certain historical phase, to be seen as private, closely-held property, withdrawn from society at large and restricted to the immediate family, the more the individual self was seen as something ultimately inexpressible and consequently difficult, if not impossible, to share.

This is an affective phenomenon we would not expect the nineteenth-century family portrait overtly to present. On the contrary, we would, if shrewd, expect the opposite: a blithe denial of anomie and, in its place, a show of hermetic closeness and chauvinistic unity. Yet as we have begun to see, this is not the case with *The Boit Children*. So let us momentarily look instead at a very fine, and I think much more representative American family portrait of the era, Eastman Johnson's *Hatch Family* (1871; fig. 22).[30] Like both the Velázquez and the Sargent this portrait is set in an elegant, wood-paneled interior in which sumptuously-appareled figures of various ages and postures are deployed. As in both other family groups, this deployment of figures is predominantly horizontal, reading along a left-right axis rather than near-far. And as in both those other works, light seems to emerge from front, back, and sides to warm and clarify what would otherwise be a thick brown darkness.

Class diversity that marked the extended family of *Las Meninas* is nowhere to be seen in *The Hatch Family*. The homogeneity of this nine-

22. EASTMAN JOHNSON, *The Hatch Family* (1871).

teenth-century group is not only signaled but proudly announced by the way in which all fifteen figures remain within a single horizontal band, with no expansive space behind them and a sizable distance in front (connoting a space between them and the world, them and us). A cultural product of a self-conscious society intent on viewing itself as democratic, *The Hatch Family* soft-pedals family hierarchy here with a manifestly egalitarian placement of figures. True, some heads are higher than others, but in a random sort of fashion that tends to prevent us from assigning predominance to any single family member. Even the mother standing out boldly against the mantel is made to share her figural rank with the eldest son on the other side of the composition; the grandfather, holding aloft his newspaper, is in a sense duplicated by the eldest granddaughter, who, although she reminds us of the grandmother by the way she is seated, recapitulates him even more by her perusal of reading matter.

The Hatch Family, as is typical of nineteenth-century family portraiture, seems to smooth over as well as it can (in this case, very well) the troubling question of with whom or with what the authority of the family was vested. Certainly that authority no longer belonged exclusively to the father, but instead was being pulled inexorably out of his grasp by internal and external rivals: by the much-touted and sentimentalized mother, who, having been kept apart from the morally suspect workaday world, was now regarded as the embodiment of morality that the father once had been; by vociferous feminists and suffragettes, who legally, politically, and socially challenged his right to rule; by workers in his factory or shop, who, like thankless children with ingratitude sharper than a serpent's tooth, rejected the limiting paternalism they had once seemed glad to accept; by educators and authors who liberally offered his offspring all kinds of necessary information and advice that he was not qualified to provide; by doctors who could cure, surgeons who could heal, lawyers and judges who could arbitrate; by scientists who could blast holes in the religious arguments that had formerly buttressed his earthly power through likening it to that of heavenly God; by inventions such as the telephone that diminished his voice to the size of all others; by corporate trusts that could drive him out of business any time they desired; by stock markets that, though a thousand miles away, could bring him to his knees with the tick of a ticker tape, and wipe out his life's savings with the transfer of a decimal point a single digit to the left or right. Such is the crisis in authority that paintings like *The Hatch Family,* by depicting Papa as a beloved, docile, and glowingly content member of the group, all too rosily evade.[31] In *The Boit Children,* however, the parents are equalized only insofar as they are both equally absent. Or so it at first appears. But upon some consideration, we realize that there is an inequality even in their respective absences. Whereas the father's absence is counterbalanced by the structural, form-producing presence of his name (Boit/boîte), the mother is exiled from the work altogether.

What of the mother: Mrs. Boit? Why up until now have I persistently avoided mentioning her? Is she so marginal that she deserves no attention? If she is marginal, is it because—and this is far from likely—she was an inessential member of the Boit household? Or because—also unlikely—Sargent deliberately wished to exclude her? Or is it because D. M. Lubin, the reader responsible for the present interpretation, happens to be a male reader, as J. S. Sargent happened to be a male painter, and thus both of us, he and I, are more attuned to the absence and presence of fathers than we are to that of mothers? Perhaps.[32]

Primarily, my reason for not finding Mrs. Boit figured in this painting is based on the absence of furniture and the sparseness of decor; none of the precious clutter or bric-a-brac that we associate with the domestic interiors of Victorian middle-class matrons is here, as it is, for example, in *The Hatch Family*, or—to take a French example from roughly the same era—the marvelous *Belleli Family* of Edgar Degas. A historian of nineteenth-century middle-class matrons living in the north of France writes:

Bourgeois women recognized the descriptive importance of their demeanor, dress, and domestic interiors. "The furnishing of a room," wrote Julia Bécour in one of her novels about bourgeois life in Lille, "describes a person. But not just any person or member of the family. Rather, it was the bourgeois woman herself, the *maîtresse de maison,* who acquired a reputation or definition from her household. Clever, neat, seductive, matronly, or even egotistical—any of these qualities and more were read from the arrangement or selection of domestic artifacts. . . . The shining interior of a home mirrored the character of its woman. . . . Mme S. renewed her interior with carpeting, drapes, objets d'art, dessert forks, fancy needlework displays, portraits, paper flowers, and liqueur glasses, among other things. . . . Basic items of furniture, purchased at marriage, were expected to last a lifetime, but they were revitalized with a constant replacement of linens and dresser scarves to disguise their declining years, and perhaps, to add to the image of freshness, youth, and fertility of the housewife.

The interior shown in *The Boit Children* is nothing if not "shining," but inasmuch as it is virtually empty of furnishings (two grand vases, a screen, a rug, and what else?), it is every bit as blank as that reflective glass in the back room, so far as concerns its having "mirrored the character of its woman." To the extent that this household's interior is articulated almost entirely by unadorned walls rather than objects on, in front of, or near those walls, the father (as structurer, law-maker, limit-definer) is portrayed, and the mother suppressed.[33]

So let us return, finally, to the matter of E. Boit/Boît(e). Boit is the name the father shares with his daughters (or, from another perspective, forces upon them), while Edward, signified by the letter E (e), is the name he keeps for himself—and by which, in this context, he is linguistically distinct from them. The E, standing for the name Edward, is his personal property within the Boit family realm; the girls, the "daughters of," are also his property, but the Edward, the E, is even more his, as it is his alone. His wife may share with him both his daughters and his family name, but not his first name; though she would have answered to "Mrs. Edward Boit," she would not have answered to "Edward." Portraiture locates the subject by representing the intersection of his general, shared characteristics with those that are personal and idiosyncratic. To put this another way, the portrayed individual is particularized by the text when his own specific development, his ontogeny, is positioned within the phylogeny of his family, his social class, his nationality, or his race.

Thus we have Edward, member of the family Boit. Yet that tells us virtually nothing about Edward; he remains unknowable to us, except as the box that gives definition to, constrains, and yet animates, to the degree they can be called animated, the four pictured females who bear his other (his family, his Other) name. Still, in a very important double sense, he—and by extension Sargent and the viewer—is the true subject of this painting. It is about him, insofar as he is alluded to in the title as the object of the possessive preposition (like Isabel in the title *The Portrait of a Lady*). Yet also, he (and Sargent and each of us) is the subject insofar as his (Sargent's, ours) is the subject-ive consciousness for whom the scene is composed and the girls displayed.[34]

Conversely, Boit's daughters are doubly denied subjecthood: they, like prisoners in Bentham's Panopticon, are the seen figures within the painting rather than the unseen-but-seeing consciousness outside it, and they, unlike him, are not accorded the privilege of having their own first names.[35] J, A, I, R we have had to label them, since the title *Daughters of Edward Boit* does not supply the individuating information. Thus, another way of accounting for the overall emptiness or lack that the painting bespeaks is that the Female Child enclosed within this geometric and ideological box is also trapped within a biological box: the lack of the father's E, his penis.

This last statement requires some immediate explaining of two very different but perhaps related matters: why in the world I have equated the Boit father's first initial, the letter E, with the male organ; and how I can be so anachronistically, Freudianly, sexist as to suggest that women are incomplete because they lack penises. Let me address the second issue first. Historian Sarah Stage has observed that "Michelet's characterization of the nineteenth century as the age of the womb, taken literally, reflected the contemporary preoccupation with woman's reproductive system, and underlined the distortion of perception, which, by placing primary emphasis on the sexual organs, enabled men to view woman as a creature apart." She then adds, "Viewing woman as 'mutilated male' enabled doctors"— and most of the rest of male society—"to judge her unfit for the demands of the larger world and thereby justify her limited domestic sphere."[36]

It was precisely the absence of the "male organ" that, historically, caused male-generated systems of knowledge to regard the female body, and, by extension, the female consciousness, as incomplete, empty, a box needing to be filled. At first it seems ironic, but, when we stop to think about it, less ironic than predictable that in French, boîte is a feminine-gender noun. Where the irony does emerge, in terms of this painting, is that almost universally in the French linguistic system, it is the letter *e*—of all possibilities—that, coming at the end of a noun or name, designates it as feminine. By coincidence(?), Sargent's portrait not only uses the devices of realist representation to depict Boit's girls as feminine, but also doubles the depiction by enclosing them within a superstructure for which the French term is feminine. Was there some principle of psychic compensation that invented for woman, who lacked the male anatomical ending, a linguistic attachment to give her? Was it an unconscious directive, a psychic sense of humor or of justice working subliminally in Sargent, that made his painting, by the interaction of its title and its boxlike form, call to our attention precisely that same attachment, the suffix *e*?

It is only reasonable to object that I have been cavalier about sliding back and forth between uppercase E and lowercase e, as though the one letter were identical with the other, which is not at all, might we say, the case. And what about the circumflex over the *i* in boîte; surely the careful reader has noticed, and accordingly been bothered, that all along I have conveniently ignored it. To remedy the situation, a little wordplay (or letter-play) is once again in order. First, what are the differences between big E and little e? To start, one is "big" and the other "little." One is all hard right angles, straight and erect, while the other contains no straight angles but is instead softly curvilinear. One outwardly projects its elements, including that smaller, centrally placed appendage without which E would be reduced to an unclosed (unmated) bracket, a "[," while the other tucks itself inward: is involuted; is, yes, womblike. (Or, if one prefers, clitoral:

Webster's phrase for the clitoris: "a small, erectile organ at the upper end of the vulva," is neatly matched by the look of the letter e.) The uppercase letter, being a capital letter, is regarded as superior to the lowercase letter, thus enacting on a typographical level not only the upper-versus-lower class differences that inhere in a capital-ist economic system, but also in a society such as the one *Boit* depicts, in which, in terms of the sexes, there is a pronounced class (or case) difference between the fathers and husbands, who possess capital (be it financial or spermatic), and the mothers and wives, who do not. Finally, E is an initiator, a letter used for starting sentences, while in French, e is a letter whose proper place, when it comes to feminine nouns, is to go behind.

In regard to the Sargent painting, what does this mean? It means nothing, but suggests a great deal. It suggests, for example, that however much property a man can bequeath his daughters, he cannot give them the socially recognized and legitimized power—the "uppercaseness"—that came to him simply because he was born anatomically male and subsequently was named, and thus socially typed and raised, male. (The name problem, of course, is a matter that the nineteenth-century authors Mary Ann Evans and Amandine Aurore Lucie Dupin, Baroness Dudevant, attempted to remedy for themselves by the appropriation of the unambiguously male pseudonym George.)

To the extent that, as we have seen, *The Daughters of Edward Boit* is a portrait, symbolically, of Sargent's patron and fellow artist, the shift from E to e might also suggest that by the late nineteenth century, not only were artists becoming increasingly boxed in and emasculated—made to feel a lack of potency—but so were paters, patrons, and patriarchs. Thus the *lack* or *void* or *absence* that at first seemed specifically an aspect of being female can also be regarded as an anxiety displacement by the male, whose once assured authority modern society has begun to erode or castrate.

What, then, of the circumflex? Where does it fit into the picture? First, let us recall how a circumflex functions. A nineteenth-century French dictionary identifies the *circonflexe* as a "signe orthographique en forme de *v* renversé (ˆ) . . . qui provien[t] de la suppression d'une autre lettre, comme hôtel pour hostel, âge pour aage."[37] Thus the circumflex is a phonetic symbol commonly used in French to mark the absence of a letter that has been suppressed, a letter that used to neighbor the character over which the circumflex now rides. In the instance of the word boîte, the circumflex signals the absence of the letter *s*. Until the sixteenth century, the French term for box had been *boiste*.

Typographically, the circumflex is formed by merging opposing accents, one hard (*aigu*), one soft (*grave*), a slash (/) and a backslash ( ), to produce what amounts to a compromise, a congress, a counterbalancing, a neutralization: (∧). The circumflex (and its sublinear cousin, the proof-reader's caret, a mark that indicates something is missing and should be inserted), is visually close to the spearhead of the "shield and spear" zo-diacal sign for Mars (♂) that in turn doubles as the medical symbol for male. A recent medical dictionary defines "male" as "designating the sex of an individual containing organs that normally produce spermatozoa."[38] When the spear of the male symbol, which normally thrusts outward toward the ("logical," "active," "masculine") right, is pulled back toward the left until vertical, it transforms into a circumflexed letter *i*, as in boîte.[39] We now stumble upon yet another linguistic and typographic oddity: the cir-cumflexed *i* of boîte marks the absence of an *s*, the letter in the alphabet that not only commences the word sperm, but also resembles the sperm cell, the spermatozoon. *Webster's Seventh New Collegiate Dictionary* de-scribes a spermatozoon as "a motile male gamete of an animal usually with rounded or elongate head and a long posterior flagellum." The description of the gamete's form could aptly be used to describe the letter *s*, with its rounded head and filiform tail. One of the roles of the letter *s* is to make a singular word into a plural; thus, not unlike sperm, *s* can have a repro-ductive function. Also, the letter *s* can be used to make a word possessive ("summer's heat"), as sperm, by instigating children, can make a man (or woman) a possessive parent. The *s*, then, of all letters, is appropriately marked missing from the term boîte, and, by extension, the household that Sargent's box portrays.

The circumflex, inasmuch as it elides letters, makes words into con-tractions—a term that, outside the realm of grammar, has its own special place in the lingo of childbirth. Indeed, the circumflex, as typographical marking, can be seen in its own right as sexual, though now in a distinctly feminine, maternal way: as a sheltering tent; a bosom; a receptacle into which the central letter of boîte,[40] the *i*, is phallically plunged. But then, the insertion is not necessarily phallic; it might also, for example, connote a mother's ready nipple entered into her infant's expectant and parted lips.

Let me now conclude what certainly will have appeared to many read-ers as a rampant and frivolous sexualizing of totally innocent typographic markings, not by trying to justify this behavior but rather by having one more go around, this time with the letter i. This letter, of course, occupies the very center of the word boîte—as indeed, the centermost daughter of the painted boîte is also an I (in terms of figural posture). But, pictorially, even more than she is an I, she is an i. That is, she literally *looks like* a lowercase i, in the way that her white face is detached from her white pinafored body by a narrow strip of black, thus duplicating the formation of an i, though with a reversal of the negative-positive polarity.[41]

In the word *boîte*, the letter *i* has lost its rounded head in exchange for a spearhead; now it bears resemblance to an erect male member, the circumflexion producing the look of a circumcision. Circumcision, of course, is not the same thing as castration, but when, as a clitoridectomy, circumcision is performed on a female child, it annihilates sexual pleasure, whereas male circumcision does not. Clitoridectomy therefore is a form of castration—a removal of genital power, a removal of the organ's capability to "reproduce" gratifying stimulation. Although clitoridectomy (a procedure conceived, needless to say, by a male physician) was not a frequent surgical operation during the nineteenth century, the abrogation of female pleasure that it sought to accomplish was more regularly achieved, anyway, through what amounted to ideological surgery performed not only by parents but also by public or private school, Sunday school, and, in the twentieth century, the school of Freud.[42] Thus we find yet another way of accounting for the absence or void that *The Boit Children* evokes: the hinted-at absence of female sexual pleasure, and whatever sense of power or completeness goes with it.[43]

In any case, whether the circumflexed i of Boit/boîte is seen as indicating that the daughter has been masculinized, sexualized, or desexualized, we can draw our current peregrinations to a close by setting down a few simple equations. First we observe that, in the case of the word boîte, $î = is$. Then we recall that $i =$ Boit's daughter in the center of the painting, and that (if you go along with me) $s =$ sperm, the male gamete. Therefore: $î =$ fertilized female, which, to the extent that a woman impregnated is a woman whose personal freedom and potential has been clipped, may also be to say $î =$ circumcised female. What is the upshot of this sexual algebra? In the present context, it is that procreation, artistic as well as biological, is now to emerge or be delivered as the central theme of *The Daughters of Edward Boit*.

* * *

A box, presumably, is meant to be filled. Similarly, the Female Child is meant to be filled, first with the rules of obedience and social propriety, then eventually with the male organ itself, and finally with a new child (who will replace the child that she, the impregnated female, no longer is). Both Isabel Archer and Pansy Osmond are receptacles in the first sense, and

Dr. Agnew's patient is, metaphorically, a receptacle in the second sense. At present we are working our way toward an understanding of how that third and final sense of female-as-receptacle is enacted by the mise-en-scène of *The Boit Children.*

But first more wordplay is in order (will it never end?), not because the activity is fun or provides amusing razzle-dazzle, but because, as is the case in the construction of this particular visual image, if not all visual images, language is an essential element, one that should not, must not, be overlooked. Let us go back therefore to the definition of boîte as "récipient de matière rigide." This phrase properly translates as "a receptacle made of rigid material," but might also be translated as "a receptacle of rigid material"—meaning, that is, a receptacle that receives into itself, is penetrated by, some material that is hard and rigid.[44] The sexual connotation is obvious. *Daughters of Edward Boit* is a visual box, every "cubic" inch of which we are invited (incited even, by such tantalizing devices as the shadow-obscured back room and the sfumato of R's face) to penetrate and animate with our hard, rigid gaze, as Boit's real-life daughters themselves, at some future point in their lives, were each meant by society to receive the procreative, life-bestowing embrace of a man.[45]

Finally, there is one last sense in which a definition of boîte seems relevant to Sargent's image, and that is in the popular, slang sense of "maison, lieu de travail"—a house or place of work. Maison is in turn given a variety of meanings, with the first among them being a structure to be inhabited, which Sargent's painting depicts. But the second meaning of maison is "édifice destiné à un usage spécial," as in a house of business— "La Maison Worth," for example—or as in house of prostitution—Maupassant's Maison Tellier being the example cited by the *Petit Robert* (1981).[46]

If the term boîte can thus be said to suggest, to a mind acquainted with French popular usage, a house of commerce (or a locale for a particular kind of commerce—a house of prostitution), and if this meaning can then be applied to the boxlike image of this painting, then the French term, *patron,* which pinpoints Boit's role in the making of this painting, takes on an additional resonance. The *Petit Robert* gives "patron" as "personne qui commande à des employés, des serviteurs"—"maître, maîtresse de maison, par rapport à ses domestiques," for example, or "personne qui dirige une maison de commerce, de petit ou moyenne importance, dont elle est généralement propriétaire," and so on. A patron, in other words, is an owner or a boss (or both): while the English usage of the term generally suggests artistic support of an almost fatherly or familial nature, the French usage stresses proprietary authority and an economic, contractual relationship.

Whereas Edward Boit was the patron of Sargent's painting, the *Edward Boit* signified by the painting's title is the *patron*—the owner and boss—of the boîte or maison the painting represents. He, the father, is thus figured in absentia as the master or boss of these young females whom the title designates as his children but who, seeming to await his slightest word or wish, might also be thought of as his servants, his domestics, and even, at the level of submerged sexual fantasy, as his harem, his congregation of wives, his jolies fillettes du bordel/maison/boîte.

Surely Sargent did not set out to liken the children of his friend and patron to well-tended slaves or pampered young courtesans lounging in the foyer of a bordello with no apparent raison d'être other than to be selected for service by their patron and source of *nom patronymique,* yet nevertheless close analysis of the painting's visual and verbal semantics makes such a reading viable. The foursquare image, with its four young females waiting and residing within, can be seen as structured, in a fundamental way, in terms of both sexual difference and class difference.

This having been said, we now are equipped to understand *The Boit Children* as a work in which the Female Child is filled in the third manner mentioned above, filled with a child of her own; she is transformed from the recipient of the patronymic (and all that it implies) to the vessel by which this patronymic is carried forth to the next generation. Reading the portrait in this way requires viewing its individual figures as representing successive stages in a life cycle, that of the generic entity we have been referring to as the Female Child.

J is the girl-child just past the point of infancy. She has attained the age at which she and a boy-child, a Little Lord Fauntleroy, might no longer be confused. The formation of her face and form establishes as much, but also, as if that were not enough, the doll in her lap announces it. A, off to the side, perhaps self-confident and content to be alone as only a not yet fully socialized adolescent can be, or perhaps only pretending to be so, is in any event the Female Child at the next stage of development. This stage is followed, the painting seems to say, by "the awkward age" that is represented in the stiff, very unrelaxed figure of I, a teenage or preteen girl who seems acutely, almost painfully, self-aware. Her central position on the canvas seems in this regard to bespeak not so much her family rank as seen objectively by others, but her own overconspicuous body and being, as she herself feels them subjectively and uncomfortably. She could be viewed as the too sensitive and too self-conscious teenager who always thinks everyone is gazing at her, surveying her, who always unpleasantly feels that she is center stage—a prisoner of society's Panopticon. R, though, can be regarded as having passed beyond that phase. She is the Female Child as exotic, mysterious young woman—the adjacent Oriental vase signifying the exotic, the shadows veiling her face indicating mystery. Indeed, as the girls grow older in this painting and recede further back into pictorial space, they become more dimly lit, as if to say that as girls turn into women, they become increasingly dark, moody, and mysterious: hard to "figure out."[47]

But if R can be seen as the female grown complex and unfathomable, she can equally be regarded as the Female Child transformed into the Young Wife, her countenance effaced as she herself is, or will be, effaced, eclipsed in importance by the man to whom she is wedded. Even more specifically, she may be regarded as that penultimate self for the Female Child, the Expectant Bride. We note the way that R stands, her shoulders back, her stomach forward, her hands slung supportively beneath, and what we see is a profiled form suggesting pregnancy. This already strong suggestion is reinforced by the huge vase to whose contours R conforms her body: the belly of the vase swells forth toward us like that of a woman with child. Note that the soaring bird glazed into the vase points directly to R's reproductive zone, as a pointing bird in early Renaissance religious iconography typically enacts the Virgin's annunciation. Indeed, a vase is a typical symbol for the womb, since it too is a vessel that bears and protects something regarded as delicate and lovely—cut flowers, for example. One might think of this picture's four pretty girls as uncut flowers; the closer they come to the age of bloom and, therefore, to the age of being clipped, the closer they come to the vase. The vase, as well as the womb it can now be seen as symbolizing, is a particular sort of boîte, vessel, or container.[48]

We have thus seen how the placement of the girls on the canvas in relation to their respective ages and stages of childhood works as a metaphor for the progression from the earliest phase at which the Female Child possesses a distinguishably nonmale identity to the final phase before which she ceases any longer to be the Female Child. Yet by encouraging the viewing eye to trace a circuit from girl to girl, the painting offers not a linear but a cyclical history of the Female Child. The story does not end with R, the Expectant Bride, but instead moves simultaneously forward and backward to J, who now is suddenly revealed to us not only as a little girl who lovingly cradles her doll, but also as a metaphorized mother who has just delivered, from the juncture of her parted legs, a baby child, an infant so newborn as not yet to appear fully human.[49] Our sense of a closed circle is heightened by the use of the mirror, which, instead of offering a window, an escape hatch, turns the world of the box back in on itself. This is a world in which everything is rebounded, everything repeated.

The question arises, is J's doll/baby male or female? The pinkish tone of the doll's cloak, according to the color-coding of pink for little girls and blue for little boys, might indicate that J's doll is female. Certainly a female doll/baby would fit neatly with our reading of the painting as stages in the life of the Female Child. However, and here for now we must rely on information wholly external to the image, the name that the real-life J gave to her doll was not feminine but masculine: "P-paul."⁵⁰ The double *p* at the start of the doll's name probably resulted from a stumbling difficulty (no doubt thought cute by adults) that the little girl experienced with that letter of the alphabet.

Why, one wonders, might this child have stumbled and stuttered over the initial phoneme of her doll's name? Might the explanation lie in the phonetic proximity of Paul, as she pronounced it, to a word of enormous and perhaps even overwhelming significance for her? The word I have in mind, of course, is "Papa." On the basis of the additional, external information of the doll's name, P-paul, almost identical in sound to Papa, our intuition is made even more literal that the ultimate purpose of the Female Child, as she is here depicted, is to transmit her p-patronymic. This suggests that the term *male* can be regarded as a noun and *female* as a transitive verb whose function is to connect masculine subject with masculine object: grandfather begets father begets son begets grandson begets greatgrandson, with the woman's role that of the "begets."⁵¹ By means of the doll, P-paul/Papa, issuing from the lap of a daughter, we uncover (or manufacture) another of the painting's several verbal-visual condensations of sexual signifiers: in a complicated variation of Wordsworth's "the child is father of the man," we arrive at "the child is mother of the father." We are encountering a condensation of linguistic signifiers as well, *pa* being the letters that commence a number of words central to our consideration of this portrait: papa, pater, patron, painter. If the Female Child is born of a patron-pater, she also, insofar as she exists on this canvas, is born of a painter (as indeed her real-life counterparts were born of Edward Boit, the artist) while at the same time she gives birth to a painter: for the artist who has gone through the labor of painting a major painting is that much more a painter for having painted it. His or her existence as an artist is reciprocally created by the art that he or she is responsible for creating. A man does not become a father until he has had a child. In a certain sense, therefore, that child gives birth to the father *as father*. Likewise, the novel is responsible for turning the person who wrote it into a novelist.

A dictionary defines *doll* as "a toy puppet representing a child or other human being." To the *Encyclopaedia Britannica* a doll is "a child's toy, modeled, however crudely, on the human form, and perhaps the oldest plaything of mankind."[52] Dolls being vestiges of mankind's earliest, most primitive figurative art, the doll in Sargent's painting reminds us that the work we are examining is itself figurative art, though now of a marvelously sophisticated sort. Thus, as a handmade, artificially rather than naturally created humanoid figure, P-paul (or simply "the doll") serves this portrait as a metaphor for itself inasmuch as the bodies in it, like the doll's, are illusionistic, artificed constructions. At the same time, the doll, as a patently artificial figure, functions twice as a metonym: it invokes, through association, both John Singer Sargent, the figurative artist who painted it, and Edward Darley Boit, the figurative artist whose offspring and household this portrait potrays. So even if we do not possess the information that the doll's name is partially homophonic with the diminutive for father, *papa,* we can still maintain a reading in which the Female Child is shown to function as a transmitter, a perpetuator, of her family's male line. The portrait shows this, however, ironically: inasmuch as these four girls are Boit's children, P-paul points up another sort of absence—Boit's lack of a son, and therefore the high probability that the father's line, rather than being perpetuated, will soon terminate. Thus again *The Boit Children* finds a way of depicting patriarchy as ubiquitously, form-bestowingly, and all-powerfully present, even as the patriarch himself is shown to be diminished, thwarted, symbolically headed toward impotence and oblivion. In so doing, the painting recapitulates aesthetically the social phenomenon of its era, in which, throughout the increasingly capitalized, federalized, and bureaucratized Western world, the patriarchal control of the individual father was being wrested out of his hands only to be reproduced, in a systematic, impersonal, formal fashion, by modern institutions of state, medicine, education, and finance.

Earlier in my reading of the painting I attributed the power of form-making and form-limiting ("boxing") not, as I have done now, to indifferent, impersonal, abstract patriarchy, but to the individual human father, to Boit, or, on a different level, to the "father" of the painting, Sargent. Yet these two distinctly different attributions are not irreconcilable. Although on one hand the painting seems to flatter the pater-patron by asserting that *he* gives all form and meaning to the life of his children, and on the other hand seems to register, through devices we have explored, a protest *against* the power of the patron, in both instances what is occurring is a sort of wishful thinking, an overcompensating fantasy, aimed at staving off a realization of the extent to which the individual father—or artist—in a market economy has lost his previously constituted authority and control. A doll, of course, is a puppet, and if this portrait, *The Boit Children,* suggests that the Female Child is treated in patriarchal society as a puppet of men, it also suggests, advertently or not, that the painter is sometimes reduced to the puppet of his cash-paying patron, and that the patron himself has become a puppet, a boxed-in puppet, of forces beyond his kith, or ken.

*   *   *

Dimly perceived in the back space of the painting is a fireplace. It is located directly above J's head, in back of I. I is the figure most closely associated with the fireplace; it is her metonymically attached signifier in the way that the doll is J's, the vase R's, and the highly polished panel A's. The interior of this fireplace is denoted by a nearly black rectangle that, were I not standing before it, perhaps would form a square instead, reproducing in miniature the shape of the canvas onto which it is painted. Either way the fireplace sets forth yet another container, another box.

If the smoothly rounded Oriental vase is a boîte that suggests fertility, this dark, cold (fireless), and angular boîte contrastingly suggests sterility, not so much in the sense of being hygienically germ free as in the sense of being genetically sperm free. It is an empty womb, a childless, impregnable womb. Compare it to the glowing fireplace boîte of Eastman Johnson's *Brown Family* (1869; fig. 23), an image in which, warmed by flickering flames, the neatly edged manteltop forms a continuous line with the benevolently shiny pate of bewhiskered, bespectacled pater, turned attentively and amusedly to his child, and mater, who sits serenely near the center, a Buddha with knitting needles. Were we still interested in reading each girl as a distinctly separate individual, we might surmise from this contrast that R is being characterized as fecund, a born mother, while I is being presented as a female without the instincts, inclinations, and potential for productivity traditionally associated with motherhood. In terms, however, of the girls as a collective entity—the Female Child—the empty fireplace represents the completion, the extinction, of the cycle: in one direction, toward J and therefore toward us, the spectators, lie life and rebirth, while in the other direction, toward that dark unknowable deep region, lies the opposite of life and rebirth, death. This is another way in which the image flatters the viewer. It suggests to "him" that in "his" direction is to be found life and regeneration, while away from it, as away from the sun, there is only coldness and void. Appropriately, the dark rectangular slab of the fireless fire-

23. EASTMAN JOHNSON, *The Brown Family* (1869).

place calls to mind yet another familiar sort of box, a coffin. Like the womb, the coffin is a protective receptacle made for holding in place the helpless human body, and in modern society, most of those who once resided in the one boîte will eventually reside in the other. But as for the Female Child, her extinction transpires not when she goes to the coffin but, instead, long before that; it occurs when her womb grows cold and permanently empty.

Freud recounts having once suddenly recalled an early memory: "I saw myself in front of a chest, the door of which was held open by my half-brother, twenty years my senior: I stood there demanding something and screaming; my mother, pretty and slender, then suddenly entered the room, as if returning from the street." Analyzing this initially inexplicable memory, Freud eventually associates it with the information he later acquired that his nanny had been caught stealing and had therefore been dismissed from service by Freud's half-brother. "This information," Freud remarks,

gave me the key to the scene from childhood, as through a sort of inspiration. The sudden disappearance of the nurse was not a matter of indifference to me; I had just asked this brother where she was, probably because I had noticed that he had played a part in her disappearance, and he, evasive and witty as he is to this day, answered that she was "boxed in." I understood this answer in the childish way, but asked no more, as there was nothing else to be discovered. When my mother left shortly thereafter I suspected that the naughty brother had treated her in the same way as he did the nurse, and therefore pressed him to open the chest.

The recollection concludes with this realization: "I also understand now why in the translation of the visual childhood scene my mother's slenderness was accentuated; she must have struck me as being newly restored. I am two and a half years older than the sister born at that time, and when I was three years of age I was separated from my half-brother."[53]

The anecdote exemplifies how a word generates an image and, years later, that image re-generates the word. For Freud, the particular word was *boxed in*. For Sargent, when conceiving this painting, might not Boit(E.) have had a similar unconscious effect, the term playing upon his artistic sensibilities, burying itself within the form and content of what was therefore not an accidental image, only to be retrieved by the analyst (in this instance, ourselves) many years later? The Freud reminiscence is of particular use to us in regard to the notion of a chest (*clothes chest* or *armoire*, which the fireplace resembles) as a symbol of a certain inimitably female, and thus alien, reality that the male has reason to fear and repress: pregnancy. When young Freud's mother suddenly departed, having gone away to give birth to another child, the boy imagined she was boxed in, which is perhaps the closest he could come at that time to imagining death. Yet in the days preceding her sudden absence, when she was full with child (and therefore not slender), might he not have looked at her and also thought the term boxed in and its root word *box* (*Schachtel* in German, a feminine-gender noun)? Could his subsequent panicked opening of the clothes box have been prompted not only by dread of his mother's disappearance (death) but also by desire to (re)enter her womb and, in so doing, displace from it whatever unborn rival he may have sensed that it harbored?[54]

In perhaps similar fashion to the chest in Freud's recollected visual image, the fireplace in Sargent's painted image amalgamates womb and coffin, pregnancy and death, generation and extinction—in each instance an audacious melding together of seeming opposites. As we think of the fireplace in this way, the slab of mirror above it becomes a sort of tombstone; but also, since it is windowlike, a hint of transmission into another plane of existence, one that lies on the other side of the fireplace crypt. The vase, meanwhile, switches its connotation in this new light, now suggesting a giant funerary urn. The painting contains four vases; might we not think of them as four urns, *memento mori* of the four girls who will have turned to ash or to dust long before this huge varnished canvas, and the pigment laid upon it, crumbles in turn?

*   *   *

Now let us examine the spatial layout of the two rooms pictured in this painting. We observe that the clearly lit front room is symmetrical and orderly, while the dark, almost indiscernible back room is vaguely asymmetrical. The juxtaposition of the back room to the front is, as Freud might put it, uncanny. Similarly, though maybe less uncannily so, there is a felt difference for the viewer between the vase on the left and the one on the right. Unlike the front room and the vase on the left, but like the back room, the right-hand vase is not clearly lit, properly proportioned, or fully revealed.

I wish to propose at this point that *The Boit Children* represents a map of consciousness, a diagram that charts the mind or psyche of the Female Child as unconsciously perceived and responded to by a particular male artist, an American in Paris, during the early 1880s. This diagram is constructed along two axes, one of them left-right, the other near-far.[55] Generally, what we find as we travel visually along each axis is that the near space and left-side space is rational, accessible, and orderly, while the recessed area and the right-side sector, exclamation-pointed by the sharp,

off-balance jag of a menstrual-red screen, is relatively unrationalized, frag-
mented, disturbed.

Were we still talking about the Female Child developmentally we could
attempt to plot along the two axes the various stages that would be represented and then give the gloss that at such and such a stage in her life
the Female Child is easy to read, while at this and that stage she is difficult
to comprehend, and so forth. But that would be a simple-minded approach,
reductive, dangerously schematic—a repression of the painting's complexity
and suggestiveness. Similar problems would occur were we to take the four
children as individuals, ranking them in terms of individual rationality or
irrationality according to their respective positions on the grid.

However, when we gather the four young females into that single unit,
the Female Child, and now regard this unit synchronically—as it is at one
given moment rather than as it develops over a period of time—what the
painting anticipates by a decade or so is Freud's initial insights concerning
the minds of the bourgeois women who were his first psychoanalytic patients, insights that the mind, the psyche, of the Female Child (our term,
not his) is an unsettling juxtaposition of reason and disorder, clarity and
obscurity, expression and repression, ease and disease. In this regard, *The
Boit Children* is a multiplanar documentation of female subjectivity, especially as it is constructed, animated, objectified, distorted, and construed
in a male system of (re)production and (re)presentation.

This matter of sexual difference should be kept in the foreground of
any further consideration given to *The Boit Children*. I would therefore
like to close this chapter by observing that *all* its axes—near-far, left-right,
up-down, lower left corner to upper right, and upper left to lower right—
converge at the spot occupying the very center of the square, the center of
the boîte: the masked genitals of the figure we have referred to as I. Might
we take this to indicate that the work is "vaginocentric," which amounts
to looking out at woman from a male perspective: the vagina as destination
or focal center—the target—of male desire? Or instead, could it be called
"clitoricentric," a looking out from woman's perspective: clitoris as the
medium of autonomous self-expression—the pointing arrow of female desire? Rather than saying disparagingly of the painting that, "typically male,"
it reifies and objectifies, fixing its sights, and thus the spectator, on female
sexuality, could we suggest instead that, atypically of male-generated art,
it strives to show reality from a female position, a woman's perspective, a
specifically feminine, "gynocentric," subjectivity? The notion is certainly
debatable, but the debate is worth undertaking, for it touches so directly
and importantly upon crucial questions of how character representation

can sometimes unbalance "the order of things," decentering absolute fixedness not by replacing it with a new, equally fixed or rigid presence, but rather by allowing it to remain, in male eyes at least, as empty, lacking, phallically incomplete.

The Boit Children, indeed, is a Pandora's box of complicated and troublesome underminings of the way things are or seem to be. The portrait becomes other than what it originally appeared. To the extent that it has generated for us so many possible interpretations, has propagated so many perceptions, has given birth to so many quickenings of our spirit and intellect, it has shown itself to be, more than simply a painting, a procreative force.

CHAPTER FOUR

The Portrait of a Lady

N OW THAT WE HAVE DISCUSSED two portraits painted in the 1880s that revolve around related questions of sexual identity and portrait-making, we shall turn to James's novelistic portrait of 1881, a work that is traversed and underpinned by the same questions. Like *The Agnew Clinic* and *The Boit Children*, *The Portrait of a Lady* proves, even on a structural level, to be about what we have been calling the act of portrayal and, in the same instance, the acting out of sexual identity.[1]

In writing and crafting *The Portrait of a Lady*, in posing and modeling the fictive construct referred to as Isabel Archer, in putting her through narrative paces, and in verbally manufacturing the physical, social, and ideological universe in which she is centered and made manifest, James not only makes a portrait but also strives, perhaps unconsciously, to assess the moral value—the benefits, the drawbacks, the psychological cost—of engaging in such an act. This novel shows itself to have been for its author (as *Agnew* and *Boit* later in the decade were for their authors) an attempt at artistic self-confrontation, a recognition that the portraitist victimizes even as he (or she) is in a correlative sense a victim. In this regard *The Portrait of a Lady*, like *The Agnew Clinic* and *The Boit Children*, is an act of expiation that, at a crucial stage in its author's career, gave him permission to continue his probings of character, probings that did inevitable violence either by the unpleasant aspects of character they revealed or by the suppression of those aspects. The psychological portraitist is always in a bind. To the extent that he pins down his subject's personality, names it, fixes it, boxes it up, he has imposed a specious unity upon it that is at best a social myth, an illusion. However, to the extent that he slices into the subject's personality, dissects it, severs the cords that help foster the illusion of unity that the subject presents to himself and society, the portraitist is liable to charges of moral vivisection.

But even as James used this novel as a vehicle for examining the functions, good and bad, of portraiture—and of the portraitist that he found himself becoming—he also, probably in an unconscious way, used it as a means of coming to terms with his own dually sexual nature. In *The Portrait of a Lady*, James seems to have subdivided himself-as-portraitist, first distributing the parts to a number of characters (primary and secondary, female and male, sympathetic and unsympathetic) and then engaging these characters in varying degrees of comradeship and conflict, as though the end result would somehow reveal to the novel's master portraitist, Henry James, how much of a man he was, how much a woman, and how acceptable was either. As Leon Edel has written, "In posing the questions: what would Isabel do with her new-found privileges? where would she turn? how behave? he was seeking answers for himself as well as for her." Whereas Edel sees *The Portrait* as an attempt by James to come to terms with his freedom to live in Europe and write fiction, I suspect motives much less consciously recognized but more basic and determining.[2]

Several characters in the book think in a manner analogous to the perceptual-conceptual processes involved in the act of portraiture. None does so more frequently or forcefully than Isabel. Similarly, though many of the novel's characters think and behave in a manner directly counter to that stereotyped for their gender—the male characters are often womanly, the females manly—no character is as much a literary transvestite as that primary fictional construct Isabel, the construct that represents the portraitist's veiled portrayal of himself.

*   *   *

In order to demonstrate how Isabel can be viewed as a portrait of a portraitist—in other words, as an instance of self-portraiture by James— it is necessary to identify her characteristic cognitive activities and show how these are the same as those employed by the artist engaged in portrayal. Throughout this book we have been regarding portrayal as a process that embodies a dialectical interaction. The interaction takes place between the artist's more or less passive observation of what appears as a pre-existent reality (the sitter: the portrait's so-called subject) and the artist's more or less active construction of a material artifact (a painting, a novel) that activates and manipulates various cultural codes in order to produce something that the viewer will read similarly to, but also differently from, how he would have read the antecedent reality. To the extent that passive observation is stereotyped by our society as feminine, while instrumental activity is characterized as masculine, the act of portrayal as it is here defined might be regarded as an activity involving dually sexual, antithetically sexual, impulses.

Before turning to *The Portrait of a Lady* itself to see how Isabel "is like" a portraitist, perhaps it would first be best to see how James conceived of literary portraiture, the activity that he performed as he proceeded to write the novel. The 1908 preface to the New York Edition of *The Portrait* starts with an account of the material circumstances involved in the production of the earlier text. Specifically, James speaks of Venice, where he wrote the latter portions of the novel, and of the difficulties he had finding his concentration in such an abundantly interesting, hence distracting, locale. He is not, at this opening point in the preface, talking about characterization; that comes later. Yet since the theory of characterization, of portrayal, is the preface's chief concern, perhaps this initial discussion of Venice is at least metaphorically related to it.

"I had rooms on Riva Schiavoni, at the top of a house leading off to San Zaccaria;" he says, then continues:

The waterside life, the wonderous lagoon spread before me, and the ceaseless human chatter of Venice came in at my windows, to which I seem to myself to have been constantly driven, in the fruitless fidget of composition, as if to see whether, out in the blue channel, the ship of some right suggestion, of some better phrase, of the next happy twist of my subject, the next true touch of my canvas, mightn't come into sight. But I recall vividly enough that the response most elicited, in general, to these restless appeals was the grim admonition that romantic and historic sights offer the artist a questionable aid to concentration when they themselves are not to be the subject of it. They are too rich in their own life and too charged with their own meanings merely to help him with a lame phrase; they draw him away from his small questions to their own greater ones; so that, after a time, he feels, while thus yearning toward them in his difficulty, as if he were asking an army of glorious veterans to help him arrest a peddler who has given him the wrong change.[3]

Just as Venice with its ceaseless human chatter and its wonderous lagoon distracts the novelist from his labor without in return supplying some right suggestion to help steady the fruitless fidget of composition, so, it might be said, does the closely observed personality of an individual subject resist artistic toil when, like Venice in all its watery depth and multichanneled complexity, it is gazed upon by the would-be portraitist as a model from which to work. "How can places that speak *in general* so to the imagination not give it, at the moment, the particular thing it wants?" James inquires. He then replies, "The real truth is . . . that [scenic locales] express, under this appeal, only too much—more than, in the given case, one has use for."[4]

Certainly James could not have continued to look out his window onto the Riva Schiavoni and still have written his novel. He had to turn away from that window; he had to shut out the view; he had to cut down the field of vision; he had to suppress. This, it seems, is what every portraitist must do: he must look away from the immensity and flux, the only too much, and turn instead to text or canvas, where an orderly, manageable, circumscribed version of reality's immensity and flux can be set forth.[5]

For James, the genuine artist views through the open window "the faintest hints of life," and then, presumably when focused again on the uncompleted page or canvas, "converts the very pulses of the air into revelations."[6] Implied in this artistic labor is a shuttling back and forth between the window from where the flux of any external reality such as the individual personality is detected, and the desk or easel where a much reduced version of that reality is put together.[7] Hence the dialectic we spoke of earlier: the productive conflict between observation and creation, between the relatively passive and relatively active modes, between taking things in (perception) and then, after changing their shape, thrusting them out again into something else (penetration). Much of the tension that animates *The Portrait of a Lady* results from a similar conflict or set of conflicts experienced by the protagonist, Isabel, who, as we shall see, yearns for reality unconstricted, uncropped, and yet at the same time for reality that is delimited, structured, graspable.

We might characterize the twin but antithetical impulses of the portraitist (whether Henry James or Isabel Archer) this way: as realism and formalism. The realist impulse, as used here, is the wish to perceive and record the object of observation, be it oneself, another person, a social formation, or whatever, as completely and with as little intervention as possible by the medium of reproduction. The formalist impulse, however, is one that finds pleasure or value not so much in what is being observed, but rather in the way that it is being observed and the way it is being reproduced. The difference here is between an impulse that favors content prior to its formalization, and another that is less interested in the "prior" content[8] than in the resulting form into which that content is artistically translated.[9]

A good example of a literary realist—using the term as given here—is the sixteenth-century French essayist Michel de Montaigne, who says of himself as self-portraitist:

> Others shape the man; I portray him, and offer to the view one in particular, who is ill-shaped enough. . . . Now the lines of my portrait are never at fault, although they change and vary. Everything goes incessantly up and down . . . both with the universal motion and with their own. Constancy is nothing but a more sluggish movement. I cannot fix my subject. . . . I catch him here, as he is at the moment when I turn my attention to him. I do not portray his being; I portray his passage; not a passage from one age to another . . . but from day to day, from minute to minute. I must suit my story to the hour. . . . It is a record of various and variable occurrences, an account of thoughts that are unsettled and, as chance will have it, at times contradictory, either because I am then another self, or because I approach my subject under different circumstances and with other considerations.[10]

Aside from the narrator of *The Sacred Fount,* no Jamesian character, not even Colonel Capadose, the title character of James's story, "The Liar," is permitted the high degree of inconsistency and moment-to-moment changeability that Montaigne perceives in himself and by extension all others. Unlike James, Montaigne shows no interest in discovering and obeying formal principles of character representation: "Could my mind find a firm footing, I should not be making essays, but coming to conclusions," he remarks somewhat waspishly at the end of the passage cited. In such open-ended works as *The Portrait,* James is certainly far from the simplistic coming to conclusions that Montaigne denigrates, yet nevertheless the very nature of his formalist imperative dictates the superimposition of closure, symmetry, and totality onto the human subject that is being portrayed.

There comes at a later point in the 1908 preface James's often-noted "house of fiction" metaphor. In this metaphor, the enterprise of literature is likened to a huge mansion with many windows, behind each of which stands a figure (a writer) who is peering through a spyglass (an individual sensibility) at the surrounding environment (reality). Since no two windows are positioned alike, no two observing figures will have the same perspective on that environment. In terms of the realist-formalist dichotomy described above, when James the portraitist is at the window of the house of fiction, "a figure with a pair of eyes, or at least with a field glass,"[11] he is the openly observing Montaignesque realist unperturbed by the inconsistency, flux, and infinite detail of the individual personalities at which he gazes.

When he is at the desk of this house, however, the formalist takes, or at least seeks, command, and in so doing strips these personalities of their immense complexity by translating them into literary concepts, categories, and effects. To some degree this conflict between what is perceived as an outside, prior reality and the subjection of that so-called reality to conventions of aesthetic form underlies virtually every act of artistic creation, not only those of portraiture, and certainly not only those of Henry James (and Thomas Eakins and John Singer Sargent). Indeed, this conflict is latent even in our day-to-day acts of selective perception, wherein we unconsciously fit sensory data to pre-established categories or, if such data will not fit, disregard it altogether: "If we had a keen vision and feeling of all ordinary life, it would be like hearing the grass grow and the squirrel's heart beat, and we should die of the roar which lies on the other side of silence," notes George Eliot, adding, "As it is, the quickest of us walk about well wadded with stupidity."[12]

But even if this conflict is inherent in virtually every artistic creation, there are certain works that particularly strive to bring it to the fore, and that includes, if not every major portrait by James, Eakins, and Sargent, unquestionably the three examined here. Already we have seen the conflict in *The Agnew Clinic*, with Eakins-as-artist seeming to ally himself most uncomfortably with both the masculine surgeon-penetrator and the feminine patient-receiver, and then seen it manifested in *The Boit Children*, with Sargent-as-artist identifying himself with the patriarchal force that encloses feminine sensibility and, at the same time, with that sensibility's resistance to patriarchy's excessively logical, symmetrical structures. Now, by looking closely at *The Portrait of a Lady*, we will see how it too is a text whose continuing life and energy is generated from the realist/formalist, feminine/masculine, reception/penetration conflicts that occur at various levels of story and discourse.

*   *   *

Isabel Archer resents being pinned down, labeled, or otherwise put in a box. She adamantly resists any conclusions that others attempt to construct for her or about her. This is especially evident early in the novel, before she is married, but it is equally true through to the end. And well she might be supersensitive to this attempt by others to narrow her down, for from start to finish almost every other character in the book is preoccupied with getting a fix on her and determining with certitude the answer to what James in the preface refers to as "the primary question"—"Well, what will she *do?*"[13]

In Isabel's first conversation with cousin Ralph, for instance, when he jokingly suggests that his mother, Lydia Touchett, has adopted her, the young woman bridles at the very thought: " 'Adopted me?' The girl stared, and her blush came back to her, together with a momentary look of pain which gave her interlocutor some alarm. . . . 'Oh no; she has not adopted me. I'm not a candidate for adoption. . . . She has been very kind to me; but,' she added with *a certain visible eagerness of desire to be explicit,* 'I'm very fond of my liberty.' "[14]

The reason for my italicizing James's notation about Isabel's visible eagerness is to call attention to this as the first of numerous occasions in the text in which her concern for how she appears to others is brought into play. Sooner or later the reader begins to see, hidden beneath each of Isabel's assertions of her desire to be free of categories and labels imposed upon her from without, a subtle, evidently unconscious bidding to others to think well of her: to pin her after all, but only as she wishes.

Again, it should be remembered that Isabel's defensiveness is not un-justified: everyone does indeed display, to one degree or another, a pro-prietary and instrumental interest in her. When Ralph first discusses Isabel with his mother, he asks, "What do you mean to do with her?" (echoing the author's "Well, what will she *do?*"). Soon afterward, Mrs. Touchett aggressively rejects Ralph's assumption that Mr. Touchett will have some say in the young woman's future: "I don't know about that. She's my niece, not his." Ralph's response is, "Good Lord, dear mother; what a sense of property!" (p. 41). Yet before long Aunt Lydia has grounds to strike back at her son's way of thinking of and speaking about their relative. "Do with her? You talk as if she were a yard of calico" (p. 44). Indeed, Mrs. Touchett, along with her husband, proves to be one of the only characters in the novel who does not attempt to take literal or epistemological possession of Isabel, or to make use of her for self-interested reasons, monetary, aesthetic, or personal. Warburton, Osmond, Ned, and even Ralph certainly do, as do Henrietta, Pansy, and of course Madame Merle, of whom Isabel says un-derstatedly at the end, "She made a convenience of me" (p. 573). Of the important characters in the novel, only the Touchetts senior and the Count-ess Gemini can get along perfectly well without her, and therefore have no need to possess her, use her, or imaginatively organize their lives around her.

"Ah, Lord Warburton, how little you know me!" Isabel gently chides when the aristocrat asks for her hand. Nonetheless she is pleased to see that she does "all so mysteriously, matter to him" (pp. 105–06). This two-stage, self-contradicting response typifies Isabel throughout: she resents attempts to pin her down, make sense of her, understand her, always viewing such attempts as misprisions, as false constructions, and yet she hungers to be admired and, in one way or another, desired. This pattern is apparent even in her dismal marriage to Osmond, where her misery stems from being saddled with a husband who not only closes off her possibilities as a free agent, but who also finds in her shamefully little to admire or desire. Perhaps there is expressed here, on Isabel's part, a narcissistic need for self-idealization; she appears to require continuing confirmations from the outside world that her ego-ideal is safe and valid, and at the same time she seems so anxious to avoid denial of this that she fights off any attempts by others to get close to her and know her in depth. My wish in describing Isabel thus is not to indulge in psychologism—the fallacy of treating a verbal, artistic construct, Isabel Archer, as though she were a flesh and blood individual who, unlike the fictional character, could undergo psychoanalysis. I do wish, however, to show how her thought and behavior within the narrative of which she is a part are analogous to the mental processes involved in James's act of portraiture (and self-portraiture). In order to accomplish this, it is necessary that we treat Isabel's (and other characters') verbal utterances and narrative behavior as though these were real acts that could be described and analyzed psychologically. Equally important, though, is never to forget that we are sliding back and forth between two disparate ontological categories—human subjects and literary characters.

Warburton to Isabel: " 'You know, if you don't like Lockleigh—if you think it's damp or anything of that sort—you need never go within fifty miles of it. . . . There's no difficulty whatever about that; there are plenty of houses. I thought I'd just mention it; some people don't like a moat, you know. Good-bye.'

'I adore a moat,' said Isabel. 'Good-bye' " (p. 110).

This banter furthers the text's construction of Isabel as a humanlike character by permitting us to see, through implied meaning and perhaps even by the use of homophony, that what she actually adores is a protective gap between herself and all others, a moat that allows her to remain *remote*.

The desire on Isabel's part not to be fixed or judged, and yet to be thought of in the best light, has perhaps much to do with that remoteness of hers that she sometimes worries makes her "cold, hard, priggish" (p. 111). So long as she is able to maintain her distance from those who attempt closeness, she remains in a protective, defensible position, because those who think well of her will not be permitted an intimacy that might sour their favorable perceptions. Moreover, those who are inclined to make judgments of her have those judgments automatically invalidated, or at least made unverifiable, by that very distance. Transferring for a moment this discussion to the real-world, historical existence of Henry James, we think of his notorious efforts to hide from others, even from so-called intimates, his inner life. Like Isabel in the text, James in the world was interested in deflecting away from himself and onto something else—in this case, his work—the judgments of others and their attempts to be close. He, like Isabel, seems to have adored moats, even if somewhat guiltily, and he made sure that he was always surrounded by one.[15]

The most direct statement of the metaphysic underlying Isabel's defensive remoteness comes in chapter 19, during the debate over the nature of personality that the young woman engages in with Madame Merle. The older woman begins by making a case that in today's terms would be described as behaviorist, inasmuch as she argues that external appearances correspond directly to internal realities, and that the internal reality may accurately be read from external appearances.

When you've lived as long as I you'll see that every human being has his shell and that you must take the shell into account. By the shell I mean the whole envelope of circumstances. There's no such thing as an isolated man or woman; we're each of us made up of some cluster of appurtenances. What shall we call our 'self'? Where does it begin? where does it end? It overflows into everything that belongs to us—and then it flows back again. I know a large part of myself in the clothes I choose to wear. . . . One's self—for other people—is one's expression of one's self; and one's house, one's furniture, one's garments, the books one reads, the company one keeps—these things are all expressive. (p. 201)

Isabel, James tells us, "was unable to accompany her friend into this bold analysis of the human personality." Her view, which is fully in keeping with her desire to be unpinned by social conventions or by people's assessment of her, can be characterized as idealist, a belief which holds that external appearances are not unimpeachable indices to internal realities, and may therefore lead an observer to entirely false conclusions about the nature of those realities. While to Madame Merle's way of thinking, the external and internal so interpenetrate or overflow one another that making distinctions between the two ultimately becomes impossible, Isabel's idealist, essentialist, Emersonian position holds that external and internal are not only distinct, but also inevitably at odds with one another.

"I don't know whether I succeed in expressing myself, but I know that nothing else expresses me. Nothing that belongs to me is any measure of me; everything's on the contrary a limit, a barrier, and a perfectly arbitrary one. Certainly the clothes which, as you say, I choose to wear, don't express me; and heaven forbid they should! . . . My clothes may express the dressmaker, but they don't express me. To begin with it's not my own choice to wear them; they're imposed upon me by society." (pp. 201–02)

In effect Isabel is saying: "No one has any right to judge me, for I am something entirely separate from the socially and environmentally mediated appearance that you wrongly, very wrongly, scrutinize, quantify, judge, and label as me."

Asserting that we cannot gain accurate knowledge of a person by regarding his appearance, his behavior, or his self-chosen appurtenances as indicators of what lies within, Isabel attacks the very premise underlying all portraiture, written, sculpted, or painted.[16] Her position rests upon an assumption that every human subject has within an inviolable and un-quantifiable essence, a soul, that remains unchangingly, uniquely, and en-tirely apart from whatever transformations time and society may enact upon habits of speaking, behaving, and dressing. This is a Neoplatonic assump-tion; it involves a conception of reality—*real* reality—as static, fixed, un-touched by history, eternally enduring. If Madame Merle claims that a person is nothing more than what one does and how one does it, Isabel thinks instead that one has a residual reality, and that this is the core reality, the true reality, the essence that not only precedes earthly existence but also cannot be reached simply through an empirical, inductive examination of that existence.

Though it would be inaccurate to describe Madame Merle as a dialec-tical materialist, her position is nevertheless historicist and anti-essentialist: she sees character not as something prior to matter and history, but rather as something that is negotiated anew, moment to moment, by the interac-tions of both material force and social relations, or, as she puts it, "the whole envelope of circumstances."[17] Thus it would seem that she speaks on behalf of the sort of portraiture James is engaged in, one that attempts to create—to show—character dynamically, developmentally, as an ongoing process rather than as a fixed, static, basically unchanging essence that is only dressed up in the clothes and ideas of time and place for the sake of local color. Earlier I suggested that, to the extent a portraitist allots priority to (material) reality over (abstract) form, he or she is realist rather than formalist. In this sense, then, Merle can be regarded as a spokeswoman for Montaignesque realism in portraiture/character depiction, while Isabel, de-valuing material reality and enshrining instead abstract essences, would seem to prefer a portraiture that imposes categorical order on the messy, recalcitrant, inconsistent material reality of human character. This idealist way of thinking causes her to regard those around her as if they were walking and talking manifestations of pre-existent forms; hence her frequent reference to other individuals as "types" or "specimens."

Yet neatly to equate Madame Merle's respect for matter with a portraitist's impulse toward realism, and Isabel's preference for intangible abstraction with the contrary impulse toward formalism, would be inadmissibly reductive. Formalism, as described above, can include not only the artist's love for the conventions, categories, and rules of an art, but also the material of it, whether that material is paint or paragraphs. In this regard, then, the artistic formalist can also be a materialist, with the material she or he prefers not so much what is being represented (the human body, let us say) as that stuff (phrases or brushstrokes) employed to build the representation. Therefore, on the formalist side, Merle might be seen representing what can perhaps best be described as material formalism, while those tendencies Isabel stands for can be termed conceptual formalism. The battle lines drawn between Isabel and Merle (first "only" ideological but later, as the plot unfolds, also sexual and proprietary) are lines that position the opposing sides, the clash of which generates James's psychological portraiture. The two major dichotomies are on the one hand between the tendencies of realism, meaning here that the imposition of order never becomes more than a secondary concern, and formalism; and on the other hand, within the formalist camp, between the proconceptual and the promaterial.[18]

To put this another way: the impulses competing with one another in James's literary portraiture are (1) the concern to be true to the human subject or subjects he is depicting; (2) the desire to manipulate not only the tools and the rules of his craft, but also the subject as he has perceived it, in order to achieve a thing of beauty; (3) his intrinsic pleasure in the materials of his trade (words, phrases, rhythmic patterns, and so forth); and (4) his high regard for the moral concepts and humane emotions that can be generated from text to reader by means of the artful arrangement, patterning—in a word, exploitation—of those same materials. Though I am not arguing that *The Portrait of a Lady* is a strictly allegorical display of various impulses battling for supremacy, I am claiming that this conflict at the aesthetic level is ultimately inseparable from the other types of conflict the text embodies.

It will be helpful to look at various characters in the novel vis-à-vis the categories introduced so far, namely, realism, formalism, idealism, and materialism. These categories sometimes blend into one another, so that it would be a mistake to think of any of them as fully isolated from the others; no one of these categories can be conceived alone. Therefore it must be remembered that when we link a certain character with realism and another with idealism, and so on, we are speaking only of general tendencies displayed by this or that particular character in word and deed.

* * *

Isabel thinks herself open and adventurous in her attitude toward herself and others. She believes she is ready to cast her gaze unflinchingly and unjudgingly upon the frailties of the human spirit. She is eager, the narrator tells us, to feed her "immense curiosity about life" and to feel "the continuity between the movements of her own soul and the agitations of the world." Following the behest of her recently deceased father, who "had a large way of looking at life," she wishes "to see as much of the world as possible." Yet because she has an imagination that is "remarkably active"— even "ridiculously" active—she possesses the often troublesome "faculty of seeing without judging." Indeed, making final judgments is, she believes, so foreign to her nature that when she was a child during the Civil War, "she felt herself at times (to her extreme confusion) stirred almost indiscriminately by the valour of either army" (pp. 33–35, 49).

It would follow, then, that Isabel's vision of humanity is fully inclusive, fully accepting, the paradigmatic mind set of the neo-Montaignesque realist to whom no human behavior is alien. As she says of herself, "I like so many things! If a thing strikes me with a certain intensity I accept it. I don't want to swagger, but I suppose I'm rather versatile. I like people to be totally different from Henrietta.... Then Henrietta presents herself, and I'm straightaway convinced by *her*" (p. 93).

Prior to this quotation, however, the narrator had already begun complicating Isabel's view of herself as an all-tolerating, all-encompassing humanist. "Isabel's chief dread in life at this period of her development was that she should appear narrow-minded; what she feared next afterwards was that she should really be so" (p. 61). How she looks to others is clearly different from and more important to her than what she "really" is. Her sense of having a genuine self distinct from external appearances paradoxically puts her in the position of manipulating the image she presents others so that she might save, not so much her integrity, but her own self-image. This is simply one of the ways in which her idealist, essentialist, Neoplatonic beliefs give rise to (or arise from) a constricting mode of perception—for certainly one who dreads appearing or being narrow-minded is not likely to perceive herself or others in a relaxed, tolerant, unrestrictive manner.

Another, and closely related, result (or cause) of her dualistic view of reality is her habit of thinking in types. She sees the people she meets not as unique, idiosyncratic individuals who are an endlessly complex admixture of psychological process and social or economic determination, but rather as flesh-and-blood embodiments of abstract qualities and pre-established categories. This is the conceptual formalism I described earlier, applied however not to aesthetic materials but instead to fellow humans. Isabel makes people fit into slots rather than making her ideological slots fit people.

Her response to Lord Warburton is a good example of this. When Ralph is about to introduce him to her, she exclaims, "Oh, I hoped there would be a lord; it's just like a novel!" A week or so later, she is still regarding him, of course with a touch of irony, as "a hero of romance" (p. 66).

Isabel had spoken [to Ralph] very often about "specimens", it was a word that played a considerable part in her vocabulary; she had given him to understand that she wished to see English society illustrated by eminent cases.

"Well now, there's a specimen," he said to her as they walked up from the riverside and he recognized Lord Warburton.

"A specimen of what?" asked the girl.

"A specimen of an English gentleman." (p. 65)

Little wonder Warburton chides that she is "always summing people up," and that her mind "looks down on us all" (p. 80), or that he can say, with Henrietta Stackpole in mind, "I never saw a person judge things on such theoretic grounds," only to have Isabel reply, "Now I suppose you're speaking of me" (p. 133).

It is not only Warburton who is the object of this stereotyping method of thinking about people. When Isabel, chatting with her uncle, discussed the neighbors, "she usually inquired whether they corresponded with the descriptions in the books." Such an inquiry as this would bring a "fine dry smile" to the old Yankee pragmatist: " 'The books?' he once said; 'well, I don't know much about the books. You must ask Ralph about that. I've always ascertained for myself—got my information in the natural form. I never asked many questions even; I just kept quiet and took notice.' " (p. 56)

Mr. Touchett, though a minor character, is more than anyone else in the novel an embodiment of that all-tolerating, fully receptive Montaignesque empirical realism that Isabel admires yet does not in any way demonstrate. When Touchett explains that he tries to look at things on their own terms instead of in categories derived from books, he is of course oblivious to the poststructuralist recognition, a century later, that all our day-to-day, common-sense perceptions of reality are unavoidably mediated by our continuous first- and second-hand exposure to "book-learning." Yet nevertheless his quiet, passively receptive approach to looking at the world and people around him is characteristic of the approach to portraiture that James conveyed years afterward by the image of himself looking out his window at "the waterside life, the wonderous lagoon spread before me." As the only genuinely disinterested character in the novel, the only one who is not engaged in an act of seeking (money, experience, freedom, a partner, an edifying or aesthetic spectacle), Touchett is the only character qualified to represent this aspect of portraiture. Otherwise, non-instrumental observation, passive reception, the valuing of things in the natural form, is present in the story only insofar as it is conspicuously absent in the lives of all the other characters.

It is appropriate of Touchett to remark, in the passage above, "You must ask Ralph about that," for like Isabel, Ralph tends to draw categories and remit people to them. "Ralph Touchett was a philosopher. . . . His father, as he had often said to himself, was the more motherly; his mother, on the other hand, was paternal" (p. 37).[19] Ralph considers cousin Isabel, as Selden considers Lily Bart, a spectacle or entertainment of a high order: " 'A character like that,' he said to himself—'a real little passionate force to see at play is the finest thing in nature. It's finer than the finest work of art—than a Greek bas-relief, than a great Titian, than a Gothic cathedral. . . . Suddenly I receive a Titian, by the post, to hang on my wall—a Greek bas-relief to stick over my chimney-piece' " (p. 63). The difference between Isabel and Ralph in this regard is that while she conceives of people in terms of familiar literary characters and types, he thinks of her in terms of lofty aesthetic objects; his manner is perhaps more sophisticated, but equally mediated. How unlike either of the elder Touchetts, both of whom seem to distrust any kind of literary portrayal, whether in a letter, a novel, or a newspaper report. Aunt Lydia, wishing to know about her several nieces, booked passage to America: "There was no need of writing, for she should attach no importance to any account of them she should elicit by letter; she believed, always, in seeing for one's self" (p. 27). Her husband amusedly reminisces about "a lady who wrote novels . . . she was a friend of Ralph's . . . she was not the sort of person you could depend on for evidence. Too free a fancy—I suppose that was it" (p. 57). As concerns journalistic portraiture, Lydia says to Isabel's friend, Henrietta, "We judge from different points of view. . . . I like to be treated as an individual; you like to be treated as a 'party' " (p. 95), the implication being that Henrietta also treats others as parties, or specimens of a type, for the sake of her reports. This is portraiture at its worst that is being mocked, a conceptual formalism exaggerated to the point of mechanical stereotype. Henrietta herself practically admits as much, ironically to be sure, when she speaks to Isabel of her latest transatlantic report: "I was going to bring in your cousin—the alienated American. There's a great demand just now for the alienated American, and your cousin's a beautiful specimen" (p. 86).

Isabel's penchant for fixing the people she knows and pinning them to pre-established categories is illuminated on one side by cousin Ralph's aestheticism and on the other by Henrietta's crassly commercial stereotyping. Taken to the extreme (as perhaps Ralph himself never takes it—unlike Gilbert Osmond), aestheticism, the ardent pursuit of "the sweet-tasting property of the observed thing in itself" (p. 41), leads to making a fetish of the personality under scrutiny, thus dehumanizing that personality, valuing it not in itself (as the Montaignesque realist might do) but for the sake of the sweet-tasting property it permits the scrutinizer to experience. Meanwhile, Henrietta's reduction of every one she meets into a type, a specimen, a party, makes her always abrasive, often comic, and thoroughly successful at her job of manufacturing for her newspaper readers stock characterizations that provide these mass consumers with merely a different, more vulgar variety of sweet-tasting property than that swallowed by the aesthete. Henrietta's manner of perceiving and representing other people commodifies them and thus is dehumanizing, but the dehumanization involved is not generically different from that which results from Ralph's aestheticism, Osmond's narcissism, and Isabel's idealism. All of these characters—from the heroine to the villain, from the faithful and kind friend to the blustery comedic one—reveal at various levels what, throughout this analysis, we have seen as the chief moral peril of portraiture: rigidification of the subject and its exploitation. Ralph's remark that "there was something in Miss Stackpole's gaze that made him . . . vaguely embarrassed—less inviolate, more dishonoured, than he liked" (p. 84) is merely a subjective statement of what it feels like to be the object of a fixing, penetrating, exploitative gaze, regardless of whether the interest that prompts the gaze is careerist (as with Henrietta), aesthetic (as with Ralph when it is turned upon his cousin), idealistic (Isabel), medical (the students in *The Agnew Clinic*), sexual (Lily Bart's observers in *The House of Mirth*), paternal (the absent father of *The Boit Children*), or artistic (that of the portraitist).

In all of these instances, the subject (the personality being gazed at) is treated as an object (the object of the gaze) and therefore as a whole, a totality, a largely immutable concretion of abstract essences (goodness, wickedness, beauty, and so forth). In their semiological study of ideology, Rosalind Coward and John Ellis observe that the function of ideology is "to fix the individual in place as subject for a certain meaning. This is simultaneously to provide individuals with subject-ivity, and to subject them to the social structure with its existing contradictory relations and powers." According to this argument, the purpose served by treating the subject as a fixed and unified whole is to hide from him (or her) the irremediable contradictions upon which both he and his society are predicated. This hiding, this repression, is the work of ideology, and its primary tool is language—an activity that, by its subject-verb format, which confers centrality and will to the I who speaks, teaches every individual in society to regard himself as a unified whole. "Ideologies set in place the individual as though he were this subject: the individual produces himself in this imaginary wholeness, this imaginary reflection of himself as the author of his actions."[20] From this perspective, then, Isabel's idealism, Henrietta's literary consumer commercialism, and Ralph's aesthetic formalism are various enactments of the main business of ideology itself, which is the fixing of the subject, or in other words, the subject's objectification: its being cemented into a seemingly noncontradictory, nondialectical, reified object.

The term "subject" makes any discussion such as this especially confusing, because the word has several meanings, all of which are involved. When we are speaking of the subject of a portrait, we might be referring to the individual agent whom the portrait represents, or to the individual who has constructed the portrait, or even to the individual who reads it. To the extent that a portrait presents Subject 1 (the individual portrayed) as a consistent whole, and thus covers over social and epistemological contradiction rather than exposing it, the portrait perpetuates our inbred notion of Subjects 2 and 3 (author and receiver) as both being fixed points of origin, of creativity, understanding, morality, and so forth, which is precisely the traditional teaching of humanism. Humanism, according to Louis Althusser, is that set of beliefs that hopes to "explain society and history, by taking as its starting-point human essence, the free human subject, the subject of needs, of work, the subject of moral and political action."[21] As defined by Althusser, humanism is the benevolent name given to subject-defining, position-fixing, contradiction-reducing ideology. A humanist text does not repress contradiction altogether, for then it would lose its credibility—people do sense, after all, that they embody contradictions, and would not accept as worthwhile anything that completely denies the lived experience—but the humanist text does make contradiction palatable and readable. It does this by its imposition of aesthetic form.

The humanist text, of which *The Portrait of a Lady* is an example, tolerates a certain amount of contradiction (*The Portrait* highlights, for instance, the contradiction between Isabel's desire to be nonjudgmental and her habitual wedging of people into categories), but presents that contradiction in an orderly, noncontradictory fashion. The balance it achieves between the inconsistency it depicts and the consistency with which it does so conveys to its reader (its final subject, Subject 3) a placating, politically liberal or progressive—and thus never revolutionary—sense that the horrible contradictions of both the individual and his or her society can be either satisfactorily resolved or tolerably accepted. Thus in a humanist text such as this early James psychological portrait, our sense of human indeterminacy is forever moderated and comforted and kept from boiling over into anything approaching radical social action by the implicit message of literary form: order shall prevail. Or, as E. M. Forster maintained, "Novels, even when they are about wicked people, can solace us; they suggest a more comprehensible and thus a more manageable human race, they give us the illusion of perspicacity and power."[22]

Yet even if *The Portrait of a Lady* reinforces and perpetuates the reigning humanist ideology of the fixed, unitary subject by such devices as (a) an implied "I–you" form of address by the narrator, (b) a relatively easy-to-understand prose style that has the effect of making the reader feel he or she occupies a privileged position to look at and understand reality, (c) the "central consciousness" point of view, (d) a heavy reliance on such melodramatic polarities as good/evil, selfish/generous, honest/deceitful, and innocent/corrupt, and (e) the normative regularity with which characters judge and label one another—even so, the text does throw out signals that contradict this dominant thrust.[23] Madame Merle's materialist challenge of Isabel's idealism is an example. True, the reader is eventually made to feel that Merle is evil, and thus is her philosophy condemned by guilt through association, but at least that philosophy, anti-idealist to the core, is enunciated fairly, and at a point in the text before the narrative has turned the reader wholly against its proponent. Similarly, the antiformalist realism of Daniel Touchett is voiced effectively and by a wholly sympathetic character, even though that voice dies with the character early in the story. The fun made of Henrietta Stackpole, who greatly exaggerates Isabel's tendency to fit people into categories, is a third way in which essentialism is opposed.

Further opposition is registered, however faintly, by the suggested weakness, loneliness, and morbidity of the book's sublime essentialist, cousin Ralph, and also by the immense dislike the reader is encouraged to feel for the villain of the piece, Gilbert Osmond. Osmond is an essentialist insofar as he partakes of empty social ritual and conspicuous displays of aesthetic consumption solely to create in others a deceptive impression of what kind of man he is within. Isabel comes to despise her husband for this essentialism without seeming to recognize how much she too is obsessed with the impression she makes. Whereas Madame Merle claims (with whatever deceit in mind) that one's internal being is inseparable from one's external situation, Osmond, again like Isabel, clearly believes that external and internal are wholly separate. Manipulating the former does not, for him, change the latter but instead only regulates outsiders' interpretation.

At the level of story and characterization, the most important of the novel's internal subversions of its dominant ideology is wrapped up in Isabel. By its frequent reiteration that her suffering and the suffering she causes those who love her is the result of her naiveté, her unworldliness, her ignoring or not seeing the contradictions in people, the text suggests to the reader, though never strongly, that fixing human subjects and assigning them to conceptual categories inevitably invites disaster. Thus the text cautions against formalism applied to humans even though, by formalizing the humanlike agents who enact the narrative, it helps inculcate in its reader the same sort of behavior.

*   *   *

By now this much should be clear: *The Portrait of a Lady* is about the act of perceiving and depicting character that we have been calling the act of portrayal. We have seen how Isabel wishes to look at others in the all-tolerating, contradiction-accepting manner that we have associated with realism, and yet also how her behavior and thought patterns, even her underlying philosophic assumptions, lead her to a formalism in which habitually she fixes (penetrates, pins down) or boxes (imposes categorical order upon) her subject. What we have not uncovered, however, is the desire that fuels Isabel's realist wish not to fix others or be fixed by them, yet at the same time motivates her formalist behavior. Perhaps in gaining some sense of that desire—observing the traces of it scattered throughout the text—we can achieve a clearer notion of the authorial desire that engendered this novelistic portrait.

There are three characters in the book who, at one time or another, are objects of Isabel's desire: Madame Merle, Gilbert Osmond, and the product of these two, Pansy. Of course the desire is different in each instance. Isabel desires Merle as a surrogate mother, Osmond as a replacement for her father, and Pansy as an idealization, a projection, of herself.

The desire that animates Isabel, and therefore the entire narrative, is one which, after Freud, we might justly call "the family romance."

Freud's brief paper "Family Romances" (published 1909) describes the ways in which a child compensates for his or her own powerlessness and inadequacy, as well as those of parents, by imagining that the parents, or their dream-substitutes, possess royal or supernatural power. Freud uses the word *romance* in the sense of the literary genre of that name, but the slightly different sense that suggests a passionate, semisexual involvement is not only applicable here but especially relevant, inasmuch as the child's romantic longing for the parent necessitates creation of a romance to insure that the parent is worthy of such tremendous longing.[24]

Isabel, who, it will be remembered, grew up without knowing her mother, is immediately drawn to the "charming, sympathetic, intelligent, cultivated" Madame Merle the "rare, superior, and pre-eminent" Madame Merle—drawn as though this woman filled a hole in Isabel's life that had been gaping for as long as she could remember. Merle becomes a screen upon which the young woman can pin her idealizing gaze, a human form through which she can Neoplatonically arrive at some prior, long-sought-after reality: her endlessly absent mother. (Ironically, as we have already seen, Merle is anything *but* a Neoplatonist.) Isabel quickly convinces herself about this older woman that she "knew how to think—an accomplishment rare in women," and, equally important, "she knew how to feel." She also concludes of Merle, however, that "Emotion . . . had become with her rather historic; she made no secret of the fact that the fount of passion, thanks to having been rather violently tapped at one period, didn't flow quite so freely as of yore" (p. 187). In this way, Merle is constructed—portrayed—by Isabel as a maternal ideal, perfect in every way. Strong (knowing how to think), tender (knowing how to feel), and serene (Serena is her first name), Merle as Isabel needs to see her is well beyond all the troublesome fears, wants, and emotions to which the wish-projecting child is vulnerable. And so goes this variation of family romance.

The narrator tells us,

Our heroine had always passed for a person of resources and had taken a certain pride in being one; but she wandered, as by the wrong side of the wall of a private garden, round the enclosed talents, accomplishments, aptitudes of Madame Merle. She found herself desiring to emulate them, and in twenty such ways this lady presented herself as a model. "I should like awfully to be *so!*" Isabel secretly exclaimed, more than once . . . and before long she knew she had learned a lesson from a high authority. It took no great time indeed for her to feel herself . . . under an influence. (p. 189)

The private garden imagery is apt; it suggests a yearning of Isabel's to regain a lost Eden—the Eden, perhaps, of the maternal womb. But the image works in another way as well. Merle, for Isabel, is less a real woman than a monumental compilation of accomplishments. To call her the "accomplished Madame Merle" is paying her a compliment, but it also characterizes her as finished, complete, no longer in a state of growth. Ralph complains of her at one point, "She is too good, too kind, too clever, too learned, too accomplished, too everything. She's too complete, in a word" (p. 251). The walled garden image therefore also bespeaks the young woman's perceptual framing—the walling in or boxing up—of Madame Merle. Isabel may feel herself shut out in one sense, but in another she is doing the shutting in, making Madame Merle the prisoner of her, Isabel's, devotional, maternal ideal, as indeed in the nineteenth century (if not since), mother-worship made prisoners of so many women, those who were willing as well as those who were not.

Whether or not Madame Merle actually wishes to be bronzed and pedestaled, Isabel automatically does it, setting herself up for immense future disappointment when she discovers that the bronze is not unblemished nor the statue perfect, which, by the way, Madame Merle admitted from the start: "If I must tell you the truth I've been shockingly chipped and cracked. . . . I've been cleverly mended. . . . But when I've to come out and into a strong light—then, my dear, I'm a horror!" (pp. 192–93).[25] The reader's sense that the older woman becomes for Isabel the long-awaited signifier of "Mother" is helped along by the continual recurrence in the text of the lady's name as "Madame Merle," the two visually prominent initials—M. M.—subtly bearing correspondence to the term of yearning learned in infancy: Mama, or, in French, *Maman*.[26]

Osmond becomes the object of a different desire, though a related one (in the context of family romance, the term *related* is especially apt). It is the desire for a father. The death of her real father offstage is the event that precipitates the happenings of the novel; Isabel's loss of her father not only makes her an orphan, which causes Aunt Lydia to bring her to England and into everyone's lives, but also makes her reject all suitors except the one man, Osmond, who is "right" to fill the void her father left.

Virtually everything the reader learns of Mr. Archer is revealed in a lengthy paragraph at the end of chapter 4, a paragraph only tangentially addressed to that subject. He is "her handsome, much loved father," an impoverished gentleman possessing "a remarkably handsome head and a very taking manner"—and then the narrator quips, "indeed . . . he was always taking something" (p. 33). This description, as it turns out, is made to order for Gilbert Osmond, also a handsome and much-loved father with "a well-shaped head" (p. 228) and ever a tendency to put his hand in someone else's pocket. Prior to marriage, Isabel is not aware, as everyone else is, of Osmond's capacity for exploiting others, but perhaps she is blind to it only because of proximity to such behavior by her father as she was growing up. From her entirely unobjective point of view, her father was admirably "indifferent to sordid considerations," but few others saw it that way: "Many people . . . held that he carried this indifference too far, especially the large number to whom he owed money" (p. 33). Osmond also appears to Isabel remarkably and exaltedly indifferent to sordid considerations, even though evidence is readily available from the start that he indeed is sordid—or at least anything but indifferent. "Had he not had the courage to say he was glad she was rich?" Isabel recalls with some fairness at a later point, after her attraction to him has soured (p. 427).

Another important congruence between Mr. Archer and Mr. Osmond is probably, for Isabel, the most significant: their father-daughter relationships. Interestingly, both men's names begin with the sound "ah," the primal sound of pleasure, of satisfaction. Although Archer had three daughters to Osmond's one, he appears to have treated Isabel as special: "his clever, his superior, his remarkable girl." True, he "wished his daughters . . . to see as much of the world as possible," while Osmond painstakingly secludes his child, yet nonetheless Archer strove to keep his girls from ever knowing anything "particularly unpleasant," so much so that it appears to Isabel in retrospect that "the unpleasant had been ever too absent from her knowledge" (p. 33). The term *knowledge* here might recall to us the fabled garden with its Tree of Knowledge, whose fruit must not be tasted. I have already suggested that Madame Merle represents for Isabel the garden of happy childhood (or even prebirth) from which she feels excluded, and I would now like to add that Osmond, in his own way, also represents that garden. Though Isabel could not articulate such a thing to herself, marrying him can legitimately be viewed as an effort to retrieve the beloved and caring, if at times overcaring, father she so recently has lost. A part of Isabel wishes to be like Pansy Osmond and live innocently and protectedly within the precincts of such a garden as Pansy inhabits; she and the girl who will become her stepdaughter regard each other as sisters, and Isabel is said to look at the child "almost in envy" (p. 318). No one is more unpoisoned by the Tree of Knowledge than Pansy: "Pansy was really a blank page, a pure white surface, successfully kept so," and it seems that a major portion of Isabel hungers all the time for this state of shelter, even as the rest of her wants to suck greedily the fruit of knowledge (p. 315).[27]

Osmond is a father figure for Isabel. Symbolically he performs the role of Father Adam in two ways: he tends the secure, seemingly Edenic garden that Isabel seeks to reenter, yet he also seems to be both a rebel against authority and a taster of knowledge. She confuses his connoisseurship of Japanese lacquer with knowledge of good and evil; she sees his private experience of suffering as firsthand experience of "the agitations of the world," and a vicarious way for her to experience them herself. Isabel desires Osmond because he seems to her a model of rebellion against the crushing authority of society; at the same time she is attracted to his authoritarian behavior as an antidote to her fear of freedom, a palliative for her persistent craving to be safe and obedient.

In the delineation of this desire Pansy Osmond plays an important role. If Isabel's obstinacy is made manifest by the way she continually outlasts stubborn and rigid Caspar Goodwood, and her typecasting tendencies are shown in comical magnification by those of Henrietta, her equally strong need to obey paternal authority is writ large in the example of Pansy, a character whose very name suggests lack of spine. It is impossible to conceive of Pansy as anything but a child,[28] and there is hardly an occasion in the book in which she appears without making a public statement of her complete devotion to the omniscient and omnipotent authority of her beloved papa ("P-paul"). Even when she has grown several years older and wishes to marry Ned Rosier, she vows she would sooner lose her suitor than disobey her father. Upon first meeting her, Isabel had admonished the child to "give pleasure to your father." Pansy's reply: "I think that's what I live for" (p. 317).

Within Isabel there are elements of a remarkably similar compulsion to be fully committed to someone or something—this despite her frequent remarks about wishing to be free, not pinned down, uncommitted. As the narrator informs us when discussing Isabel's decision to accept (or is it take?) Osmond in marriage, "The desire for unlimited expansion had been succeeded in her soul by the sense that life was vacant without some private duty that might gather one's energies to a point."[29] The passage continues:

What had become of all her ardours, her aspirations, her theories, her high estimate of her independence and her incipient conviction that she should never marry? These things had been absorbed in *a more primitive need*—a need the answer to which brushed away numberless questions, yet *gratified infinite desires*. It simplified the situation at a stroke. . . . There was explanation enough in the fact that he was her lover, her own, and that *she should be able to be of use to him*. (p. 352. Emphasis added.)

This last phrase, an echo of Pansy's "that's what I live for," is almost immediately followed by an extended discussion first of and then with the young girl, reinforcing for us the similar functions these two young females wish to fill in Father Osmond's life. Learning of the impending marriage, Osmond's biological daughter astutely remarks to his new symbolic one, "Oh, then I shall have a beautiful sister!" (p. 353).

Late in the novel, when Isabel defies Osmond by heading for England to visit Ralph on his deathbed, she first goes to see Pansy, who is sequestered in a Roman convent that creates in Isabel "the impression of a well-appointed prison; for it was not possible to pretend Pansy was free to leave it" (p. 549). In terms of plot motivation, Isabel stops to visit Pansy because, having just discovered that the girl is the illegitimate child of Madame Merle, she wishes to "reach out a hand." But on the level at which the portrait of Isabel is drawn by the implicit comparison and contrast to other characters, she comes here to confirm for the reader her internal similarity to Pansy, and, in so doing, to provide an understanding of why she will return to Osmond, whom she now hates, rather than stay away. She will return not because of the promise she makes to Pansy—Isabel has reneged on other promises or half-promises during the course of the book—but because underneath all her show of defiance, Mrs. Osmond is terrified of freedom. She is thus inwardly compelled, like Pansy, her "sister," to prostrate herself (however bitterly and obstreperously) before the magnificent authority of her/their "papa."

"I'll do anything—I'll do anything," said Pansy. Then, as she heard her own words, a deep pure blush came into her face. Isabel read the meaning of it; she saw the poor girl had been vanquished. . . . The collapse of the girl's momentary resistance (mute and modest though it had been) seemed only her tribute to the truth of things. . . . She had seen the reality. She had no vocation for struggling with combinations. . . . She bowed her pretty head to authority and only asked of authority to be merciful. (pp. 556–57)

Isabel is somewhat better at struggling with combinations, but not much; her dualistic, a priori mode of perceiving experience makes it too difficult for her to entertain dialectical opposites at the same time, and so she must always suppress what complicates things or people and would make them less easy to fit into pre-arranged categories or positions. In the case of her unhappy marriage, this can be seen in her oscillating behavior: she alternates between defying Osmond and martyring herself to his authority. Philosophically as well as psychologically, she seems unable to conceive of marital equality or compromise. Her logic is that of the excluded middle; the middle ground of anything is territory she is incapable of occupying. Nothing condemns Isabel to that bleak future at which the narrative abandons her more than her fixed, dualistic notions, which cause her to conceive of existence as pre-established, completed, authorized (by a transcendent authority—the Law of the Father), as always already accomplished. Hence her deep-rooted passivity, her consequent inability to rebel, and the necessity of her being able only to complain and remain ineffectually miserable. Her belief that there is a single, noncontradictory truth of things, an immutable reality that can finally, determinably be seen, traps her into a locked position even as she, by experiencing life in rigid categories, falsely positions others.

Listening to a remark made by Madame Catherine, one of the nuns who has charge of Pansy at the convent—another sister, so to speak—Isabel notes that the very tone of the woman's speech "seemed to represent the surrender of a personality, the authority of the Church" (p. 555). The Roman church can be seen as the ultimate formalizer of human life, displacing idiosyncrasy and self-contradiction with ritualized behavior that reduces the formidable combinations of morality into a simple dichotomy of good and evil. Isabel finds the institution crushing in its effect upon individuality and yet thinks in a similar manner. Therefore, even though the repressive Church is associated with Osmond (especially when Pansy speaks in this place of her papa, which in Italian can signify the Pope, the ultimate earthly father, law-giver, and figure of authority), it is also a symbolic expression of Isabel's repressed and repressive consciousness. In psychoanalytic terms, Osmond, the Church, and Isabel's superego are interchangeable: they are the enemy, but the enemy is she. Isabel can no more escape Osmond and Rome (the Church) and the dualistic, dichotomizing, patriarchal authority they embody, then she can—or fully wishes to—escape from herself. Her return from (Protestant) England is inevitable.[30]

We have spoken above briefly of garden imagery in relation to Isabel's being drawn to Merle and Osmond as parent substitutes. We should recall that when Isabel first strides onto the stage of the novel, back at the very beginning, it is at a place called Gardencourt. The beautifully gardened convent at the end of the book where the Rappaciniesque Osmond keeps his obedient daughter, Pansy, could be termed by us, for the sake of contrast, "Gardenconvent." There in the lonely but immaculately ordered habitation where Pansy feels so much at home is "a collection of wax flowers under glass" (p. 549), which suggests how lifeless and entrapped are the so-called blossoms of this asocial garden. Gardencourt, however, by its very name implies a different sort of garden: a court is a securely sheltered but not inaccessible open space, or it is a place where sometimes pleasant games are played, or it is a place where people come to resolve their civil disputes in a fair, socially structured fashion. The text sets these two gardens in opposition and makes Isabel choose which she shall inhabit.

This is not to say that Gardencourt is set up as a perfect good to Gardenconvent's perfect evil, for within the confines of the former two men (Ralph and his father) die, two men (Warburton and Goodwood) court Isabel—that is, "seek to gain or achieve" her, according to one definition of the word—and Madame Merle comes fatefully into the heroine's life. Though this locale is more promising of individual freedom than Gardenconvent, it is no more than an illusion, for in neither garden is Isabel free of her own deterministic notions and desire.

* * *

What, finally, does this have to do with Henry James's aesthetic act of constructing a portrait? How does our understanding of Isabel's desire to renounce her orphanhood and the insecure freedom that goes with it enable us to fathom the desire that gave form and movement to this novel? And how can this family romance be seen by us as an embodiment of the portraitist's unconscious drive to locate his various internal energies and contradictory impulses in terms of sexual identity? Indeed, what grounds can we have for even thinking that such a drive operated within this portraitist James? After all, if the only possible firsthand witness to an alleged phenomenon—in this case, a psychic drive—is said to have been largely if not entirely unconscious of its existence, how in the world can we know that it actually did exist?

To this last question, the answer is that we cannot know. We can only speculate. Speculation in and of itself is neither good nor bad; to paraphrase Shakespeare, only thinking makes it so. It is how we use the speculation that counts: to what ends, with what effect, and in what manner. Here the purpose of speculation is to enrich the meaning of the text both in terms of our better understanding what organizes and propels the narrative and the characters who are a part of it, and the history of the portraitist, his craft tradition, and his social culture. Inasmuch as neither artistic texts nor levels of history can be circumscribed within (boxed into) fully determinate, complete, or, as Isabel would say, accomplished, meanings, speculations of the sort suggested here are worthwhile to the extent that they help keep open our critical and historical horizons. It is when these horizons start to narrow to one sort of dogma or another that we should be worried, and not, to the contrary, when the vistas of indeterminacy open before us.

So let us entertain the speculation, elaborated upon in chapter 1 above and treated in different contexts in chapters 2 and 3, that Eakins, Sargent, and James were American artists of the 1880s who possessed idiosyncratically different, as well as culturally shared, reasons to attempt to work out through their portraits of women (and men) profound and dismaying questions of sexuality. With *The Portrait of a Lady,* what do we see?

We see a novel in which one character perceives his father as "the more motherly," while "his mother, on the other hand, was paternal"; in which a manly character like Caspar Goodwood plays the more traditionally woman's role of waiting years for a desired marriage partner to have done with adventuring about and settle down into a domestic arrangement; in which someone with a woman's name (Henrietta—a variant of James's own first name, Henry) displays none of the traditional female virtues of tenderness, modesty, and soft-spokenness, but is instead pushy, loud, and brash, in the manner more normally reserved in realist fictions of the era for young men on the make, like Howells' Bartley Hubbard or, during the next decade, Norris' McTeague, Dreiser's Drouet, or Crane's Henry Fleming. We also have in *The Portrait of a Lady* a sickly, often bed-ridden hero (if he can be called that) who is tender, modest, and quiet, plus a villain whose aestheticism makes him seem effeminately morbid and insular.[31] Yet of all these reversals of sex-role characteristics, none is more significant for our purposes than "Lady" Isabel's fixing, pinning, structuring, boîte-forming, dualistic, and idealist mode of thinking.

Once again, this is not to claim that only men practice instrumental ways of thinking, or that only women can be quietly passive receptors—experiencers rather than doers. But whatever gender labels we may give to these differing modes of living and thinking about life, *The Portrait of a Lady* tests them out on various levels, levels that include having the protagonist lean more toward one form of behavior than the other and having her, and therefore the reader who has been made to identify with her, suffer because of it. If Gardencourt is a locale symbolizing, within this context, the impulse we described earlier as realist, and Gardenconvent represents the formalist impulse at its worst, then Isabel's story is the story of movement from one sphere to the other, a movement that is like an individual's or a society's movement from the mother to the father, from nature to knowledge, from reception to penetration, from matter to idea, from freedom to law, from feeling to form.

Recall James's anecdote about the writing of this novel in Venice, when he was forced to choose, from moment to moment, between standing by the window taking in all the rich, overabundant, unreproducible beauty and complexity of the world outside, or sitting at the desk, struggling with

combinations: language, categories, and aesthetic form. What resulted—
and still does result—is a portrait in which his attempt to be faithful to
the given, the out there, is in conflict with his wish to be the giver, the
form-maker. It is a question of original presentation and second generation
re-presentation: a question of reproduction. And that, finally, is a sexual
question. Isabel's rigid formalism, her obsessive abstraction or translation
of experience, embodies the opposite and yet the counterpart of what the
novel's discourse tends toward when it tirelessly reports the ups and downs,
the ins and outs, the aberrations, the convolutions, and the contradictions
of Isabel's enormously—and realistically—complex consciousness.

The union of these two contraries, and the struggling with combinations implied, is in a very profound sense a union, and a struggle, of sexual
valence. The child that results is the text. This text, this portrait, like a
child, grows and changes, is manifold, never simple, never a false, easy
totality, never without contradiction. Like a child, it can, by definition,
never be entirely accomplished, finished, complete.

CHAPTER FIVE

Conclusion

A CONCLUSION SHOULD BE COOL, quiet, and colorless, summoning a sterile array of precision tools to complete the operation by stitching up the patient—either the texts considered or the readers—with the neatest, most elegant of sutures. But here there is no conclusion, only inconclusion.

If this is not as it should be, it is how I would prefer it to be, for sometimes a conclusion is an occlusion, a blocking from view. It does this by the very way that it orders and unifies and tries to hold to account the disorder, disunity, and ultimate unaccountability of those secondary texts we call readings, texts that spring dialectically from the painting or novel as it meshes with the reader's historically situated response/imagination/desire. So here there will be no tying together of all the loose strings, no tidy superimposing of a conceptual, definitional grid. Likewise, no careful, systematic pinning down the edges of the fly-away subjects we have looked at, and no last-ditch attempts to squeeze into transparent, panoptic boxes, for surveillance and display, the ideas and half-ideas (some as elusive as barely recollected dreams) that have slithered and slipped through the preceding pages like St. George's dragon.

The painting is not yet completed, the book not closed. There is always more to come. No matter what determinisms we hold sacred, no matter how prefigured—psychologically, sexually, economically, ideologically, racially, historically, biologically, intertextually—we believe the world to be, no individual within it is finished in advance, epistemologically packed up: signed, sealed, and delivered. A portrait cannot be a fait accompli either, for the surface of a mirror held up to cracks, fissures, and diffusion will also appear cracked, fissured, and diffused.

When does repetition become redundant? Certainly by now the point, a word that calls to mind the sharp tip of Dr. Agnew's lancet, has many times over been made (been thrust, penetrated) that each one of the three portraits embodies a conflict, indeed numerous conflicts, between passive and aggressive impulses, verbal and visual, formative and reflective, formalistic and realistic, those that would condense and those that would dispense, some that our society deems feminine, others masculine . . . the combinations go on and on. Unlike Pansy Osmond, who has no vocation for struggling with combinations, the close examiner of portraits as texts must have that vocation more than any other. But one needs to be careful. Powerful as the combinations may be, they can all too easily wither, or at least withdraw from sight into the uncanny shadows, into the askew, irretrievable, barely discernible back room that is guarded on one side by an enormous China vase and on the other by a mysterious screen, red as blood.

But there comes a time to stop. Combinations, of course, will continue, but these words are about to cease. Thus now, as author, I permit myself to shirk the control, the restraint, the cool surgical neutrality that I, like each portrait, have sought after and fought against from the start.

Notes

NOTE TO THE READER

1 "The facts of history never come to us 'pure,' since they do not and cannot exist in a pure form: they are always refracted through the mind of the record-er" (E. H. Carr, *What Is History?* [New York: Alfred A. Knopf, 1962], 22). Or, "it should be realized that the past, in its real, alive form, is not the same past which was the present when the incidents occurred. The past, as past, is the past as it appears to us *now:* what happened then as it speaks to us now" (J. H. van den Berg, *The Changing Nature of Man: Introduction to a Historical Psychology,* trans. H. F. Croes [New York: W. W. Norton, 1961], 37). In a more radical, contemporary mode: "History is substitution, signifier, figure, difference, text, fiction" (Vincent B. Leitch, *Deconstructive Criticism* [New York: Columbia University Press, 1983], 58).

2 "On Some Pictures Lately Exhibited" (1875), in *The Painter's Eye,* ed. John L. Sweeney (Cambridge: Harvard University Press, 1956), 88.

CHAPTER ONE: INTRODUCTION

1 I use the term *writing* here and elsewhere in the generic sense—writing as an act of marking or inscribing upon a surface, encompassing the art of the paintbrush as well as that of the pen. Likewise, *reading* is used here to signify an act of interpretation of materials printed *or* painted.

2 See Charles Feidelson, Jr., *Symbolism and American Literature* (Chicago: University of Chicago Press, 1953), 8–9, 14–15 for a contrast of the allegorical and symbolic modes in Hawthorne. See also p. 176, an extract from a letter

of Melville's to Mrs. Hawthorne emphasizing "the part-&-parcel allegorical-ness" of *Moby-Dick*.

3 As Henry Adams was to put it, looking back at the early 1860s, "Henry James had not yet taught the world to read a volume for the pleasure of seeing the lights of his burning-glass turned on alternate sides of the same figure. Psychological study was still simple." Adams then adds, "Under a very strong light human nature will always appear complex and full of contradictions." *The Education of Henry Adams* (New York: Modern Library, 1931), 163. By the 1880s, the art of James, as well as that of Eakins and Sargent, was seriously devoted to the application of precisely the very strong light Adams describes.

4 The word "portrait" occurs frequently in James's work and correspondence and in a variety of critical and biographical writings about him. It returns over and over, for example, in Leon Edel's *Henry James: The Middle Years* (Philadelphia: J. B. Lippincott, 1962), which, extending through and beyond the 1880s, describes the period immediately after the publication of *The Portrait* (1882), includes James's becoming friends with Sargent (1884), his gathering several of his important literary essays together in a volume entitled *Partial Portraits* (1888), and his crafting of *The Tragic Muse* (1889), a novel whose protagonist is a lonely but dedicated portrait painter who, Edel persuasively contends, stands for James himself. That the novelist-essayist conceived of himself as a prose painter there can be no doubt, and each characterization he limned in words, whether inspired by a single model or a composite, was for him a task of portraiture. Taking as he did an empirical, inductive approach, James differed from those earlier American fiction writers whose characterizations tended toward the deductive, as in the artificial character constructions of the allegorists, the fantasy embodiments of romancers, the dimensionless mouthpieces of social propagandists, and the straw men of satirists. See Edel, *The Middle Years,* 260, 373.

5 Sometimes our reading of a portrait may alter or broaden our perception of human reality, but more often it simply reconfirms it, as for example when we "see" in one of Rembrandt's old men the "nobility and dignity of age" that we have been trained to pick out and value by our culture (humanism and sentimentalism) and by our personal psychological motivations (such as dread of aging, fear of death, craving for purpose, or need to posit a higher, fatherly authority).

6 I use the term *political* in the broad sense of being concerned with the distribution of power in any society of two or more individuals.

7 William Dean Howells considered the average adult to be more an onion than a nut: "Nothing but hulls, that you keep peeling off, one after another, till you think you have got down to the heart at last, and then you have got down to nothing." *A Boy's Town* (New York: Harper & Brothers, 1890), 171.

8 P. 12.

9 P. 249.

10 For a theoretical justification of this approach, see chapter 1 of Peter Gay's *Art and Act* (New York: Harper & Row, 1976), to which much of my thinking on this subject is indebted.

11 "O, what a satisfaction it gave me to see the good Spanish work, so good, so

strong, so free from every affectation. In Madrid I have seen big work every day and I will never forget it," Eakins wrote his father. The letter is quoted in Margaret McHenry, *Thomas Eakins Who Painted* (Oreland, Pa.: privately printed, 1946), 17.

12 See Richard Ormond, *John Singer Sargent* (New York: Harper & Row, 1970), 16, 27.

13 Balzac's mode of literary portraiture seldom, however, went beyond a notion of *le personnage typique*. See "Balzac and the Zoologists: A Concept of the Type" in *The Disciplines of Criticism*, ed. Peter Demetz (New Haven: Yale University Press, 1968), 397–418.

14 In the late eighteenth century, while many American poets, philosophers, and preachers were viewing character typologically, as an individual's fixed and immutable private property, his socially identifiable *essence*, Benjamin Franklin considered character to be nothing more than an appearance, not an essence but a floating image to be manipulated before the public at will for pragmatic purposes. In this regard, as in so many others, Franklin was a man ahead of his time. When during the nineteenth century Americans in general became aware of how in business, politics, and even in religion, a man or woman's "character" was not necessarily what it appeared to be, the impulse to "delve within" became a moral imperative. Hence the greater interest in a psychological, as opposed to typological, approach to portraiture.

15 *Symbolism and American Literature*, 89. See also Sacvan Bercovitch, *The Puritan Origins of the American Self* (New Haven: Yale University Press, 1975), 1–35, his *American Jeremiad* (Madison: University of Wisconsin Press, 1978), 93–131, and Karl Keller, "Alephs, Zahirs, and the Triumph of Ambiguity: Typology in Nineteenth-Century American Literature" in *Literary Uses of Typology from the Late Middle Ages to the Present*, ed. Earl Miner (Princeton: Princeton University Press, 1977), 274–314.

16 Flaubert's Emma Bovary, created within the same decade as Hester Prynne, can be viewed as the European paradigm. She hides her adulteries behind an honorific class title, *Madame,* which it is the portraitist's role to unmask: "Her existence," writes Flaubert, "was a continuous string of lies, in which she wrapped her love as if in layers of veiling in order to hide it." *Madame Bovary,* trans. Mildred Marmur (New York: New American Library, 1964), 256. Though the European portraitists may have regarded themselves as unveilers, they seem not to have questioned the desire or need for veiling.

17 According to Daniel Boorstin, "Historians of journalism date the first full-fledged modern interview with a well-known public figure from July 13, 1859, when Horace Greeley interviewed Brigham Young in Salt Lake City, asking him questions on many matters of public interest, and then publishing the answers verbatim." (*The Image: A Guide to Pseudo-Events in America* [New York: Atheneum, 1961], 15). See also pp. 45–76. Greeley's "invention," the journalistic interview, could be considered a type of portraiture, in that it focuses upon—and tries to convey the presence of—a particular individual. However, in its emphasis only on ideas, feelings, and behavior that are easy to prepackage and predigest for potential consumers, it is a travesty of a psychological portrait. Concerning portraiture, 1859 is nevertheless a significant year,

for that is the date that marks the publication of Darwin's *Origin of Species,* a work that may be seen as symbolizing the birth of those modern scientific studies of man (biology, psychology, anthropology) to which, in its empiricism, the new style of artistic portraiture was something of a counterpart.

18   Karen Halttunen analyzes the sentimental and theatrical aspect of American life at midcentury in *Confidence Men and Painted Women: A Study of Middle-Class Culture in America, 1830–1870* (New Haven: Yale University Press, 1982). By examining documents of the period such as etiquette guides, fashion books, and mourning manuals, she explores the ways that "within the middle-class home and, more specifically, within the social sphere defined by the parlor, an intricate system of social forms had been hammered out within which middle-class men and women might place tentative confidence in one another without relying on each other's perfect sincerity. Polite society, they were beginning to recognize, could never rest on the sincere adherence to Christian law of all its participants. But it could insist that all members assume an *outward appearance* of virtue" (p. 187; emphasis added).

19   The psychological portrait also provides an externalization—it makes the invisible visible, the inapparent apparent—but since it is chiefly concerned with leading the viewer deeper into others and himself, it gives to the term *externalization* a notably different inflection from that used above.

20   Alexis de Tocqueville, *Democracy in America,* trans. George Lawrence (Garden City, N.Y.: Anchor Books, 1969), 508.

21   Thomas L. Haskell, *The Emergence of Professional Social Science* (Urbana: University of Illinois Press, 1977), 38–39.

22   Introduction to *The Land of Contrasts: 1880–1901,* ed. Neil Harris (New York: George Braziller, 1970), 6.

23   P. 247. Daniel Touchett, Isabel Archer's benefactor in *The Portrait of a Lady,* made his fortune, and thus Isabel's, as a banker. In a certain sense, therefore, investment capital is the absent clockmaker responsible for winding the springs that set in motion the narrative of which Isabel is the principal performer.

24   P. 241.

25   One might object to this: what of Rembrandt and Hals, psychological portraitists par excellence? As it happens, both of these artists painted their most powerful portraits *after* and not before severe financial reversals impoverished, if not embittered, them. Thus both Rembrandt and Hals, to an extent far beyond that generally experienced by their contemporaries, knew firsthand the loss of autonomy that was to become a commonplace of the late nineteenth century.

26   "The pattern," observes Burton J. Bledstein, "manifested itself everywhere, in popular culture, the academy, and spectator sports, indeed in the ordinary habits of a middle-class life as an individual learned the hygienic ways to bathe, eat, work, relax, and even have sexual intercourse. . . . Americans after 1870, but beginning after 1840, committed themselves to a culture of professionalism which over the years has established the thoughts, habits, and responses most modern Americans have taken for granted" (*The Culture of Professionalism* [New York: W. W. Norton, 1976], 80).

27   "James seems discomfitted by undergoing the same sort of scrutiny that he

directed at others as a matter of course," Carter Ratcliff remarks upon analyzing a letter James wrote shortly after having "sat to" Sargent for the oil
portrait of 1913 (*John Singer Sargent* [New York: Abbeville, 1982], 195).
Certainly, though, it was years earlier that the novelist understood what it must
be like to be subjected to another portraitist's entrapping gaze. See Edel, *The
Middle Years,* 332–35, on James's reaction to Vernon Lee's satirical portrait
of him in her short story "Lady Tal." Even prior to that incident, the novelist
had placed in *The Tragic Muse* this observation about a James-like dramatist
who was having his portrait painted: "He was so accustomed to living upon
irony and the interpretation of things that it was strange to him to be himself
interpreted, and (as a gentleman who sits for his portrait is always liable to
be) interpreted ironically."

28 *In the Cage and Other Tales,* ed. Morton Dauwen Zabel (New York: W. W.
    Norton, 1969), 108.

29 Along the same lines, see Boorstin's *Image* for a twentieth-century study of
    how we have come to prefer the media-conveyed picture of an individual to
    the individual himself (or, for example, to prefer someone else's news coverage
    of an event to our own on-the-spot witnessing of that event). Browning is more
    pungent, but Boorstin elaborates with an array of examples.

30 See John Higham's pamphlet *From Boundlessness to Consolidation: The
    Transformation of American Culture, 1848–1860* (Ann Arbor: Walter Clem-
    ents, 1969) on the early moments in this national centralization. For a detailed
    look at consolidation in the specific period with which this book is concerned
    see Alan Trachtenberg, *The Incorporation of America: Culture and Society in
    the Gilded Age* (New York: Hill and Wang, 1982) and also Robert Wiebe,
    The Search for Order, 1877–1920 (New York: Hill and Wang, 1967). John A.
    Garraty's *New Commonwealth, 1877–1890* (New York: Harper & Row,
    1968), is a rich, readable compilation of data that illustrates the swift and
    powerful changes occurring in American industrial, agricultural, financial, and
    political life during this time.

31 Adams, *Education,* 240.

32 Ibid., 111.

33 Edmund Wilson, *Patriotic Gore: Studies in the Literature of the American
    Civil War* (New York: Oxford University Press, 1962), 620–21.

34 Ibid., 668; George M. Fredrickson, *The Inner Civil War: Northern Intellectuals
    and the Crisis of the Union* (New York: Harper & Row, 1965), 175–76.

35 Wilson, *Patriotic Gore,* 632.

36 Ibid., 654; Fredrickson, *Inner Civil War,* 159. The James quotation is from
    Notes of a Son and Brother (New York: Charles Scribner's Sons, 1914), 379–
    80.

37 See Leon Edel, *Henry James: The Untried Years* (Philadelphia: J. B. Lippincott,
    1953), 173–79; Gordon Hendricks, *The Life and Work of Thomas Eakins*
    (New York: Grossman, 1974), 14; Charles Merrill Mount, *John Singer Sargent:
    A Biography* (New York: W. W. Norton, 1955), 17, 23.

38 Eakins' passionate commitment to rugged sporting activities—sculling, shoot-
    ing, wrestling, boxing, baseball—is well known, but the fact of his assiduous
    participation, either as player or spectator, does not of itself prove anything.

He might have been, to use twentieth-century parlance, overcompensating, like the present-day academic who runs marathons or idolizes the Red Sox as a sort of psychic refusal of the muscleless bookworm role that society has reserved for him.

39 To twentieth-century minds it is certainly no secret that the world of Victorian male privilege was actually anything but hale and hearty. For a recent and provocative examination of that world in crisis, see T. J. Jackson Lears's *No Place of Grace: Antimodernism and the Transformation of American Culture, 1880–1920* (New York: Pantheon, 1981), particularly ch. 1.

40 Simone de Beauvoir, *The Second Sex,* trans. H. M. Parshley (New York: Alfred A. Knopf, 1953), xix.

41 Barbara Ehrenreich and Deirdre English, *For Her Own Good: 150 Years of the Experts' Advice to Women* (Garden City, N.Y.: Doubleday Anchor, 1978), 14–15.

42 On the cult of domesticity in late nineteenth-century America, and the critique of it by one of that era's leading feminists, Charlotte Perkins Gilman, see William O'Neill, *Everyone Was Brave* (Chicago: Quadrangle Books, 1969), 32–44.

43 James met Sargent in Paris the year after *The Boit Children,* which he greatly admired, was exhibited at the Salon of 1883. The two may very well have been introduced by their mutual friend, Mrs. Boit (Louisa Cushing Boit), whom James affectionately referred to as "shepherdess of the studios" (Edel, *The Middle Years,* 107–08). Besides becoming good friends for the rest of their lives, the men established something of a professional relationship: James wrote for *Harper's Magazine* an exultant piece on the painter in 1887 and later revised it for a collection of his own art essays (*Picture and Text*); Sargent drew a profile of the writer in 1886 and in 1913 completed the now famous oil portrait that was slashed with scissors at the Royal Academy the following year by a suffragette who was incensed, probably neither by James nor Sargent, but rather by the sexist institutions she perceived them to represent. (Ratcliff, *Sargent,* 195, 231 n203; Evan Charteris, *John Sargent* [New York: Charles Scribner's Sons, 1927], 79, 161.) James seems to have been unaware of Eakins even when he visited Philadelphia in 1904, and most likely would not have responded favorably to that painter's work. When Sargent, on the other hand, was paying a visit to Philadelphia at about the same time, his host inquired whom he would most like to meet. Sargent named Eakins—or so the story goes—but the host, Dr. J. William White, did not recognize that name, even though only a decade and a half before he had been included by Eakins as one of the main figures in *The Agnew Clinic* (Mount, *Sargent,* 256–57). Mount indicates that the two artists met, and more than once, but offers neither documentation nor details of the implied meetings. Goodrich, *Thomas Eakins* (Cambridge: Harvard University Press, 1982), 2:222, has the two portraitists becoming frequent companions during the spring of 1903, but notes that when he interviewed Eakins' widow half a century ago, she did not confirm the story. Many years earlier, the first time Sargent ever visited Philadelphia, in fact the first time he ever crossed the Atlantic to see his homeland, he attended the Centennial Exhibition of 1876. It is highly probable, his father having for

some years been a doctor in Philadelphia, that he wandered through the medical section at the Exhibition, and thus encountered Eakins' monumental realist portrait, *The Gross Clinic,* which had been banished there by a Centennial jury too squeamish to exhibit it in the art section. Whether or not twenty-year-old Sargent saw the painting, and if so, what he thought of it, remains unknown. There is one last Sargent-Eakins connection hardly worth noting save for its curiosity value. As a doctor, Sargent's father had served until shortly before John's birth at Wills Eye Hospital, the first hospital in the Western hemisphere specifically devoted to the eye. David Hayes Agnew, of Eakins' later portrait, was an attending surgeon at Wills from 1864–68, some eight years after FitzWilliam Sargent had moved away. Nevertheless, it is possible that the two Philadelphia physicians, both involved in the fledgling field of ophthalmology, were acquainted, thus allowing us to imagine a historical link—very tenuous, as are the other "links" contrived above—between the one painter and the other.

44   James set fire to his personal diaries and letters; the two painters possibly never had any diaries or intimate letters to destroy.

45   To this list of anxiety-provoking challenges to male confidence and authority should be added the rise of social science "expertism," with its well-intended but demoralizing intrusion of credentialed authorities into family life. See Christopher Lasch's angry appraisal of how the traditional male-run family has been undermined by the very "experts" assigned to better it (with no one, male or female, any the happier), in *Haven in a Heartless World: The Family Besieged* (New York: Basic Books, 1977). See also his *Culture of Narcissism: American Life in an Age of Diminishing Expectations* (New York: W. W. Norton, 1979), concerning what he refers to as "the social invasion of the self." Lasch and others (Jackson Lears, for example, in *No Place of Grace*) have depicted a late nineteenth- and early twentieth-century American society in which cultural authority passed from fathers in the home, the pulpit, and the seat of government to quasi-fathers in executive boardrooms, hospital operating rooms, and university classrooms, and yet brought no gain—rather a loss—in the sense of well-being experienced by those involved (including the many women who seemingly benefited from this loosening of the reins of patriarchy).

46   Seymour Chatman, *Story and Discourse: Narrative Structure in Fiction and Film* (Ithaca: Cornell University Press, 1978), provides a general summary of narrative theory that distinguishes between story and discourse. For a particularly suggestive analysis of modes of duration in the novel, see Gérard Genette's *Narrative Discourse: An Essay in Method,* trans. Jane E. Lewin (Ithaca: Cornell University Press, 1980).

47   There is also the implied duration of the character's fictive life, of which only a segment is being given. We unreflectingly assume that Isabel, Dr. Agnew, and the Boit daughters each had time-bounded experiences prior to the incidents shown, and had, or will be having, others afterward.

48   When we pick up a novel a day or two after setting it aside, we start up again where we left off, thus reconnecting a discourse that was interrupted. When we come back to a painting, however, we go again to the beginning of the

discursive chain. That is, our eye starts off more or less by retracing the path it took during the earlier viewing. But now, because of that prior experience, certain forms and combinations are likely to receive more attention than before, and others less. This process of adding to and subtracting from the discourse as it was engendered on the initial occasion is, as with the novel, a continuation of the discourse and not a mere repetition of it.

49   Even in classical realist fiction, reader attention shuttles back and forth between the scene being read and previously read scenes brought to mind, but the overall movement of the narrative is forward and linear.

50   A familiar example of this phenomenon is the male consumer's reaction to a commercial photograph of a sleek, sexually attractive woman draped across the shiny hood of a sports car. He translates the visual image, or so the advertiser hopes, into a quasi-verbal internal directive that says, "Behind the wheel of a car like this, I could command the attention and desire of a woman like that, and the admiration and envy of other men like myself." That the potential consumer does not actually hear himself thinking these words is not surprising; out of the low, murmuring background noise in our head we are always receiving semiverbal messages without realizing it, since the vast majority of these messages slip back into the general, hardly hearable haze before we can get a grasp on them and consciously remember encountering and being moved by them, although moved in one way or another we usually were—and are. Excellent accounts of this process are to be found in John Berger, *Ways of Seeing* (Harmondsworth, Eng.: BBC and Penguin, 1972), 129–54; Judith Williamson, *Decoding Advertisements* (London: Marion Boyars, 1978); and in Jean Kilbourne's short film, *Killing Us Softly* (Cambridge, Mass.: Cambridge Documentary Films, 1980).

51   The two classic texts are Rudolph Arnheim, *Art and Visual Perception: A Psychology of the Creative Eye* (Berkeley and Los Angeles: University of California Press, 1954; rev. ed., 1974), and E. H. Gombrich, *Art and Illusion* (Princeton: Princeton University Press, 1960).

52   Eisenstein's theory of montage can be found in a collection of his essays entitled *Film Form,* trans. Jay Leyda (New York: Harcourt, Brace & World, 1949). As for Pudovkin, see *Film Technique and Film Acting,* trans. Ivor Montague (New York: Bonanza Books, 1949). Two appropriate extracts from these books are contained in *Film: A Montage of Theories,* ed. Richard Dyer McCann (New York: E. P. Dutton, 1966), 23–37. See chapter 2, below, for a more detailed discussion.

53   See Bill Nichols, *Ideology and the Image* (Bloomington: Indiana University Press, 1981), 52–68, for a helpful, well-illustrated discussion of how the editing we automatically perform on the images we look at bears the hidden mark of ideology.

54   Bryan Jay Wolf, *Romantic Re-Vision: Culture and Consciousness in Nineteenth-Century American Painting and Literature* (Chicago: University of Chicago Press, 1982), xv.

55   As David L. Minter has observed in perusing James's collected prefaces, "Repeatedly [James] insists that the adventures of his protagonists parallel and are analogous with his own technical adventures in rendering them" (*The Inter-*

preted Design as a Structural Principle in American Prose [New Haven: Yale University Press, 1969], 166).

56 Quoted in Edel, *The Middle Years,* 20–21; taken from James's *Notebooks,* ed. F. O. Matthiesen and Kenneth B. Murdock (New York: Oxford University Press, 1947), 23.

CHAPTER TWO: *THE AGNEW CLINIC*

1 Rudolph Arnheim, *Art and Visual Perception,* 33–36.
2 We will have to leave aside here the questionable status of any metaphor as "natural." It should at least be noted, however, that even the most apparently obvious comparisons of one type of visual form to another can only occur within language and its categories. Because that language and those categories have been socially constructed and are ideologically sustained, the comparisons that are the most natural perhaps seem that way by virtue of their adherence to the dominant values of the society that generates them. If a pair of female breasts is likened by members of our society to a pair of eyes, that might be not only because of the ubiquity of sexual desire, but more specifically because patriarchal values and masculine fears of femininity are somehow served or expressed by comparing nonmale physical characteristics to features that males do possess. Freud's attempt to account for *scopophilia*—sexual gazing—was introduced in *Three Essays on the Theory of Sexuality* (1913), then further explicated in his 1915 paper "Instincts and Their Vicissitudes." Recently, the feminist theoretician Laura Mulvey has elaborated in psychoanalytic-cinematic terms upon the process by which, through castration anxiety, the male spectator makes a fetish of the female form. See Mulvey, "Visual Pleasure and the Narrative Cinema," *Screen* 16 (Autumn 1975), 6–18. A discussion specifically concerned with the breast as object of visual pleasure is found in Robert T. Eberwein, "Reflections on the Breast," *Wide Angle* 4, no. 3 (1980): 48–53.
3 I refer to later images by other artists not because of a desire to trace artistic lines of descent, but rather to suggest the intertextuality of all Western paintings, perhaps even of all Western cultural productions, when looked back at from the present.
4 A concise review of psychophysiological and psychoanalytic studies of symmetry and asymmetry perception in vision can be found in Maureen Turim, "Symmetry/Asymmetry and Visual Fascination," *Wide Angle* 4, no. 3 (1980): 38–47. Here in the backdrop of *Agnew,* the interplay between the symmetrical positioning of the figures and their various asymmetrical postures is a compositional enactment of the order/disorder, economy/excess, active/passive, and male/female antinomies carried on at other levels in this portrait and our other two.
5 Goodrich, *Thomas Eakins,* 2:42.
6 Lloyd Goodrich, *Thomas Eakins: His Life and Work* (New York: Whitney Museum, 1933), 180.
7 David Hayes Agnew was born in Lancaster County, Pennsylvania, in 1818, graduated from the medical department of the University of Pennsylvania twenty years later, and soon after joined his in-laws running an iron foundry.

When the business failed in 1846, Agnew started work as a country doctor, then eventually moved back to Philadelphia, where he began teaching, practicing as a surgeon, and contributing prolifically to medical literature. He became nationally known in 1881 for his attempts—unsuccessful, finally—to save the life of wounded President James A. Garfield. In 1888, the year before the Eakins portrait, Agnew was elected Emeritus Professor of Surgery at the University of Pennsylvania. He died in 1892. Francis R. Packard, *History of Medicine in the United States* (New York: Hafner, 1963), 393–94.

8   Richard Selzer, *Mortal Lessons: Notes on the Art of Surgery* (New York: Simon and Schuster, 1976), 15–23.

9   Quoted in Goodrich, *Eakins: Life and Work,* 48–49.

10 *Thomas Eakins* (Boston: Little, Brown, 1967), 40.

11 *Selected Stories* (Harmondsworth, Eng.: Penguin, 1963), 53.

12 "The Agnew Clinic [sic] was obtained by a class of students of a certain year, who desired a portrait of their beloved teacher, sought Mr. Eakins and agreed to pay seven hundred and fifty dollars for the single figure. Mr. Eakins delighted with the opportunity to paint a man whom he both admired and respected, determined to give the boys a great composition—'The Agnew Clinic.' Mr. Eakins never regretted that the students could only pay him the sum originally agreed upon for a single portrait of Dr. Agnew." From a letter by Susan MacDowell Eakins quoted in Goodrich, *Thomas Eakins,* 2:322.

13 Certainly not all surgeons felt the same as Agnew concerning the matter of visible blood, but then, not all surgeons worked in Philadelphia. The English physician Sir Frederick Treaves, according to Lewis Mumford, "remembered how the surgeons of Gay's Hospital boasted of the incrustations of blood and dirt on their operating coats, as a mark of long practice!" (*Technics and Civilization* [New York: Harcourt, Brace, 1963], 171).

14 For an exceptionally complete and valuable study of *The Gross Clinic,* or *Portrait of Professor Gross,* as well as information about Dr. Gross himself, the state of medicine at the time the portrait was painted, and comparisons to Rembrandt's *The Anatomy Lesson of Dr. Tulp,* F.-N.-A. Feyen-Perrin's *The Anatomy Lesson of Dr. Velpeau* (1864), and *The Agnew Clinic,* see Elizabeth Johns, *Thomas Eakins: The Heroism of Modern Life* (Princeton: Princeton University Press, 1983), ch. 3.

15 Quoted in Hendricks, *Eakins,* 100.

16 Ibid., 98.

17 Not only penlike, the instrument also resembles a penknife, as suggested by the graffiti artist in the top row.

18 *Naked Masks,* trans. Eric Bentley (New York: E. P. Dutton, 1952), 231.

19 This matter of the viewer's infinite capacity for projection is one that has been dealt with brilliantly on numerous occasions by E. H. Gombrich. See, for instance, "Meditations on a Hobby Horse" and "On Physiognomic Perception" in *Meditations on a Hobby Horse* (London: Phaidon, 1963) and "The Mask and the Face: the Perception of Physiognomic Likeness in Life and Art" in Gombrich, Julian Hochberg, and Max Black, *Art, Perception, and Reality* (Baltimore: Johns Hopkins University Press, 1972).

20 *Eakins: Life and Work,* 125.

21 *Thomas Eakins*, 106.

22 Eakins himself may have shared with Goodrich, Schendler, and us these qualities and feelings, but at this particular point in our inquiry we are interested
less in the consciousness of the original constructor of meaning (the artist)
than in that of the belated constructor: the viewer. Later, we will try to discern
from the painting Eakins' sensibility (personality? character? desire?) as it
reacted in terms of visual, compositional form to the individual he was commissioned to portray. Yet however much insight the painting and our interpretation of it may allow us either into our own minds or into the mind of
this artist who worked a century ago, it cannot give us anything of substance
about the real-life Agnew other than a physical, professional, and at best general biographical description.

23 *Film Technique and Film Acting*, 140.

24 McHenry, *Eakins*, 17.

25 Peale, by his frontality, would seem to be more like Velázquez in authority and
self-confidence than like Agnew-as-Eakins, even though Peale is considerably
closer to his fellow Philadelphian in time. Peale's period was not, however,
closer in terms of certain fundamental social and economic factors, the earlier
artist having painted not only in pre–Civil War America, but also in a pre-
Jacksonian America. His society, at least in comparison to the one Eakins
struggled in, was substantially less troubled by industrialism, urbanization, and
reckless capitalism; by the assaults of organized feminism and organized labor;
and by the emotional burdens of a civil war that had been dubiously successful,
in contrast to the unequivocally successful Revolution. Called "the Athens of
America," Peale's Philadelphia was, indeed, a satisfying place to be an artist:
"It led all other cities in reputation, size, and magnificence. Profiting from its
years as national capital, it contained a brilliant cosmopolitan society and a
flourishing port; it was home for many famous writers, artists, attorneys and
physicians [and] was known for its university, its free library and its art academy" (Neil Harris, *The Artist in American Society: The Formative Years,
1790–1860* [New York: Simon and Schuster, 1966], 108).

26 All the more significant now is the penknife in the upper left corner of the
painting, for it is a cutting blade used as an instrument of inscription. Other
major Eakins paintings such as *The Gross Clinic* and *Between Rounds* (1899)
contain a "scribe," who, like this student with the penknife, can be regarded
as an observer leaving some record, testament, or account of the event that he,
like us, is witnessing.

27 Recall William Dean Howells' description of the personality as "nothing but
hulls, that you keep peeling off, one after another." Later in the passage from
which that quotation is taken he observes that "every boy is two or three boys,
or twenty or thirty different kinds of boys in one; he is all the time living many
lives and forming many characters." In this regard, the Eakins portrait is like
Howells' "every boy."

28 Jack the Ripper, it is interesting to note, carved his victims holding his blade
in his left hand. What is also interesting is that, in the *Study of Dr. Agnew* at
Yale, Eakins used bright red paint—a good deal of it—to sign his name and
the title of the picture. The signature almost seems to drip from the surgeon's

scalpel-wielding hand. Could this have been Eakins' private way of getting back at the doctor for his insistence that the blood be expunged?

29   On the back cover of the fall 1982 issue of *Diacritics* the editors superimposed an oversized Cross pen into the lance of a fourteenth-century St. George, thus visually and wittily making a similar connection between critic and dragon-slayer.

30   Agnew's name is proximate to the noun *agnate,* which stands for "a relative whose kinship is traceable exclusively through males . . . a paternal kinsman," according to *Webster's Seventh New Collegiate Dictionary.* As an adjective, agnate means "related through male descent or on the father's side." By the very sound of his name, then, Agnew is typified as paternal or patriarchal, and so might be this "agnate" clinic painting that bears the doctor's name.

31   "The most moving mirror of . . . response is the face of Nurse Clymer." Schendler, *Thomas Eakins,* 107.

32   *Female Complaints* (New York: W. W. Norton, 1979), 69.

33   *Male Practice: How Doctors Manipulate Women* (Chicago: Contemporary Books, 1981), 30–31. Mendelsohn's italics. Concerning Dr. Gilliam's remark that female castration "pays," one would like to ask, *pays whom?*

34   *Vaginal Politics* (New York: Quadrangle Books, 1972), 128, 134. Also, on the history of breast cancer operations, see Edward Shorter, *A History of Women's Bodies* (New York: Basic Books, 1982), 244–45.

35   *Thomas Eakins,* 107.

36   A rewarding discussion of such paintings in terms of their narrative ingenuity may be found in Nelson Goodman's "Twisted Tales; Or, Story, Study, and Symphony" in *On Narrative,* ed. W. J. T. Mitchell (Chicago: University of Chicago Press, 1981).

37   I received information about the first practice from Dr. Norman Simon, Professor of Medicine at Mt. Sinai Hospital, and learned about the second from Dr. Albert M. Dibbins, a pediatric surgeon at Maine Medical Center.

38   It is hardly surprising that the passive/active tension would be a matter of central importance during these decades that saw the transition from a society celebrating the gospel of self-reliance to one that, while continuing to pay lip service to that gospel, promulgated the new creed of consumerism instead. On the development of the consumer ethos in America, see *The Culture of Consumption: Critical Essays in American History, 1880–1980,* ed. Richard Wightman Fox and T. J. Jackson Lears (New York: Pantheon, 1983). Particularly relevant are the essays by Lears, Christopher P. Wilson, and Jean-Christophe Agnew. See also Stuart Ewen and Elizabeth Ewen, *Channels of Desire: Mass Images and the Shaping of American Consciousness* (New York: McGraw-Hill, 1982), 72–77.

39   I maintain my earlier contention that masturbation is not a mentally passive act, though *instrumentally*—in the realm of pragmatic effect upon the world—it is indeed passive. Those readers interested in masturbation and desiring a firmer grasp of the point may enjoy looking at G. J. Barker-Benfield, "The Spermatic Economy: A Nineteenth-Century View of Sexuality," in *The American Family in Social-Historical Perspective,* ed. Michael Gordon (New York: St. Martin's Press, 1978), 374–402; and John S. Haller, Jr., and Robin M.

Haller, *The Physician and Sexuality in Victorian America* (Urbana: University of Illinois Press, 1974).

40 François Truffaut, *Hitchcock* (New York: Simon and Schuster, 1967), 159.

41 John Canady writes, "The operation itself and the people performing it are described as noncommittally as a factual report . . . an enumeration of facts rather than a response to them." He terms this "dryness," "downright stubborn objectivity," and "uncompromisingly flat statement" (*Mainstreams of Modern Art* [New York: Holt, Rinehart, and Winston, 1959], 319–20).

42 When the eyes are veiled by hooded lids and the hands hidden by apparel, we the viewer are *encouraged* to speculate, to project, to use our imagination. This technique of veiling, which Eakins employs so often and so well, has a long tradition in art history going back to the sfumato of the portraitist/anatomist/experimenter who was Eakins' earliest spiritual predecessor, Leonardo. "No wonder," Gombrich observes in *Art and Illusion*, "that the greatest protagonist of naturalistic illusion in painting, Leonardo da Vinci, is also the inventor of the deliberately blurred image, the sfumato, or veiled form, that cuts down the information on the canvas and thereby stimulates the mechanism of [viewer] projection" (p. 221).

43 Peale in his museum again: the artist as showman, shaman, magician, prestidigitator, manipulator, masturbator.

44 A suggestion from Elizabeth Johns made me think about the term *clinic,* which derives from the Greek *klinē,* the word for bed. *Klinē* in turn derives from *klinein,* to lean or recline: the patient reclines naked upon her bed. I might add that *klinein* also happens (happens?) to be the root of the word climax, a synonym for culmination as well as for orgasm. The male gaze culminates here with the woman; Dr. Agnew is at the peak, the summit, the culmination—the climax—of his career. *The Agnew Clinic/Klinein/Climax:* Agnew's Bed/Culmination/Orgasm. Agnew, as we have already noted, leans back; he too is reclined. *Klinein.*

45 Act 3, sc. 5.

46 *Man and People,* trans. Willard R. Trask (New York: W. W. Norton, 1957). See pp. 115–17. Ortega pays particular attention to the sort of look that is emitted from heavily-lidded eyes. This is the look that Americans term "bedroom eyes," the French call *les yeux en coulisse,* and that, according to Ortega, characterizes "the painter when he steps back from the canvas to judge the effect of the brushstroke he has just made." We can see exactly this look on both A and Agnew. Ortega says that its effect on the person looked at is "like an arrow."

47 *The House of Mirth* (New York: Charles Scribner's Sons, 1969), 134.

48 *The Novel of Worldliness* (Princeton: Princeton University Press, 1969), 16–17.

49 *Discipline and Punish,* trans. Alan Sheridan (New York: Pantheon, 1977), 200. The Panopticon disciplines the prisoner by denying him freedom from observation. Foucault writes: "Discipline fixes; it arrests or regulates movements; it clears up confusion; it dissipates compact groupings of individuals wandering about the country [or, we might add, the canvas] in unpredictable ways; it establishes calculated distributions" (p. 219). We should not hesitate to notice

that the present reading of *The Agnew Clinic,* in its efforts to catch hold of and analyze, or otherwise control, every stray detail and meaning, is itself an attempt to be panoptic.

50   *Ways of Seeing,* 62.

51   *On the Rationalization of Sight* (New York: Da Capo Press, 1973), 9.

52   Berger, *Ways of Seeing,* 62.

53   See Walter Benjamin, *Illuminations,* trans. Harry Zohn (New York: Schocken, 1969), 241.

54   See L. J. Jordanova, "Natural Facts: A Historical Perspective on Science and Sexuality," in *Nature, Culture, and Gender,* ed. Carol P. MacCormack and Marilyn Strathern (Cambridge: Cambridge University Press, 1980).

55   If in *The Gross Clinic* the female observer shrinking back in horror had proven to be prophetic of Philadelphia's response to the painting, here with the nurse Eakins may have inadvertently conjured the public audience for *The Agnew Clinic:* cool, impassive, indifferent.

56   Yet recent psychoanalytic approaches to cinema have shown how the shot/ reverse-shot structure of classically edited films securely sutures (an appropriately surgical term in this context) the viewing subject into the narrative, enabling "him" to occupy a privileged position of authority—phallocentrism all over again. So perhaps the nurse's reversal of Agnew's gaze does not ultimately work in an antiauthoritarian fashion after all. See Daniel Dayan, "The Tutor-Code of Classical Cinema," and William Rothman, "Against 'The System of the Suture' " in *Movies and Methods,* ed. Bill Nichols (Berkeley and Los Angeles: University of California Press, 1976). See also Stephen Heath, "Notes on Suture," and Jacques-Alain Miller, "Suture" in *Screen* 18 (Winter 1977–78). Heath's article has been reprinted in his collection entitled *Questions of Cinema* (Bloomington: Indiana University Press, 1981).

57   *The Sweet Cheat Gone,* trans. C. K. Scott Montcrieff (New York: Vintage, 1970), 54.

CHAPTER THREE: *THE BOIT CHILDREN*

1   *Theory of Literature* (New York: Harcourt, Brace, 1970), 221.

2   "Honoré de Balzac," in *French Poets and Novelists* (Freeport, N.Y.: Books for Libraries Press, 1972), 118.

3   Despite Madame Gautreau's self-presentation, her apparent packaging of herself as hard, cold, and calculatingly mysterious, she transcends the vacuity one can easily read into her, and offers in its place a genuinely sphinxlike mystery, an indecipherability. The exhibition title of the painting, *Madame X,* was, I think, wholly appropriate and properly theatrical.

4   On the basis of the image itself, as opposed to ancillary information, the precise place (Paris) and date (1882–83) are not recoverable.

5   Unfortunately, most reproductions of the painting black out almost the entire back region. It is visible, however, in the color postcard sold by the Museum of Fine Arts, Boston.

6   Ormond, *Sargent,* 30.

7   "The blue and white vases have survived sixteen ocean voyages between the

Paris apartment in which they here appear, and their Boston home. They still belong to a member of the family, Mrs. E. Mauran Beals, Jr." David McKibbin, *Sargent's Boston* (Boston: Museum of Fine Arts, 1956), 30.

8 "The Square Format and Proto-Modernism in American Painting," *Arts* 50, no. 10 (June 1976): 73. The phrase "the four-corners game," is from Henry Houssaye, "Le Salon de 1883," *Revue des Deux Mondes* 57 (1883): 616.

9 *Webster's Seventh New Collegiate Dictionary*, 1967, s.v. "box."

10 *Micro Robert: Dictionnaire du français primordial*, 1973, s.v. "boîte."

11 "*Ces jolies fillettes réunies par M. Sargent dans une cadre un peu trop vaste et parfois un peu vide.*" ("Le Salon de 1883," *Gazette des Beaux-Arts* 28 [1883]: 9.)

12 *Mrs. Edward D. Boit* is painted with the loose and broad brushwork, the facial mobility, and the richly contrasted tonalities that are associated with the portraiture of Frans Hals, an artist Sargent had avidly studied in a visit to Holland in 1880. One almost hears in this depiction of Mrs. Boit the "merry laugh" that Henry James attributed to her in a notebook entry made five or six months before Sargent painted *The Boit Children* (Edel, *The Middle Years*, 44).

13 The fact that, like his friend Sargent, the real-life Boit was a painter is all the more reason to draw this connection between the two.

14 The painting is also known as *The Daughters of Edward Darley Boit,* the middle name lending that much more weight and authority to the father for whom it was painted.

15 To try to arrange these various pairs so that the feminine half always appears first (or always second) would be reductively to suggest neat parallels between all the first members of the pairs and all the second ones. Instead I have arranged each pair according to the preference of my ear. It should nonetheless be noted that the ear, like the eye, is not ideologically innocent; if one syntactical arrangement sounds better than another, there are sociocultural as well as idiosyncratic reasons why this is so.

16 *Sargent,* 30.

17 See the entire opening chapter of Foucault's *Order of Things* (New York: Random House, 1970), 3–16.

18 What Sargent's mirror does provide is an implied passageway, an escape hatch out of the pictured world into another world that is adjacent to it but as yet unknowable. In this sense, the mirror is a window or door, equivalent perhaps to that open door which, at the back of the Velázquez image, is filled by a figure who posturally and gesturally bears a resemblance to the artist's depiction of himself: a suggestion that portraitists act as "transitioners," mediators, who provide passageways from one room to another, one life to another, one reality to another.

19 Yet however much it is a methodological problem as to what particular permutations of Western family history these two family representations can, on their own, reveal, deny, or confirm, what is less a problem is to regard them as texts in the history of representation. Should it not be clear by now, it certainly soon shall be that *The Boit Children,* every bit as much as *Las Meninas,* is a metaportrait, a portrait about portraiture, a painting about the painter's relationship to the painted. And like *The Agnew Clinic* and *The*

Portrait of a Lady, its discourse is a performance of what it is discoursing: the text's attempts at patriarchal control over its characters and, simultaneously, its attempts at disrupting that control, that order. The modernity of these three portraits in contrast to the one by Velázquez is that in them we see the order/disorder antithesis at various levels of aesthetic form and narrative content, while in the much earlier work, order and control are, so far as I can tell, visually delineated, accepted, and celebrated, but not also resisted.

20 In front of the painter and behind him in the temporal sense as well as the spatial, if one assumes that the canvases hanging on the wall are works that this painter has previously completed. From external information we know, however, that in the chamber depicted here, Velázquez's studio in the Alcazar, hung replicas of Flemish works as copied by the artist's son-in-law, Juan Bautista Martínez del Mazo.

21 "As parenthood has become more voluntary, children are coming to be wanted more conspicuously as expressions of the creative and affection-giving potentialities of their parents," note Nelson Northrup Foote and Ruben L. Hill in *Encyclopaedia Britannica,* 1973, s.v. "family."

22 "By splitting society between 'work' and 'life', proletarianization created the conditions under which men and women looked to themselves, outside the division of labour, for meaning and purpose," observes Eli Zaretsky, including among those affected by his umbrella term "proletarianization" not only working-class individuals but also alienated bourgeoisie. "Introspection intensified and deepened as people sought [in themselves, their families, their children] the only coherence, consistency, and unity capable of reconciling the fragmentation of social life" (*Capitalism, the Family, and Personal Life* [New York: Harper & Row, 1976], 66).

23 Such indeed is exactly what *The Portrait of a Lady*'s Gilbert Osmond attempts to achieve with his daughter, Pansy, and though many readers would claim Osmond is motivated not by a subjective need for self-expression but rather by a need to manipulate, through her, the way he will appear to others, I think that the one position is not entirely different from the other.

24 On the positioning of figures within the pictorial space of *Las Meninas,* and the question of determining the picture's focal center, see Leo Steinberg, "Velázquez' *Las Meninas,*" *October* 19 (1981): 45–54.

25 Bernard Bailyn et al., *The Great Republic* (Lexington, Mass.: D. C. Heath, 1977), 105.

26 *Centuries of Childhood: A Social History of Family Life,* trans. Robert Baldick (New York: Random House, 1962), 403–04.

27 "What counted most of all was the emotion aroused by the child, the living image of his parents." (ibid., 364.)

28 Ibid., 375.

29 *The Making of the Modern Family* (New York: Basic Books, 1975), 205.

30 I cannot stress enough the importance of remembering that portraits do not in any confirmable way unlock the past for us, nor can they be used to prove (though it is attempted all the time) any thesis about the past. As we saw in the last chapter, an image can readily be adapted to illustrate virtually any preselected meaning, even when the preselection is unrecognized. This said, I

can now proceed in good conscience to find in these paintings social-historical, rather than simply art-historical, differences, knowing, at least, that the reader has been forewarned that these findings are interpretations or suggestions, not statements of fact.

31 "Rosily" is indeed the proper term, for the predominant color here is a warm, rosy red. This rose color suffuses and softens the painting. Like rosewater taken after a bath, it lends a sweet scent and refreshing tingle.

32 Among Sargent's biographers there is no debate as to which parent figured more significantly in his life—father was recessive, mother domineering—and one could certainly argue that the elimination of mother from *The Boit Children* and the building up of father to near-cosmic proportions was in some sense an act of psychic compensation or wish fulfillment on the part of an artist who unconsciously harbored resentment for the one parent who had been too weak, or for the other who had been too strong.

33 See Bonnie G. Smith, *Ladies of the Leisure Class: The Bourgeoises of Northern France in the Nineteenth Century* (Princeton: Princeton University Press, 1981), 66–68.

34 Recently the argument has been made with increasing frequency that any realist, perspectival visual (or verbal) representation flatters its spectator by accommodating itself to his vantage point, thus treating him, in a manner that ultimately reinforces society's status quo, as a centered subject. See Jean-Louis Baudry, "Ideological Effects of the Basic Cinematographic Apparatus" in *Apparatus,* ed. Theresa Hak Kyung Cha (New York: Tanam, 1980), 25–37, and Stephen Heath, "Narrative Space" in *Questions of Cinema,* 19–75.

35 Their family name, of course, has been passed down to them patrilineally, further instancing the subjecthood that is awarded their father but denied them.

36 *Female Complaints,* 68.

37 E. Littré, *Dictionnaire de la langue française,* 1874.

38 *Melloni's Illustrated Medical Dictionary,* 1979, s.v. "male."

39 "Society and the whole universe have a side which is sacred, noble and precious, and another which is profane and common; a male side, strong and active, and another, female, weak and passive; or, in two words, a right side and a left side." ("The Pre-Eminence of the Right Hand: A Study in Religious Polarity" [1909], in Robert Hertz, *Death and the Right Hand,* trans. Rodney Needham and Claudia Needham (New York: Macmillan, 1960), 98.

40 The phrase "letter of *boîte*" suggests the French *boîte aux lettres* or mailbox, which in the present context inevitably puns into "male box."

41 Not only in her visual but also in her psychological appearance is the figure as we have described her an *i*, a dependent female or child, rather than a fully formed independent consciousness, an I.

42 "There had been a brief fad of clitoridectomy (removal of the clitoris) in the [eighteen-] sixties, following the introduction of the operation by the English physician Isaac Baker Brown. Although most doctors frowned on the practice of removing the clitoris, they tended to agree that it might be necessary in cases of nymphomania, intractable masturbation, or 'unnatural growth' of that organ. (The last clitoridectomy we know of in the United States was performed

in 1948 on a child of five, as a cure for masturbation.)" (Ehrenreich and English, *For Her Own Good*, 123; on the ideological clitoridectomy performed on twentieth-century women by influential followers of Freud, see pp. 270–74).

43   This raises a point-of-view question. Whose sense of lack, whose feeling of being deprived, does the painting register: That of the female herself? Of the male husband-father? Of the artist? Of the viewer? My inclination would be to argue "all of the above," inasmuch as the social atrophying or nullification of desire, whether male or female, is a problem that affects us all.

44   In both the French and the English languages, the preposition *of* translates ambiguously. For instance, a *coffret de bois* can mean either a box made of wood or a box made for containing wood. Likewise, "the portrait of a lady" can mean either an artistic depiction of a certain woman or an artistic depiction that a certain woman happens to possess.

45   The viewer's gaze travels in this painting from figure to figure circularly or in a sawing motion back and forth. These visual patterns have motile counterparts in the intercourse behavior of the male who, once he has penetrated the vaginal box, experiences pleasure by gyrating or by sawing rapidly forward and back. This description of intercourse from the male perspective is indeed graphic, but that is precisely the point: male sex, like looking, is a graphic, a linear, activity; during intercourse, man scrawls his lines (and sometimes his lineage) with that first of all pens, the penis. The penis enters into the dark, unseeable box where the eye cannot go, but the penis has no eye of its own; hence, perhaps, that powerful, ever-yearning, never-quenched relationship between the male's organ of sex and his organ of sight. This is the phenomenon of scopophilia, which, despite Freud's attempt, has yet to be convincingly explained.

46   The third classification of meaning for *maison* (like boîte, a feminine noun) is "les gens qui vivent ensemble, habitent la même maison," referring to the individuals who live together in the physical proximity of the house or in the genetic proximity of the family. One might speak, for example, of the Habsburgs as "la maison d'Autriche."

47   For a historical, demographically based examination of adolescence as a modern American concept, see Joseph F. Kett, *Rites of Passage: Adolescence in America, 1790 to the Present* (New York: Basic Books, 1977). Although the four Boit daughters occupy a different class position from that of most of the adolescents Kett describes and happen to be living in France, not the United States, the book is instructive in this context because it shows how the notion of an intermediate phase of life, a phase that marks a transition between childhood and maturity, was "an expression of a mélange of nostalgia and anxiety, and in its crudest mold an embodiment of Victorian prejudices about females and sexuality" (p. 143).

48   "Her reproductive system," writes Sarah Stage of the nineteenth-century female, "came to be seen as a sacred trust, one that she must constantly guard in the interest of the race. The uterus, considered 'the controlling organ in the female body,' took on an importance which reduced woman to simply a vessel, an organ bearer" (*Female Complaints*, 69).

49   The doll might also at first look like a lapdog, calling to mind the moment in
      The Rape of the Lock when, her "sacred Hair" [hymen] dissevered, Belinda
      emits a scream. Pope writes, "Not louder Shrieks to pitying Heav'n are cast, /
      When Husbands, or when Lapdogs breath their last, / Or when rich *China*
      Vessels, fal'n from high, / In glitt'ring Dust and painted Fragments lie!"
      (canto 3, 153–60). China vases no less!

50   McKibbin, *Sargent's Boston*, 85. The children are identified, reading left to
      right, as Mary Louise (whom we have called A), Florence (R), Jane (I), and
      Julia (J).

51   In her study of the late nineteenth-century bourgeois woman of northern
      France, Bonnie G. Smith speaks of the tendency modern-day critics have had
      to regard such a woman as "a culpable reproducer of babies to insure the
      transmission of private wealth." Smith is right in cautioning historians who
      are attuned to feminist concerns and eager to glorify the exceptional women
      of the nineteenth century not to ignore the subjectivity of the nonrebelling
      woman of that period, or deride her as a baby machine. Still, that does not
      rule out the fact that this non-exceptional nineteenth-century woman was most
      valued by her contemporaries, and often by herself, very much in terms of her
      ability to insure the transmission of private wealth—and of course the moral
      precepts, family name, and social rank that this private wealth underwrote
      (*Ladies of the Leisure Class*, 57).

52   *The New Century Dictionary,* 1927; *Encyclopaedia Britannica,* 1973,
      s.v. "doll."

53   *The Psychopathology of Everyday Life,* trans. A. A. Brill (New York: Mentor,
      1981), 35–36.

54   Elsewhere, Freud recounts a case (interesting term for us, since it also means
      box) that merits extended quotation: "In the course of a longish dream, [the
      female patient] imagined that she saw her only, fifteen-year-old daughter lying
      dead 'in a case.' She had half a mind to use the scene as an objection to the
      wish-fulfillment theory, though she herself suspected that the detail of the 'case'
      must point the way to another view of the dream. In the course of the analysis
      she recalled that at a party the evening before there had been some talk about
      the English word 'box' and the various ways in which it could be translated
      into German—such as *'Schachtel'* ["case"], *'Loge'* ["box at the theater"],
      'Kasten' ["chest"], *'Ohrfeige'* ["box on the ear"], and so on. Other portions
      of the same dream enabled us to discover further that she had guessed that the
      English 'box' was related to the German *'Buchse'* ["receptacle"], and that she
      had then been plagued by a recollection that *'Buchse'* is used as a vulgar term
      for the female genitals. If some allowance was made for the limits of her knowl-
      edge of topographical anatomy, it might be presumed, therefore, that the child
      lying in the case meant an embryo in the womb. After being enlightened up
      to this point, she no longer denied that the dream-picture corresponded to a
      wish of hers. Like so many young married women, she had been far from
      pleased when she became pregnant; and more than once she had allowed herself
      to wish that the child in her womb might die. . . . Thus the dead child was in
      fact the fulfillment of a wish, but of a wish that had been put aside fifteen
      years earlier." *The Interpretation of Dreams* (1900–30), trans. James Strachey

(New York: Avon Books, 1965; repr. from the *Standard Edition*, London, 1953), 187–88. At a period relatively contemporary to that during which *The Boit Children* was produced (that is, Edward Boit's daughters were reproduced), the word and concept *box* generated in Vienna a similar series of unexpected and unconscious allusions: to the female genitalia; to the womb, which houses generation; and to a coffin, which houses the body's degeneration.

55   The third axis, up-down, is for the purposes of this present discussion the same as near-far, since we are talking about the image in terms of its illusional three-dimensionality rather than its literal two. In other words, a point placed high on the canvas is read in this instance as a point deep in space.

CHAPTER FOUR: *THE PORTRAIT OF A LADY*

1   *The Portrait of a Lady,* unlike the two portraits examined in the previous chapters, has been at the center of so much good critical writing that I have thought it best to refrain from citing any of it in the following pages, so that the reader may travel unburdened by cumbersome bibliographic luggage. Permit me, therefore, to check all of the luggage into this one bulky note. On James's strategies for constructing character in his fiction, see Martin Price, *Forms of Life: Character and Moral Imagination in the Novel* (New Haven: Yale University Press, 1983) and Mary Doyle Springer, *A Rhetoric of Character: Some Women of Henry James* (Chicago: University of Chicago Press, 1978). On James's notion of portraiture as a visual enterprise, see Viola Hopkins Winner, *Henry James and the Visual Arts* (Charlottesville: University Press of Virginia, 1970). On James's fiction in terms of the pressures exerted on the formation of his characters by exigencies of the marketplace and newly arising consumer sensibilities, see Jean-Christophe Agnew, "The Consuming Vision of Henry James" in Fox and Lears, *The Culture of Consumption,* and Laurence B. Holland, *The Expense of Vision: Essays on the Craft of Henry James* (Baltimore: Johns Hopkins University Press, 1964). Leo Bersani, in *A Future for Astyanax: Character and Desire in Literature* (Boston: Little, Brown, 1976), illuminates, as his subtitle suggests, the formative (and deformative) effect of desire upon literary characters and characterization. Charles Feidelson, "The Moment of *The Portrait of a Lady,*" *Ventures* 8 (1968): 47–55, Dorothea Krook, *The Ordeal of Consciousness in Henry James* (Cambridge: Cambridge University Press, 1962), and Richard Poirier, *The Comic Sense of Henry James: A Study of the Early Novels* (New York: Oxford University Press, 1967), all provide model readings of *The Portrait* in which the characters are described and analyzed with rare discernment. Although I doubt that any of the authors mentioned above would find (or would have found) the following chapter in complete concurrence with their own approach to *The Portrait of a Lady,* all of them contributed to it by showing me possible ways that I might go.

2   *Henry James: The Conquest of London* (Philadelphia: J. B. Lippincott, 1962), 422–23. Here is a good opportunity for me to state that throughout this chapter (unlike with the introduction), "Henry James" primarily refers to that

site of meaning signified by the written text as its author, and only secondarily to the historical individual who lived from 1843 to 1916. The relationship between the one Henry James and the other is highly problematic. Valuable discussions concerning the role of the author can be found in Roland Barthes, "The Death of the Author" in *Image-Music-Text*, trans. Stephen Heath (New York: Hill and Wang, 1977), 142–48, and Michel Foucault, "What is an Author?" in *Textual Strategies*, ed. J. Harari (Ithaca: Cornell University Press, 1979), 141–60.

3   Preface to *The Portrait of a Lady* (Harmondsworth, Eng.: Penguin, 1971), v. The Penguin, which I am using here and throughout this chapter, is based on James's revision of the novel for the New York Edition. Though my concern is with portraiture of the 1880s, I feel obliged to work from the later, altered version because the other two portraits I have examined also have been altered, even if only by the impersonal processes of time and dust and the nonauthorial interventions of museum conservationists. And if I cite from an inexpensive, almost universally available paperback edition of the 1908 revision rather than from the costly hardcover set housed in university libraries, the choice reflects my desire to avoid regarding *The Portrait* as some sort of holy writ, or the New York Edition as a sacramental relic preserved for priestly scholars while generally inaccessible to all others. (Similarly, although grateful to the University of Pennsylvania and the Boston Museum of Fine Arts for the excellence with which they have preserved *The Agnew Clinic* and *The Boit Children*, I resist any notion that these texts, as ever-active signifying systems, belong to the institutions that own them.) Whatever convenience for scholars may be achieved by citing from the New York Edition, the subtle foregoing of intellectual freedom that may occur from such adherence to uniformity is not worth the price.

4   *Portrait*, vi. This passage is echoed at the end of the preface when, having to draw his remarks to a close, the ever-so-verbal James is forced to concede, "There is really too much to say" (p. xviii).

5   The verbal style of late James, an attempt to track this immensity and flux by means of increased complexity and nuance, can legitimately be viewed as having more, rather than, as is often supposed, less fidelity to reality. During the period of *The Portrait*, however, not only the prose but also the categorization of characters and the relatively clear-cut structure of the narrative seem less interested in reproducing the complexity of the world than in clarifying and simplifying it.

6   "The Art of Fiction," in *Henry James: Selected Fiction*, ed. Leon Edel (New York: E. P. Dutton, 1953), 594.

7   From "the lips of Ivan Turgenieff" James learned that after an initial "vision of some person or persons, who hovered before [the artist], soliciting him . . . just as they were and by what they were," the artist must then go to work "to imagine, to invent and select and piece together the situations most useful and favourable to the sense of the creatures themselves, the complications they would be most likely to produce and feel" (*Portrait*, vii).

8   Prior is put in quotation marks because it is debatable whether or not there can be such a thing as content unmediated by conventionalized codes of lan-

guage or vision. For a recent and helpful discussion of this point as it has been debated within philosophic and literary-critical traditions, see Terry Lovell, *Pictures of Reality* (London: British Film Institute, 1982), 9–28.

9 Contradictory impulses of a similar sort underlie the debates in book review sections between traditionalists who view criticism as, at best, only a handmaiden to the text, and deconstructors, for whom the text serves as a springboard by which to launch forth a new and also rewarding creation, a new text.

10 *Essays,* trans. J. M. Cohen (Harmondsworth, Eng.: Penguin, 1978), 235.

11 *Portrait,* ix.

12 . *Middlemarch* (Harmondsworth, Eng.: Penguin, 1971), 226.

13 *Portrait,* xiv. "Was will das Weib?" Freud was later to ask in bafflement, "What does woman want?"—a strikingly similar question to James's "What will she *do*?" As pointed out by Edel ("He was seeking answers for himself as well as for her") the question also mirrors James's internal questions about his own future, about what it is that he will, or should, do. Such questions were not, in the mid- to late nineteenth century, the sole property of would-be portraitists. As a twenty-year-old, Charles William Eliot, later the stalwart president of Harvard, wrote to a friend, "What a tremendous question it is— what shall I be?" Quoted in Bledstein, *The Culture of Professionalism,* 159.

14 *Portrait,* 20–21. Emphasis added.

15 In *The Middle Years,* Edel discusses the price paid by James for maintaining this unbreachable distance from others. The biographer leaves us with a sense that it was this, finally, that drove James's friend Constance Fenimore Woolson to suicide after years of loving him unrequitedly. (See pp. 356–72.)

16 H. W. Janson writes of Plotinus, the second-century Greek philosopher responsible for Neoplatonism, that he "was so contemptuous of the imperfections of the physical world that he refused to have any portrait made of himself. The body, he maintained, was an awkward enough likeness of the true, spiritual self; why then go to the bother of making an even more awkward 'likeness of a likeness'?" (*History of Art,* 2d ed. [Englewood Cliffs, N.J., and New York: Prentice-Hall and Harry N. Abrams, 1977], 176.)

17 Let us set aside here the question of Madame Merle's duplicity, and for the time being take her at her word concerning her philosophic view of the world.

18 Although such literary theorists as Roland Barthes (in *S/Z*) have demonstrated the enormous extent to which realism is a highly codified, conventionalized system of representation, we must bracket that information to the side in hopes of keeping the present argument clear.

19 In terms of the issue of gender identity that we will be examining, it is noteworthy that James has here typified the embodiment of quiet, passive reception as a motherly figure, while Mrs. Touchett, an embodiment of sharp, penetrating consciousness—"as honest as a pair of compasses" (p. 220)—is deemed paternal.

20 *Language and Materialism: Developments in Semiology and the Theory of the Subject* (London: Routledge & Kegan Paul, 1977), 76.

21 Louis Althusser, "Est-il simple d'être marxiste en philosophie?" *La Pensée,*

October 1975, 27. Quoted in Coward and Ellis, *Language and Materialism,* 81.

22 E. M. Forster, *Aspects of the Novel* (New York: Harcourt, Brace, 1954), 64.

23 The first device mentioned above is exceptionally pervasive, common to most writing in our culture, including, of course, this book. The second device is characteristic of premodernist and realist fiction (and many other types of discourse as well), while the third, theorized and perfected by James, helped open the gates for stream-of-consciousness, subjectivist, arch-modernist authors such as Woolf, Kafka, and Joyce. For discussions of James's reliance on codes of melodrama, see Peter Brooks, *The Melodramatic Imagination* (New Haven: Yale University Press, 1976) and William Veeder, *Henry James: The Lessons of the Master* (Chicago: University of Chicago Press, 1975).

24 Sigmund Freud, "Family Romances," in *The Sexual Enlightenment of Children,* ed. Philip Rieff (New York: Collier Books, 1963), 41–45.

25 A chipped or cracked bowl in Victorian fiction and painting often symbolizes a fallen woman. At the close of chapter 49 in this novel, when Osmond fingers such a piece while talking to Madame Merle, or in James's *The Golden Bowl* more than two decades later, it goes beyond that to suggest the inherent imperfection of all human beings, male or female, and of all human relationships.

26 Recall here the suggested equation in chapter 3 of "P-paul" with "Papa"— again, a double syllable of infant desire.

27 Especially relevant here is the conversation Isabel has with Ralph early in the book, in which she admits she is "very fond of knowledge," but does not wish to nor think she needs to suffer in exchange for that knowledge. (See p. 48.)

28 "That she would always be a child was the conviction expressed by her father" (pp. 352–53).

29 This is a theme taken up in full by James's brother William some years later in his famous essay "The Moral Equivalent of War" (1910). See Fredrickson, *Inner Civil War,* 229–38 for an illuminating discussion of the theme and its relevance in post–Civil War America.

30 From a different angle, one might argue that Isabel's decisive return to Osmond and authoritarian Rome is an expression of what Lears, in *No Place of Grace,* terms *antimodernism.* Although at first it may seem preposterous to see Gilbert Osmond as a Jamesian equivalent to Henry Adams' Virgin of Chartres, a good case could be made that Isabel's continuing, if cynical, choice of Osmond above all others is an act of resistance against disturbingly modern industrial, capitalist, and liberal values, as embodied by Goodwood, the Touchetts, and Warburton.

31 Significantly, what causes Isabel to recognize finally that there is an unpropitious connection between her husband and her accomplished former friend is her having glimpsed Osmond sitting while Merle stood—an inversion of proper sexual etiquette suggesting perversion of moral order, which the rules of etiquette are meant to signify.

Bibliography

Adams, Henry. *The Education of Henry Adams.* New York: Modern Library, 1931.

Agnew, Jean-Christophe. "The Consuming Vision of Henry James." In *The Culture of Consumption: Critical Essays in American History, 1880–1980.* Ed. Richard Wightman Fox and T. J. Jackson Lears. New York: Pantheon, 1983.

Althusser, Louis. "Est-il simple d'être marxiste en philosophie?" *La Pensée* (October 1975).

Ariès, Philippe. *Centuries of Childhood: A Social History of Family Life.* Trans. Robert Baldick. New York: Random House, 1962.

Arnheim, Rudolph. *Art and Visual Perception: A Psychology of the Creative Eye.* Berkeley and Los Angeles: University of California Press, 1954; revised, 1974.

Bailyn, Bernard, et al. *The Great Republic.* Lexington, Mass.: D. C. Heath, 1977.

Barker-Benfield, G. J. "The Spermatic Economy: A Nineteenth-Century View of Sexuality." In *The American Family in Social-Historical Perspective.* Ed. Michael Gordon. New York: St. Martin's Press, 1978.

Barthes, Roland. "The Death of the Author." In *Image-Music-Text.* Trans. Stephen Heath. New York: Hill and Wang, 1977.

Baudry, Jean-Louis. "Ideological Effects of the Basic Cinematographic Apparatus." In *Apparatus.* Ed. Theresa Hak Kyung Cha. New York: Tanam, 1980.

Beauvoir, Simone de. *The Second Sex*. Trans. H. M. Parshley. New York: Alfred A. Knopf, 1953.

Benjamin, Walter. *Illuminations*. Trans. Harry Zohn. New York: Schocken, 1969.

Bercovitch, Sacvan. *American Jeremiad*. Madison: University of Wisconsin Press, 1978.

————. *The Puritan Origins of the American Self*. New Haven: Yale University Press, 1975.

Berg, J. H. van den. *The Changing Nature of Man: Introduction to a Historical Psychology*. Trans. H. F. Croes. New York: W. W. Norton, 1961.

Berger, John. *Ways of Seeing*. Harmondsworth, Eng.: BBC and Penguin, 1972.

Bersani, Leo. *A Future for Astyanax: Character and Desire in Literature*. Boston: Little, Brown, 1976.

Bigot, Charles. "Le Salon de 1883." *Gazette des Beaux-Arts* 28.

Bledstein, Burton J. *The Culture of Professionalism: The Middle Class and the Development of Higher Education in America*. New York: W. W. Norton, 1976.

Boorstin, Daniel J. *The Image: A Guide to Pseudo-Events in America*. New York: Atheneum, 1961.

Brooks, Peter. *The Melodramatic Imagination*. New Haven: Yale University Press, 1976.

————. *The Novel of Worldliness*. Princeton: Princeton University Press, 1969.

Canaday, John. *Mainstreams of Modern Art*. New York: Holt, Rinehart, and Winston, 1959.

Carr, E. H. *What Is History?* New York: Alfred A. Knopf, 1962.

Charteris, Evan. *John Sargent*. New York: Charles Scribner's Sons, 1927.

Chatman, Seymour. *Story and Discourse: Narrative Structure in Fiction and Film*. Ithaca: Cornell University Press, 1978.

Coward, Rosalind, and Ellis, John. *Language and Materialism: Developments in Semiology and the Theory of the Subject*. London: Routledge & Kegan Paul, 1977.

Dayan, Daniel. "The Tutor-Code of Classical Cinema." In *Movies and Methods*. Ed. Bill Nichols. Berkeley and Los Angeles: University of California Press, 1976.

Demetz, Peter. "Balzac and the Zoologists: A Concept of the Type." In *The Disciplines of Criticism*. Ed. Peter Demetz. New Haven: Yale University Press, 1968.

Eberwein, Robert T. "Reflections on the Breast." *Wide Angle* 4, no. 3 (1980): 48–53.

Edel, Leon. *Henry James: The Conquest of London*. Philadelphia: J. B. Lippincott, 1962.

————. *Henry James: The Middle Years*. Philadelphia: J. B. Lippincott, 1962.

————. *Henry James: The Untried Years*. Philadelphia: J. B. Lippincott, 1953.

Ehrenreich, Barbara, and English, Deirdre. *For Her Own Good: 150 Years of the Experts' Advice to Women*. Garden City, N.Y.: Doubleday Anchor, 1978.

Eisenstein, Sergei. *Film Form*. Trans. Jay Leyda. New York: Harcourt, Brace & World, 1949.

Eliot, George. *Middlemarch*. Harmondsworth, Eng.: Penguin, 1971.

Ewen, Stuart, and Ewen, Elizabeth. *Channels of Desire: Mass Images and the Shaping of American Consciousness*. New York: McGraw-Hill, 1982.

Feidelson, Charles. "The Moment of *The Portrait of a Lady*," *Ventures* 8 (1968): 47–55. Reprinted in *The Portrait of a Lady*. Ed. Robert D. Bamberg. New York: W. W. Norton, 1975.

————. *Symbolism and American Literature*. Chicago: University of Chicago Press, 1953.

Flaubert, Gustave. *Madame Bovary*. Trans. Mildred Marmur. New York: New American Library, 1964.

Forster, E. M. *Aspects of the Novel*. New York: Harcourt, Brace, 1954.

Foucault, Michel. *Discipline and Punish*. Trans. Alan Sheridan. New York: Pantheon, 1977.

————. "What is an Author?" In *Textual Strategies*. Ed. J. Harari. Ithaca: Cornell University Press, 1979.

Frankfort, Ellen. *Vaginal Politics*. New York: Quadrangle Books, 1972.

Fredrickson, George M. *The Inner Civil War: Northern Intellectuals and the Crisis of the Union*. New York: Harper & Row, 1965.

Freud, Sigmund. "Family Romances." In *The Sexual Enlightenment of Children*. Ed. Philip Rieff. New York: Collier Books, 1963.

————. *The Interpretation of Dreams*. Trans. James Strachey. New York: Avon Books, 1965; reprint from the *Standard Edition*, London, 1953.

————. *The Psychopathology of Everyday Life*. Trans. A. A. Brill. New York: Mentor, 1981.

Garraty, John A. *The New Commonwealth, 1877–1890*. New York: Harper & Row, 1968.

Gay, Peter. *Art and Act*. New York: Harper & Row, 1976.

Gerdts, William H. "The Square Format and Proto-Modernism in American Painting." *Arts* 50, no. 10 (1976): 70–75.

Gombrich, E. H. *Art and Illusion*. Princeton: Princeton University Press, 1960.

————. "The Mask and the Face: The Perception of Physiognomic Likeness in Life and Art." In E. H. Gombrich, Max Black, and Julian Hochberg, *Art, Perception, and Reality*. Baltimore: Johns Hopkins University Press, 1972.

————. "Meditations on a Hobby Horse." In *Meditations on a Hobby Horse*. London: Phaidon, 1963.

————. "On Physiognomic Perception." In *Meditations on a Hobby Horse*. London: Phaidon, 1963.

Goodman, Nelson. "Twisted Tales; Or, Story, Study and Symphony." In *On Narrative*. Ed. W. J. T. Mitchell. Chicago: University of Chicago Press, 1981.

Goodrich, Lloyd. *Thomas Eakins*. 2 vols. Cambridge: Harvard University Press, 1982.

————. *Thomas Eakins: His Life and Work*. New York: Whitney Museum, 1933.

Haller, John S., and Haller, Robin M. *The Physician and Sexuality in Victorian America*. Urbana: University of Illinois Press, 1974.

Halttunen, Karen. *Confidence Men and Painted Women: A Study of Middle-Class Culture in America, 1830–1870*. New Haven: Yale University Press, 1982.

Harris, Neil. *The Artist in American Society: The Formative Years, 1790–1860*. New York: Simon and Schuster, 1966.

————. Introduction to *The Land of Contrasts: 1880–1901*. New York: George Braziller, 1970.

Haskell, Thomas L. *The Emergence of Professional Social Science: The American Social Science Association and the Nineteenth-Century Crisis of Authority*. Urbana: University of Illinois Press, 1977.

Heath, Stephen. "Narrative Space." In *Questions of Cinema*. Bloomington: Indiana University Press, 1981.

Hendricks, Gordon. *The Life and Work of Thomas Eakins*. New York: Grossman, 1974.

Hertz, Robert. "The Pre-Eminence of the Right Hand: A Study in Religious Polarity." In *Death and the Right Hand*. Trans. Rodney Needham and Claudia Needham. New York: Macmillan, 1960.

Higham, John. *From Boundlessness to Consolidation: The Transformation of American Culture, 1848–1860*. Ann Arbor: Walter Clements Library, 1969.

Holland, Laurence B. *The Expense of Vision: Essays on the Craft of Henry James*. Baltimore: Johns Hopkins University Press, 1964.

Howells, William Dean. *A Boy's Town*. New York: Harper & Brothers, 1890.

Ivins, William, Jr. *On the Rationalization of Sight*. New York: Da Capo, 1973.

James, Henry. "The Altar of the Dead." In *In The Cage and Other Tales*. Ed. Morton Dauwen Zabel. New York: W. W. Norton, 1969.

————. "The Art of Fiction." In *Henry James: Selected Fiction*. Ed. Leon Edel. New York: E. P. Dutton, 1953.

————. "Honoré de Balzac." In *French Poets and Novelists*. Freeport, N.Y.: Books For Libraries Press, 1972.

————. *Notebooks*. Ed. F. O. Matthiesen and Kenneth B. Murdock. New York: Oxford University Press, 1947.

————. *Notes of a Son and Brother*. New York: Charles Scribner's Sons, 1914.

————. "On Some Pictures Lately Exhibited." In *The Painter's Eye*. Ed. John L. Sweeney. Cambridge: Harvard University Press, 1956.

————. *The Portrait of a Lady*. Harmondsworth, Eng.: Penguin, 1971.

Janson, H. W. *History of Art*. 2d ed. Englewood Cliffs, N.J., and New York: Prentice-Hall and Harry N. Abrams, 1977.

Johns, Elizabeth. *Thomas Eakins: The Heroism of Modern Life*. Princeton: Princeton University Press, 1983.

Keller, Karl. "Alephs, Zahirs, and the Triumph of Ambiguity: Typology in Nineteenth-Century American Literature." In *Literary Uses of Typology from the Late Middle Ages to the Present*. Ed. Earl Miner. Princeton: Princeton University Press, 1977.

Kett, Joseph F. *Rites of Passage: Adolescence in America, 1790 to the Present*. New York: Basic Books, 1977.

Kilbourne, Jean. *Killing Us Softly*. Cambridge, Mass.: Cambridge Documentary Films, 1980.

Krook, Dorothea. *The Ordeal of Consciousness in Henry James*. Cambridge: Cambridge University Press, 1962.

Lasch, Christopher. *The Culture of Narcissism: American Life in an Age of Diminishing Expectations*. New York: W. W. Norton, 1979.

————. *Haven in a Heartless World: The Family Besieged*. New York: Basic Books, 1977.

Lears, T. J. Jackson. *No Place of Grace: Antimodernism and the Transformation of American Culture, 1880–1920*. New York: Pantheon, 1981.

Leitch, Vincent B. *Deconstructive Criticism*. New York: Columbia University Press, 1983.

Lovell, Terry. *Pictures of Reality*. London: British Film Institute, 1982.

McCann, Richard Dyer, ed. *Film: A Montage of Theories*. New York: E. P. Dutton, 1966.

McHenry, Margaret. *Thomas Eakins Who Painted*. Oreland, Pa.: privately printed, 1946.

McKibbin, David. *Sargent's Boston*. Boston: Museum of Fine Arts, 1956.

Mendelsohn, Robert S. *Male Practice: How Doctors Manipulate Women*. Chicago: Contemporary Books, 1981.

Minter, David L. *The Interpreted Design as a Structural Principle in American Prose*. New Haven: Yale University Press, 1969.

Montaigne, Michel de. *Essays*. Trans. J. M. Cohen. Harmondsworth, Eng.: Penguin, 1978.

Mount, Charles Merrill. *John Singer Sargent: A Biography.* New York: W. W. Norton, 1955.

Mulvey, Laura. "Visual Pleasure and the Narrative Cinema," *Screen* 16 (Autumn 1975): 6–18.

Mumford, Lewis. *Technics and Civilization.* New York: Harcourt, Brace, 1963.

Nichols, Bill. *Ideology and the Image.* Bloomington: Indiana University Press, 1981.

O'Neill, William. *Everyone Was Brave.* Chicago: Quadrangle Books, 1969.

Ormond, Richard. *John Singer Sargent.* New York: Harper & Row, 1970.

Ortega y Gasset, José. *Man and People.* Trans. Willard R. Trask. New York: W. W. Norton, 1957.

Packard, Francis R. *History of Medicine in the United States.* New York: Hafner, 1963.

Pirandello, Luigi. *Naked Masks.* Trans. Eric Bentley. New York: E. P. Dutton, 1952.

Poirier, Richard. *The Comic Sense of Henry James: A Study of the Early Novels.* New York: Oxford University Press, 1967.

Price, Martin. *Forms of Life: Character and Moral Imagination in the Novel.* New Haven: Yale University Press, 1983.

Proust, Marcel. *The Sweet Cheat Gone.* Trans. C. K. Scott Montcrieff. New York: Vintage, 1970.

Pudovkin, V. I. *Film Technique and Film Acting.* Trans. Ivor Montague. New York: Bonanza Books, 1949.

Rothman, William. "Against 'The System of the Suture.'" In *Movies and Methods.* Ed. Bill Nichols. Berkeley and Los Angeles: University of California Press, 1976.

Schendler, Sylvan. *Thomas Eakins.* Boston: Little, Brown, 1967.

Selzer, Richard. *Mortal Lessons: Notes on the Art of Surgery.* New York: Simon and Schuster, 1976.

Shorter, Edward. *A History of Women's Bodies.* New York: Basic Books, 1982.

———. *The Making of the Modern Family.* New York: Basic Books, 1975.

Smith, Bonnie G. *Ladies of the Leisure Class: The Bourgeoises of Northern France in the Nineteenth Century.* Princeton: Princeton University Press, 1981.

Springer, Mary Doyle. *A Rhetoric of Character: Some Women of Henry James.* Chicago: University of Chicago Press, 1978.

Stage, Sarah. *Female Complaints.* New York: W. W. Norton, 1979.

Steinberg, Leo. "Velázquez' *Las Meninas*." *October* 19 (Winter 1981): 45–54.

Tocqueville, Alexis de. *Democracy in America.* Trans. George Lawrence. Garden City, N.Y.: Anchor Books, 1969.

Trachtenberg, Alan. *The Incorporation of America: Culture and Society in the Gilded Age.* New York: Hill and Wang, 1982.

Truffaut, François. *Hitchcock.* New York: Simon and Schuster, 1967.

Turim, Maureen. "Symmetry/Asymmetry and Visual Fascination." *Wide Angle* 4, no. 3 (1980): 38–47.

Veeder, William. *Henry James: The Lessons of the Master.* Chicago: University of Chicago Press, 1975.

Warren, Robert Penn, and Wellek, René. *Theory of Literature.* New York: Harcourt, Brace, 1970.

Wharton, Edith. *The House of Mirth.* New York: Charles Scribner's Sons, 1969.

Wiebe, Robert. *The Search for Order, 1877–1920.* New York: Hill and Wang, 1967.

Williamson, Judith. *Decoding Advertisements.* London: Marion Boyars, 1978.

Wilson, Edmund. *Patriotic Gore: Studies in the Literature of the American Civil War.* New York: Oxford University Press, 1962.

Winner, Viola Hopkins. *Henry James and the Visual Arts.* Charlottesville: University Press of Virginia, 1970.

Wolf, Bryan Jay. *Romantic Re-Vision: Culture and Consciousness in Nineteenth-Century American Painting and Literature.* Chicago: University of Chicago Press, 1982.

Zaretsky, Eli. *Capitalism, the Family, and Personal Life.* New York: Harper & Row, 1976.

Index